WATERS UNDER THE BRIDGE

WATERS UNDER THE BRIDGE

TWENTIETH CENTURY TOLLCROSS, FOUNTAINBRIDGE AND THE WEST PORT

written and compiled by
Tollcross Local History Project

ABERDEEN UNIVERSITY PRESS
Member of Maxwell Macmillan Pergamon Publishing Corporation

First published in 1990
Aberdeen University Press

British Library Cataloguing in Publication Data

Waters under the bridge: twentieth century Tollcross,
   Fountainbridge and the West Port.
   1. Great Britain. History
   I. Tollcross Local History Project II. Easton, Drew
   941.34

   ISBN 0 08 040906 7

Cover illustration: The Queen's Visit to Freer Street, 1953
(Painting reproduced by permission of the artist, George Brown)

PRINTED IN GREAT BRITAIN
THE UNIVERSITY PRESS
ABERDEEN

Contents

List of Illustrations

Acknowledgements

Many thanks are due to the following people and organisations for their assistance and information: Edinburgh City Libraries, Huntly House Museum, Dean Education Centre, History of Education Centre, Alexanders (Edinburgh) Limited, Royal Commission on Ancient Monuments (Scotland), the Fountainbridge Reunion Group, Ian McMurtrie (Honorary Curator, Lothian and Borders Fire Brigade Museum), Mr A Jeffries (Lothian and Borders Police), Major MacEachan (Territorial Army HQ), Catherine Toall, Dr D H McVie, Andrew F Hay (Ethicon Ltd), Kenneth Neal (Headteacher, Tollcross Primary School), Margo McVicar (Senior teacher, Tollcross Primary School), Tollcross Community Council, Lister Housing Cooperative, Fountainbridge Housing Association and the Community Education Service of Lothian Regional Council.

The members of the Local History Project are: Betty McAnna, George Brown, Liz Allan, Gillean Somerville-Arjat, Mary Macdonald, Allison Young, Jane Curr, David Fisher, Margaret McArthur and Drew Easton.

List of contributors and their years of birth

William Anderson	1875	Andrew Lynch	1922
Mrs Henrietta Johnstone	1895	Mrs Betty McAnna	1922
Mrs Chrissie Borthwick	1899	Mrs Margaret Weddell	1923
The Very Rev Dr R Leonard Small	1905	Mrs Janet Dow	1924
Dr Alistair C McLaren	1907	George R Ramage	1924
AHR	1908	Mrs Grace Suttie	1925
Mrs J Plenderleith	1909	Mrs Nancy Barclay	1926
John Walker Blanch	1911	Mrs Iris Munro	1927
The Rev Dr R Stuart Louden	1912	MB	1927
Mrs Grace Taylor	1912	Mrs Ina Begbie	1928
Mrs Nellie Rogers	1912	Alexander A Alexander	1928
Mrs Helen Louden	1915	George McMillan	1928
Mrs Margaret Downie	1916	Andrew Laing	1928
Tommy Lang	1917	Robert Stuart	1929
Mrs Mary Cruickshank	1918	Stan Player	1931
Mrs I D Graham	1918	Mrs Betty Lennox	1933
Mrs J D Thomson	1919	John Wilson	1934
Jack Gillett	1919	Mrs Frances Waddell	1935
Mrs Annie Hepburn	1919	Mrs Margaret Smith	1935
John G Webster	1919	Mrs Alice Burt	1937
Miss Olwen Anderson	1919	Jim Alexander	1937
Mrs Ruby Clifford	1921	Mrs Josephine Black	1937
Mrs Lexie Lang	1921	Miss Margaret Wilson	1939
Alex Kitson	1921	Willie Thompson	1940
Mrs Margaret Mowat	1921	George Robertson	1941
Mrs Jane Moore	1921	Ms Liz Allen	1942
Mrs Annie Kitson	1921	Mrs Irene Kinder	1945
Dr W Grant McIntosh	1922	Mrs Andrea Shaw	1950
Mrs Netta Thomson	1922		

Introduction

This book could be described as a sequel to *By the Three Great Roads, a History of Tollcross Fountainbridge and the West Port*; or it could be called an expansion of that book's last chapter, 'Tollcross and Fountainbridge Remembered'.

By the Three Great Roads, written by the Tollcross Local History Project and published in 1988, dealt with aspects of the area's history going back to the thirteenth century. In its last chapter former residents gave their memories of life in the area before the exodus of the 1950s to 1970s when many houses were demolished. It was well received. In particular it aroused great interest among former residents, many of whom had been meeting regularly since 1981 in a reunion group organised by Mrs Betty McAnna. There was a keen demand for a further book which would draw on the memories and talents of this group.

The Tollcross Local History Project was reconvened; some former members were unable to rejoin, but others took their place. The project was publicised, bringing in further offers of contributions. An open day at Tollcross Primary School generated interest and contributions from former pupils and staff. In all over fifty people gave interviews.

The wealth of high quality material produced by these interviews would fill volumes. Our contributors have thought much about their experiences and have brought it alive in vivid narrative. For us—the project members—the main task was to make a selection and to offer some further interpretations of the material. We can only hope that we have done at least some justice to it.

Tollcross today is a different area. Fewer people live in it, more people come to it for entertainment. It is cosmopolitan. In Fountainbridge industry has largely taken over from housing, and new developments are planned which will further change its character. Yet it could have changed even more—indeed as a housing area it could have been destroyed—if the grandiose development plans of the 1960s had taken effect. Chapter 9 describes how these plans were abandoned, largely as a result of pressure by the people affected.

So there is still a community in the area, a different community, whose story must await the next instalment—perhaps it won't prove to be so very different?

'What I like most about living in Tollcross is the way you can go into the shop and say, "I'll pay my papers", and they don't say, "What's your name?"'.

ANDREA SHAW, Tollcross Community Councillor

Our warmest thanks are due to all who cooperated in this work, and most of all to our contributors.

31 January 1990   MARY MACDONALD

CHAPTER ONE

Living at Home

Mary Macdonald

Living at home—in one of hundreds of individual homes, all differing according to the family's personalities and relationships, their employment, housing, antecedents, and place in the social hierarchy.

Some common features appear, all with exceptions. There is a neighbourly closeness, a sense of being 'all in the same boat', a system of mutual help—but this has its limitations, people can still feel isolated. Housing conditions range from inadequate to appalling—but the range is wide; there are even some commodious residences at the top end of it. Home finance, very near the bone, relies much on the pawn shop and on credit schemes—but some people make a point of avoiding debt. A great fund of energy and organising ability is put into maintaining cleanliness—but there are some failures.

The people who have told their stories are survivors. Most of them look back with affection on the place where their youth was spent. This place was not 'Tollcross': it was a street, part of a street, or even a stair—a little village community:

> Everybody knew everybody, from one end of Fountainbridge to the other. It was a closed community.
>
> Mrs Betty Lennox

> Grove Street was like another village really, I mean you knew the people because they went to school with you. To me Grove Street was like another place, although it was down the road and round the corner.
>
> Mrs Annie Kitson

> Innumerable people after I had left Wright's Houses have spoken about it and have said it was like a little village—you know there was outside wooden stairs . . . It had the Barclay Church as a background . . . I just loved Wright's Houses.
>
> AHR

> This [showing her picture of Glen Street as seen from above] is number one . . . this was our corner window. I'm going to do this all over again and make these figures bigger. That's what we called the soor dook man . . . and believe it or not, they still put goal posts on the church at the foot of the street, because I passed not so long ago and there was goal posts painted on.
>
> Mrs Grace Taylor

Houses

For a few single people, home could be a bed in a hostel; for most families it was a single end or room and kitchen, with or without internal water supply or toilet, maybe one or two extra rooms; for the privileged few, it was a house with a bathroom. In Lauriston Place there were some large houses where, in its time, the full ceremonial of Edwardian middle-class life was carried on. In a later chapter one such house is described.

Grove House . . . it was all cubicles. And it was about three flats high, it must have housed quite a few men . . . They were all working men.

ALEX KITSON

The flat on Freer Street Terrace was built on top of Andrew Waddell's stables, so it came complete with horse stink, rats and mice. The other things that came with the two-room flat were one black iron sink with one cold-water faucet, one gas lamp and one coal-burning fire place. The second room, which was much smaller, had one gas lamp only. Toilet facilities were down the hall, a little room with no window, no light fixture, shared by four families, all with kids . . . I remember the flat as being very dark, cold and cramped.

GEORGE RAMAGE

If you had a child not there in your Sunday School class on Sunday then you went and visited, and some of us were quite frightened to go along . . . The Terrace was the one most people hated . . . there were no lights and it was like a rabbit warren, you got one passage on one floor but then there were ever so many different bits branching off and their doors just opened straight on to the passages. Quite a lot of people took a torch if they were visiting, but I think you were better off without one as long as you could knock on one door and ask because you quite frequently saw rats in the corridors. That was quite a shake-up . . . very often in the houses you found the three generations all living together in a room and kitchen and some of the houses were spotless.

MRS HELEN LOUDEN

Our house in High Riggs was a room and kitchen and a recess. We were lucky, we had inside water, the rest of the stair had water outside on the landin'. The toilet was shared by all five houses on the landin'. I slept in the recess, being the only boy. My five sisters slept in the big bedroom. And my mother and father, they slept in the kitchen.

JOHN WEBSTER

My mother said I'd been her thirteenth child, but I can only go back aboot eleven o' them and I know o' two that she lost . . . quite well spread out, but in a room and kitchen that's a lot of children . . .

MRS INA BEGBIE

We were a maindoor house and we felt we were a little above people who lived in

1   Fleming's Stores in Earl Grey Street, showing part of the Ironmongery Department.
Courtesy of St Bride's Community Centre.

stairs. For some reason it was quite something to be in a maindoor. We were about
half way up the street, and there seemed to be a distinction, at the bottom of the
street people were poorer, the flats were not quite as good . . . we had hot water
which the houses below us didn't have, and further up the street the stairs were
pleasanter, cleaner and lighter . . . the people right at the bottom didn't have
inside toilets.

Ms LIZ ALLEN

Then we shifted down to Grove Street . . . It was a revelation! . . . they were good
rooms, high ceilings wi the old cornicing round, oh it was a substantial house. And
we had a bathroom and a bath, which was an unknown quantity in that area, no
just in Fountainbridge but in that area.

ALEX KITSON

At 149 Fountainbridge there was about eight families on a landing, four on each
side, and there was three landings. And there was two toilets, one on each side,
so that was one toilet between two families. But it was dark, there was no lights.
And we lived in, well it was more or less just a single end, with a boxroom that my
sister and I slept in . . . my dad was working as a labourer and he was always
coming in wet, you know, his clothes all soaked, and trying to dry them in a wee
house like that, quite a problem, there always seemed to be wet clothes hanging
about . . . he had to retire, I think he was about 58, with osteoarthritis.

MRS ANNIE KITSON

When I was first married I stayed with my mother for about two years. Then there was up 149 Fountainbridge, the lassie Galbraith, it was her mother's house I got, up on the top flat, she was leaving a huge end. But there were four laddies and two lassies in that big single end that I was going into and she was going into a room and kitchen just next door. You went down a wee lobby and the toilet was between Mrs Galbraith and I, but we had a lamp inside and Mrs Galbraith bought the oil one week and I bought it the next, she was a grand neighbour . . . I had a big double bed and I'll tell you where I got it. These American people that Johnnie worked for, I went out with Betty in the pram tae see them and whenever I went into that house I said 'Oh . . .' and the woman must have seen the expression on my face—oh, what a beautiful bed, ye know. It was like . . . the frame was green but down there was like brass and it was like a harp, it was beautiful, and the brass knobs were like that. And I always mind when they were going back, they said tae Johnny 'Dae ye think yer wife would like that bed, John?' So I wanted tae pay for it but no they wouldnae take nothing. Well, I had that in ma kitchen and at the bottom o' that I had ma cot for Ian, because he was just a baby, then there I had a basket for keeping dirty clothes, and up there was my meter for putting money in for the gas, I got a cane and two wee nails and I got a bit cretonne and I thingmied that off wi' the cretonne. Then there was ma sideboard, and in front of ma sideboard was ma gate-legged table . . . then over there wis a settee and I had a lovely, big old-fashioned fire, but I had it tiled and ma mantelpiece was up there. I had a beautiful house along there, a lovely house. I'm maybe no so houseproud now but when I was younger I was awfie houseproud.

MRS CHRISSIE BORTHWICK

No carpets on the floor, only lino. There was a kitchen table, a double bed in the bed recess, scrubbed chairs, but no chair at all with a soft seat. It was all just wooden chairs. We eventually got a bed settee and that was the most wonderful piece of furniture.

MB

Finance

For most people resources were counted in pennies, and it was hard to make them last till the end of the week. For many the pawnshop was in regular use. As long as the man was in work things could be kept going, unless (as happened in some cases) the money went on drink before reaching the house. The hardest times came with unemployment; relief was obtainable but it was barely sufficient and, by some, was felt to be degrading.

It was generally Mother who took charge of the budget and she had recourse to various credit or savings schemes, especially for expensive items such as clothing. She, or one of her friends or workmates, might start a 'menage': a group whose members each paid a fixed sum each week and took turns to spend the kitty. For working girls, this might even make possible some luxury such as a perm. At the Coop there was the 'Store Club'—a saving scheme—and the 'Store Book'—a form of credit—as well as the twice yearly dividend which was a useful form of saving. There were also friendly societies and insurance schemes.

My first week's pay was ten shillins. In those days every boy went home and gave his mother the pay. I gave my mother the ten shillins and she gave me half a crown, which was two and sixpence, an I thought I was well off.

TOMMY LANG

It seems like the only time my father was home was to sleep. The rest of the time he was either working, or he was in the pub. He never had a day's unemployment . . . but the money never came into the house.

GEORGE RAMAGE

My mother, aye, she would get the wages. And she'd pay the rent, insurances, penny policies or something. Still they had to be paid. And they hadnae, at that time, any electricity bills because it was gas mantles and I can remember, if the gas mantle was broken, well it would maybe stay broken for a wee while, till my mother felt she could afford that penny or whatever it was, because a penny was a lot. The rent man came, I think it must have been every week. I can remember the gas man came and counting out the pennies . . . You always heard about going to the pawnshop but we never, my mother never done that. She was very proud . . . Oh no, my parents didn't save at all, not until I would say we were working maybe, they hadnae that kind of money.

MRS ANNIE KITSON

My father was about the best paid man in the stair. How we helped each other then. On a Monday or a Tuesday a lot o' the other people were skint, and they used tae come tae my mother borryin' an egg, maybe borryin' sugar, borryin' tea, but regular on a Friday without fail everythin' was paid back, and that's how we lived. There were never any defaulters at all. Everybody paid their dues.

JOHN WEBSTER

The pawnshop? Oh aye, everybody—it was a way of life. The people had to live from one week to another, they got it out on Saturday, Monday they hadnae money so it went back in. And you werenae alone, I mean it wisnae a stigma, what you was pawning was your own and nobody else's . . . The menage, oh aye, that was a way of life as well. People had to, and then you had your societies as well. You had your Friendly society you paid a penny, get up to ten bob, come back from ten bob to a penny, but these people that were, well I would say careful, that was their holiday money.

MRS ANNIE HEPBURN

We went to the pawnshop. But I came to an agreement after I started work . . . I said to my mother, 'Now look, I have managed to save up a few shillings and instead of going to the pawnshop, you know you have to pay for redeeming and pay for your ticket and things like that, you take money out of that drawer, Ma, and at the end of the week you'll put that money back'. But invariably you know when you said to her, 'You owe me three shillings' or 'four shillings', 'Oh, do I owe you as much as that?'

AHR

Pawn shop! Oh that was one place I wouldn't go! I took more leatherings for that . . . Joanne went. She was a bit older than me. They wouldn't serve you unless you were fourteen. So I had to kneel on the pawnshop floor and she stood on my back, to make her taller, and she was swayin' from side to side. We got away wi' it a few times, but then the man came round wonderin' why she was always trippin' back and forth. He wouldn't serve us and oh, we went back without the money. I kept out o' the way . . . My mother was always in a menage. My grandfather had never heard o' such a thing . . . he thought it was a lucky draw.

MRS J PLENDERLEITH

Oh aye you had menages, I would pay two shillings a week and my turn to get a perm would be in the third week. Say one of the women would say 'I'm going to take twenty people, or maybe ten people to make a menage', so she got the ten names and we'll say it was five shillings a week, well we paid that five shillings and you took a turn, and maybe a shoe menage—we'd go to Bennet's the shoe shop . . . you did dress, I mean you might be working in the mill but when you came out at night you went and you dressed, you didnae go about in the same things.

MRS MARGARET DOWNIE

The Store book was just a form of—well you got your messages then you paid at the end of the week, like tick . . . you had a share in the store, so it was your money you were spending . . . in these days they were getting about four shillings in the pound, in their divi, which again paid for a lot of things, by the time the divi came.

MRS ANNIE KITSON

My father and the other doctors always sent out their accounts when the Store divi was due. So we got some payment.

DR A C McLAREN

Mother used to have a club going, it was a shilling a week, and that's what she clothed us on. That was another thing, when I started work I started in a club as well, and it was a shilling a week. But when I got to seventeen I thought, 'There's going to be no more clubs for me. I'll do without a costume or do without a coat this year, and next year I'll have ready money to go and buy where I want'.

AHR

Lots of people were in the clubs and got things on tick, but my mother never never got anything like that at all. She had to be jolly sure. She had to have the money in her hand, and to spare, before anything was bought. The rent and the coal and the tokens for milk for that week. These things were purchased before anything else . . .

It was the days of the depression and like many people my father was unemployed . . . if my memory serves me well, I think a couple got something like one pound five shillings per week and two shillings for each child. It was always referred to as 'the dole' . . . almost constant deprivation, but then we didn't realise it was deprivation, not when we were too young anyway.

MB

My dad was always lucky to be in a job. But . . . his old war wounds affected him to such a degree that he was off for a while with that. With the result that my mum couldn't make ends meet. So my mum had to go to the parish, cap in hand. There was no shame in it at all . . . so at that time you got your school dinners. You got your wee ticket from the parish.

Mrs Betty Lennox

The parish was dreadful. You didn't get any money, you got a ticket. A white card. You had to say how many was in your family. One part of the ticket said, 'bread, groceries', no butcher meat, and 'meal'. You felt degraded. We had to go to Adam's in Dundee Street, the grocer's. You could have kippers, broken biscuits—no whole ones—bacon, eggs, the necessities. It was marked how much. Maybe a pound. It was terrible. My father was in the Deaconess Hospital for eight months . . . there was no rent paid . . . the factor that came for the money wasn't nice, he had no sympathy for anyone. That was the only time you felt different to other people.

Mrs J Plenderleith

Food

Soup and porridge were the mainstays. They can be made over an open fire. So too can various stewed dishes, such as tripe—which requires laborious preparation—and sheep's heid. Some families had a coal range or, later, a gas cooker, which gave scope for baking. Some could afford extras such as a cooked breakfast, or treats such as a tripe supper or fish and chips. Those on hard times had recourse to cheap lines, old bread, stale fruit, chipped eggs. There are few reports of actual hunger, though some frugal meals are described.

It was all big pots of everything. They were always on the side of the fireplace.

Mrs Ruby Clifford

This is our family [shows her picture] sitting in front of the range . . . That's my youngest sister, my young brother, myself and my eldest brother. Two of them are toasting bread. And my elder brother—I put him opening the oven door for my mother, who was a great baker, she's putting a cake in the oven.

Mrs Grace Taylor

The house I lived in when I was married was just a single end in Freer Street . . . I didnae have a gas stove at first. I just had a gas ring, but I had a coal fire and I used to put the kettle on and then later I got a cooker. And I loved it, because then you loved to cook and you liked to try everything, oh there was the oven and it made you—made you want to do things, it was like, oh the greatest thing on earth.

Mrs Margaret Downie

My mother made good soup out o' sheep's heids and all that, and it was an ever open door, the police, and even the doctor, Labenjoh, used to come in if they were in the area and have a bowl o' soup. It was always there for them. My mother's soup was well known . . . Your main food then was soup and porridge. My mother used tae tell us 'There's a shillin' which was quite a lot then. You went down to the butcher's and asked them for either a marry bone or a sheep's heid to make the soup with. And with the sheep's heid you always told him tae keep the eyes in it to see you over the weekend! If you got a marry bone, which was good as well, then you went over to Dunsmore and got thruppence worth of mixed vegetables . . . We had the old fashioned range. My mother polished it every morning. There was a bracket for the big pots . . . you had an oven each side where your mother done the baking and all that, scones, three cornered scones, treacle scones, everything.

JOHN WEBSTER

2   A Rathie, Tobacconist in East Fountainbridge, 1963. Courtesy of Richard W Cowell.

When they got sheep in they used to cut the wee tails off them, they made the most gorgeous potato soup. My mother always made sheep's heid broth, you could dance on it, it was lovely. Then she used to take all the meat off the head, put it in a bowl, a plate on it, and press it with a big iron overnight. So for your dinner you got the soup, and then you got the slices of meat with potatoes and turnip. We put the peas from the soup at the side of our plates and then put them in paper pokes to eat like sweets!

Mrs Grace Taylor

My mother gave us what she calculated good wholesome food, and I can remember her doing the best that she could. I remember we bought sheep's bags, I think they were about tuppence. We had to do what my mother called 'plooting' them, that was dipping them into boiling water and scraping, and that was my job. I did this on a wooden table . . . it was a long thing—and then my mother cut it up when I had finished with it and she cooked it, and she used part of it to make a haggis. It was made with liver, mince, oatmeal and onions, and suet. Invariably that was our Sunday dinner.

AHR

They used tae come round the streets wi' cheap bags tuppence, thruppence, that was for tripe—it was an awful cleaning right enough but it was a good wholesome meal.

Mrs Chrissie Borthwick

Sometimes for breakfast we would have porridge and a kipper and maybe sausages or an egg . . . and the fish man used to come, Tammy Smith, he had a cart and horse, he used to stop at my granny's window and they used to get a lump of cod, thruppence worth of cod, he just cut it, it wasn't weighed or anything. My granny used to get it for all her daughters and would get the money back from them.

Mrs Annie Kitson

Then there was Meldrum's up Home Street. They sold the most gorgeous tripe suppers. You took your jug up and you got your tripe with the white sauce and the boiled potatoes. It was really lovely.

Mrs Grace Taylor

Because it was Saturday night we might have fish and chips from the chip shop round the corner, which was quite something, and a bottle of juice, and later on a snowball each from the Italian shop.

Ms Liz Allen

We used to go to the High Riggs and buy chippit eggs. At Rankin's at the end of the night when they were clearing out, you used to get bananas that were going a bit soft. You got them a lot cheaper. It was first come first served. If you were in the front of the queue you got the best. Otherwise you got the rubbish.

Mrs Betty Lennox

There was a baker at the corner of Gillespie Crescent called Murdoch and we took the pillow case—took it off the pillow, you know, we wouldn't have a spare pillow case—we went over and sat at the baker's, sat and blethered, quite a crowd had accumulated there waiting on the baker opening. We paid I think about thruppence for the old bread or teabread.

AHR

Everyone was on the dole . . . I can remember being sent up to Smiths, much to my disgust, with a big enamel jug for chipped eggs and broken kippers. But having said that it didn't mean we were living in poverty. Looking back now I can mind sitting having my dinner . . . we always got good soup, and always got well fed, and saying to my mother, 'Are you not having your dinner Ma?' 'Oh I've had mine hen' . . . but I often wondered if she'd had anything. My faither aye being connected with the fisher folk, he used to trot away to Leith and he used to come back with flounders and all that kind of thing. And I would say that if half the kids nowadays were as well fed as I was on unemployment they'd be doing fine.

Mrs Peggy Weddell

There was a butcher at the corner of Fountainbridge and Freer Street . . . he was really an angel as far as lots of unemployed people in the district were concerned. He made an excess of pie gravy for his weekend steak pies, so that he'd have all this left over and the unemployed people, one member from each family, could queue on Thursday night after closing time with a pitcher, a large jug, and it was filled with this lovely rich pie gravy, meaty, thick pie gravy. It was our staple Thursday night tea—a soup plate with a slice of bread soaked in this pie gravy. It was very tasty and I'm sure quite nourishing.

MB

We used to go out and get old rolls and loaves of bread and things like that from the bakers. We also used to steal milk off the doorsteps. They'd leave a bottle of milk and some rolls, and I'd be so damn hungry that I would go out and steal a bottle of milk and eat some rolls.

George Ramage

Clothing

Hand-me-downs, second-hand shops, Asa Wass's rag store—all these were made use of, but there were variations. Some children went barefoot, but others, with the aid of a menage, could be provided with new party frocks. Working girls (as Margaret Downie recounts above) could aim at being dressy. Clothing had also another aspect: once acquired, it was an asset which could be pawned, especially boots or a man's suit.

We always had a new dress for the Sunday School picnic, and a new blazer and things like that. I can remember, looking back, that my mother didnae have an awful lot herself, new clothes . . . they were kept for Sunday, if you got new things. I mean we'd maybe get a pair of shoes, but oh they were put aside, you couldnae wear them to the school, looking at it it's silly isn't it, because those shoes must have got tight on us.

Mrs Annie Kitson

My dad had a war pension. In these days it was about five shillings a week but it made a difference and I don't think I ever went to a Sunday School picnic or party or anything like that where I didn't have a new frock. There was always the menage from Parker's . . . She did insist that I got a panama hat which I once managed to throw over the canal bridge! I telt her that the wind had blowed it off my heid! She said how could it blow off your heid, you've got elastic under your chin.

Mrs Peggy Weddell

Sometimes I got my cousin's clothes—I always say I was 'second hand Rose', but that didn't matter. And at school if your mother was able to buy material the sewing mistress would make up a dress, you know we were all working on a dress in our class.

AHR

There was a shop owned by two sisters, 70 West Port, you could go in there if you were going to a big dance, and rest assured that you would get a really good evening dress, because she bought off all the actors and actresses that were playing in the Palladium. I got some lovely stuff there, the most I ever paid was two shillings. That was for a coat.

Mrs Janet Dow

My mother bought an awful lot o' stuff from Asa Wass, with working there, and if it was a frock that went to your feet, she just turned it up from our feet. And it stuck out like a crinoline. Oh, it was a bonny sight goin' to school! If they'd been takin' pictures at the time, I would've been saw in the books! . . . I mind one day—this was really funny—we seldom had shoes on our feet because we seldom had the money. So this day was my birthday and she says, 'I'd better get you a pair o' shoes'. You'd think I was away to one o' those high class shops. I was away to Paddy's Market in the West Port, now he had a great big mountain o' shoes from the floor to the ceiling and you just looked for one, and if it fitted you, you looked for the neighbour. She'd say, 'How much is this pair?' 'Oh they're sixpence . . .' 'Put them away. Find the neighbour for that one. How much are they?' 'Thruppence'. 'Well, look for the other one'. And you started to look. Anyway, it was my birthday, and a woman stops outside Stewart's pub in Semple Street and says, 'Hullo Maggie, my goodness, I've not seen you for ages!' And she says, 'Well you wouldnae have seen me the day either, only it's this yin's birthday and I'm takin' her for a new pair of shoes'. And who was standin' on the left o' me but the wee Italian woman with her monkey and her wee hurdy gurdy organ, and it had its wee red fez and its wee green coat on, runnin' up, chitterin' and chatterin', and it had a tin in its hand for anybody giein' it a ha'penny or a penny. And this woman says, 'Oh it's your birthday hen! Oh my goodness!' And she gave me a silver thruppenny in my hand and I put it in the monkey's tin. I was delighted to be able to dae this. And my mother she went over, she pulled the tinny oot the monkey's hand and she slapped its face and emptied the thruppenny and gave it its tinny back! I never got the shoes. I never saw the thruppenny again. Back to Freer Street.

She telt *everybody* aboot me giein' a monkey thruppence. 'And it kept me on gas for a week', she says. And I was in my barries for another year. That was my birthday!

Mrs J Plenderleith

Also about the police station up the High Street, if ye were supposed tae be hard up, once a year you could put in tae get police boots, but ye couldnae pawn them, because there were five holes pierced in the upper part o' the boot, which meant 'DO NOT PAWN THESE BOOTS'.

John Webster

Well my dad had to be dressed for his job. That was all weekend work. So his suit would go in on the Monday. They never even opened the parcel and he got his money back.

Mrs Ruby Clifford

Keeping Clean and Tidy

Even keeping oneself personally clean was a chore, though it had its cosy aspect, the zinc bath by the fire. House cleaning, which included many now unheard-of tasks such as blackleading the grate and beating the rugs, called for organisation, with mother and daughters playing their parts. It varied though—some mothers took on most of it themselves, in some families the boys helped too. Father helped in a few cases, but of course he had to think of his reputation when it came to a job that could be seen from outside, such as window-cleaning. Some families were not capable of keeping to these exacting routines.

The sink was outside . . . there was nae light in it . . . you had a candle . . . you'd take your hot water inside and you'd do half and work your way down. On the water tank above was where the nail was . . . you could take the wire off and stop the water from going to anybody. When you are waiting for the water coming you've got the soap on your face and they keep on using it, and you canny get it. So that's what you did to get your own back—turn it off!

Mrs Nancy Barclay

And a Friday night we always got our bath in a big zinc bath in front of the fire . . . one of us getting washed and my dad sitting drying us and getting us a cup of cocoa or something after, sitting on his knee . . . you know these wee things all come to mind.

Mrs Annie Kitson

It was the zinc bath in front of the fire . . . I never remember seeing my mother or father having a bath there. They used to go up to the Infirmary Street Baths, then when I got older that's what I used to do as well. I went to Infirmary Street and you could get a private bath there with carbolic soap and I still like the smell of carbolic soap.

We had to do quite a lot of housework because my mother was working. We had

3 Smith's Provision Stores at 72 Fountainbridge, taken probably in the early 1960s. Smith's was an independent firm owned by Mr John Smith who eventually had six branches in the city, with a Head Office in Grindlay Street. There was an average staff of fifteen at the Fountainbridge shop. Anonymous donation.

our set chores on a Saturday, my brother and I, Mum used to take the message line in to the Coop in Morrison Street in the morning, then we used to go down and collect the messages and certain jobs we had to do, like sweep the floor, clean the grate. I remember it was black lead but it also had brass on it and stainless steel, and I had to scrape that with an emery board and Brasso, that was our job on a Saturday morning.

MRS ALICE BURT

Of course they [her seven children—she was a widow and went out working] were beginning to grow up too, and then I had always the age when they could help a bit in the house, and help with the shopping and things like that. Oh, I had everything organised. You had to be organised or you would get in a mess . . . Cleaning the house wasn't difficult—you just took it all in your stride. As I say if you were organised, you couldn't slack up on anything or it was worse for yourself.

MRS HENRIETTA JOHNSTONE

Well I'll tell you one thing, we were never allowed out on a Friday night. That was cleaning night. Us three girls, we all had our turn to do maybe the brasses, or the spoons—we'd all to do something, and I used to love doing the carpets. We rolled the carpets up, took them down to the street, and beat them and swept them down there. Well very few of the teenagers got out on Friday nights, the girls, and my chums used to bring their mothers' carpets down and have a caper and blether at the foot of the stair. We held them against the wall and beat them, then you brushed them, if the pavement was clear you laid them on the pavement, knelt down on them and swept away. Rugs, doormats, things like that.

MRS GRACE TAYLOR

We used to have some rare fun, because we were in a bigger house, we had the parlour ye see, and ma pals would come up and on would go the record player and everybody would get the old bits o' blanket on their feet and we would be dancing to polish the parlour floor.

MRS INA BEGBIE

I used to plead with my mother, oh please let me wash the stair. She used to say, you'll get to do these things soon enough . . . My dad was very good in the house. He helped quite a lot. He would clean the brasses or he would sweep the floor and things, I can see him doing things like that. Well maybe it was unusual, but you see at the time we never thought anything about it, because he was that type of man, you know, he was a good father really.

MRS ANNIE KITSON

Cleaning the windows was a terrible job . . . I used to say to my dad, 'Why don't you clean the windaes for my mother?' and he used to say, 'My Union doesnae allow me'—he would have been too proud to sit oot the windae!

MRS NANCY BARCLAY

There was a man across the street who cleaned his wife's windows for her, and people looked down on this man. I can remember women standing gossiping in the shops and saying, 'I know who wears the trousers in that house' . . .

There were one or two families in the street that were terribly dirty, when you went into their houses they smelled, newspaper on the table—I was appalled because my mother prided herself on setting a good table. Looking back on it, I think in a lot of the houses where things were not kept properly, the mother perhaps was a little simple, maybe the parents weren't quite up to looking after the families.

MS LIZ ALLEN

One of the biggest chores was washing clothes. Very few people did it at home, where there was generally no hot water and no space for drying. Fortunately the Town Council operated a chain of public wash houses. The Ponton Street or Lochrin wash house was opened in 1921 and gave valuable service till there was a phased programme of closures (hotly contested since it was first mooted in the early 1960s, but finally approved in the mid 1970s) because of decreasing usage. At the wash house you paid by the hour for the use of washtubs and driers—clothes horses which pulled out from the wall and then were pushed in again so that the clothes were dried in a heated chamber. Some of the customers came from quite a distance, trundling their washing on prams or trolleys.

The washing I did in the house at first, until they built Tollcross wash house, which we knew an awful difference, because we could get away earlier from our work— we worked on a Saturday then too, and all us married women, we all got away early. Soon as ever we did something we had to do we got it done, and we could all get over to the wash house. And in there you see you got it washed and dried and all the wringing done and boiled—which was the most particular thing, especially for girls, the whites you know . . . we missed the wash house when it went, no slittering in the house, boiling things.

Mrs Henrietta Johnstone

Ponton Street . . . they had high old times in there in those days I think. They seemed to have good times in the wash house doing things and all helping one another.

Mrs Frances Waddell

My mother used to say, 'Now when you come from the school come straight to the wash house', and you had to be there to help her. In the wash house you had your tub and your boiler. It was a double tub and your boiler had taps, just at the back, and you put your washing in. Then you had the horse that came out from the wall. Everything had to be ironed so you had to take your turn. And then my dad, the collars and everything had to be starched . . . Portsburgh Square . . . it was all more or less room and kitchens or single ends, and it was balconies . . . they wouldn't have facilities for washing in the house, they went to the wash house at Tollcross. And everybody had what they used to call their wheels, which would be an old pram or an old go-cart, anything they could get that had wheels, and they used to borrow the wheels back and forward. What they said was, 'I've left the wheels on the balcony, so when you're ready if you've got some washing the morn the wheels are there'.

Mrs Janet Dow

There was a wash house opposite Tollcross School . . . That's where we used to make a bob or two, goin' over there and hingin' about when you come out o' school, and a woman, she might have a basket o' washin', and she would ask you tae help her tae carry it home. You usually finished up gettin' a penny or tuppence fae her.

John Webster

Oh the steamie was brilliant. I came out here [to Drumbrae] and for the first three Hogmanay days that I lived in this house—and I'm going back thirty-five year— I went in on the first bus in the morning tae the wash hoose tae get a' the wash— it was just one o' these things, your place had tae be done for the New Year and there was no way you could cope if the weather was bad. I liked the wash house I must say, for the simple reason that you could come home and put them on the pulley, air them and that wis it, they were ready tae go away. Ye dried them on

the clothes horses . . . ye used to pay one and six to go through the door and I think
it was aboot a shilling an hour or ninepence an hour, and if you came out before
your two hours was up, then you got your change back. You took your own
powder or soap or whatever, your washing stick and a' the rest of it.

Mrs Ina Begbie

Public Behaviour

Of crime in the area there are only isolated reports: a family given to house-
breaking, and a sinister disappearance, recalled by several people, that might
have been accident or crime. Serious outbreaks of vandalism were unusual. On
alcohol there are varying accounts, reflecting individual experiences, but little
on alcohol-related crime. The police had time to spare for keeping an eye on the
behaviour of children and teenagers. They were kenspeckle figures in the area,
known by name and personality and in general, it would seem, not disliked,
although their methods could be summary. One of them, Basher Thomson, was
a notable local worthy and is described in chapter 3.

There was one family in particular which I'm no going to mention. They were . . .
forever breaking into houses and if you were going out for the day, the whole
family, two of you went out the front door and two went out the back, so that they
didn't realise the whole family had gone out together.

A young boy across from us disappeared . . . Ian Aitken was his name. He came
in from the school one day and his mother wasn't in which was very unusual . . .
told a neighbour to tell his mum he was going along to see the horses . . . he never
got to the stables and they never found him to this day.

Mrs Alice Burt

Simon Henderson's bakery . . . when they closed down all the young kids broke
in, and of course they went to town! They threw flour down the lift, and one of
them fell down the lift and broke his leg! But ye didn't get them breaking windows
and setting fire to things. This made the news round here because it was so
unusual. Normally, if you broke a window you run for your life . . . Actually crime
was very very small there. You got the odd drunk, perhaps hitting his wife or
something like that, but even that was very very few.

Tommy Lang

My dad took a drink . . . I daresay most of the men did. I think it was to get oot the
hoose.

Mrs Ruby Clifford

I'd say that many many people, many husbands, spent all the time in the taverns.

George Ramage

There was maybe the odd scuffle on Saturday night. But having said that I don't
think it was the Fountainbridgers that done the fighting.

Mrs Peggy Weddell

I can't remember any crime related to alcohol. We lived right opposite a pub, but my father never drank and we never really knew people who did. I suppose men did go out for a pint and that, but I don't remember hearing that any of the neighbours got hammered or anything because their husbands had been out drinking.

MRS ALICE BURT

When we were wee the police would cuff your lug, but then there wisnae the crime for the police tae spend their time on there is now

MRS INA BEGBIE

4   Richard Cowell in the back green of Freer Street in the 1950s.
Courtesy of Richard W Cowell.

The beat policeman was Tommy, he was a great big man and the way he used to speak to the kids, they daren't do anything . . . they seemed to keep an eye on the kids, you know they'd even get a telling for stepping out into the road, and there wasn't the amount of traffic then that there is now.

MRS JANET DOW

We used to call him 'the Giant Marshmallow' because he was a great big tall man, six foot two inches. His name was Gordon and he was a well known character. The minute you seen that man walking down the street you ran like hell, whether you were doing anything or not. He knew everyone from one end of Fountainbridge to the other, and . . . he used to clout you across the lug or he'd give you a boot up the backside. And you never went home to tell your mum or dad you got a kicking from the policeman. But he was well respected.

MRS BETTY LENNOX

When we got a wee bit older, round about fifteen or sixteen, and got our first long trousers we used to stand at the corner of Grove Street . . . we didn't know what to do with ourselves. And the police'd come along and say 'Now come on lads, break it up'. There wasn't any argument then. You just drifted away and waited till they were away and you came back and you congregated again. They were never rude and it never bothered you.

TOMMY LANG

Oh they were all big polismen then, no like nowadays, they're all young laddies. Oh some o' the old polis were characters. Danny, we used to cry him Lumpy Dan. And then Basher Thomson . . .

ANDREW LAING

Weddings and Funerals

The chamber pot, full of salt for good luck, is an old-established wedding ritual. The theme was elaborated, with decorations and a procession, expressing friendship among fellow workers. Similarly, the strict observance of funeral rites gave opportunities for fellowship between neighbours.

Nobody ever had a hall wedding. It was all done in the hoose. Curled up sandwiches. You were awfy well off if you got the Store to do it, but otherwise you did it yourself. Before my wedding I was dressed up. I was done up with balloons and Christmas decorations, doon the back and the front, and a great big chamber pot. I wish I had it now, to sell it. It had pink roses and everything, and they filled it wi' salt, and that was for good luck . . . And you always had the wee man. A wee bride and groom stuck in the middle.

MRS J PLENDERLEITH

You used to see them coming out of McKays, and the brewery and the mill, coming out and wheeling them in a barrow, dressing them up, and a potty full of salt, dolls, and us as kids used to rush out to see them because there was usually crowds of folk with this person that was getting married . . . aw the placards and things on them, hanging wi streamers, coming up Fountainbridge . . . I cannae remember any kind of honeymoon, they seemed to just move into their houses. You knew a person that was newly married, because they all had new linoleum on their floors, and new bits and pieces they had got . . . a bit fae one place and a bit fae another, what anybody could afford to give. But of course they always had the sort o' showing o' the presents. And I can remember when I was working in St Cuthbert's there was two or three of the girls that were getting married and you were invited round to their house . . . the mother put on a nice tea for you.

MRS ANNIE KITSON

If you went to a funeral you could never go in white, there was a shop in Earl Grey Street that was cried the mourning shop, and you'd to go and get a black dress, all black. And even after the funeral, oh aye I mind that, a man would never have went unless he had a black band, even a woman had a black band on her coat . . . it was only the near relatives that got all mourning . . . and that's how you used to know, 'Oh she's lost somebody', because they were in mourning. And now there's a thing, if anybody died they came round the doors for money for a wreath, you know, well that's what you cry 'neighbours'. And at the graves, there was a globe—ken those stone things they put on graves—and that's from neighbours . . . they didn't ask for a lot of money, just what you could give, a shilling or so, but it always bought them a flower . . . For funeral expenses they were in an insurance, the Jacobites I think they cried it. And then when I was young like it was the horses, then after that it was the motors . . . there was the hearse and then there was the next one. I think four of them went in it . . . Even when my mother died (when I was a child) I had to be all in black, nothing light was to be put on me.

MRS MARGARET DOWNIE

When the hearse went by the men just fell into lines, and not a man would wear brown boots. He would have blackened them with black lead if he couldn't have got anything else. It was all walking funerals. And no women. Not at the funerals.

MRS J PLENDERLEITH

Our kitchen was in the basement so you could look up on to the street, and with the mortuary of the Infirmary being just a few steps along the road, every day there was funeral after funeral, and I remember them well, these wonderful Flemish horses with their hooves all polished with black polish and plumes on their heads and the white froth from their mouth flecking all over. It was a wonderful sight and many of them were walking funerals with the people walking behind . . . this girl [maid from Shetland] gave notice after a very short time, said she couldnae stay here, 'Ah cannae stand it, there's ower mony deid cairts passing every day'. So she left.

DR A C McLAREN

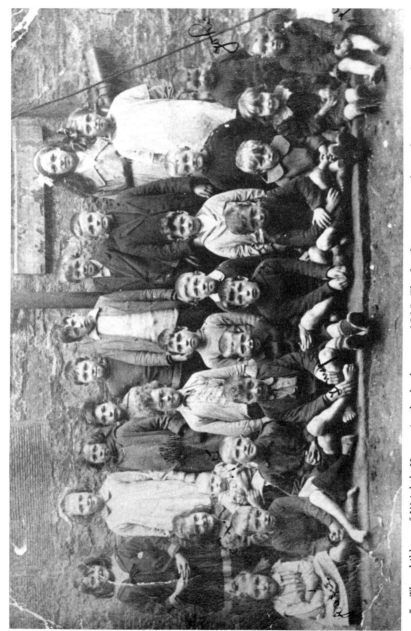

5   The children of Wright's Houses in the back green, 1918. The families represented are the Jamiesons, the Wisharts, the Sinclairs, the Watsons, the Rentons, the Shankies, the Clarks, the Tramnents, and the McIllwricks. Courtesy of AHR.

Neighbours

A network of communities—family communities intertwined with communities of neighbours. People needing each other. A system of cooperation, largely run by the women and extending to everyday help—lending the wheels for washing—as well as to the life and death emergency help in which some women were specially skilled. A friendly environment, unmarred by sectarianism. This was how most people saw it, and many felt bereft when removed from it. Something very precious was lost by the break up of these communities. Yet there were limitations to neighbourliness. Except when help was needed, most people didn't go much into each other's houses. It was mainly on the back greens that the women congregated, passing the word round as to who needed help. Some people, members of a family network, would have a lot of comings and goings while incomers—although said to have generally received a friendly welcome—had fewer contacts. There were social gradations—between streets, or even parts of streets; some of the numerous little village communities, of which the area was composed, felt themselves to be superior to others. Disability, disease, extreme poverty could produce isolation.

The communities have broken up—but the will to be neighbourly has not quite departed from the area, as Mrs Nellie Rogers has found. And some have found it also in their new surroundings.

> The neighbours were first class citizens. You could run to them for help. Any of them. And this is a thing that makes me very, very angry. I had a loan of a book from Mrs White next door, and it said that Freer Street was the worst slum in Edinburgh, and it made me so angry. But we were all in the same boat, and we were happy. I never knew the same comradeship again. It was hame.
>
> Mrs J Plenderleith

> That was our happy days when we were all together in Dundee Street. Neighbourliness was all there. This was a big upheaval coming out here. You have all the conveniences and everything but there's still something missing that you'll never get in the new houses . . . we were all in the same boat. You made the most of what you had. And all the Catholics and all the Protestants. We all got on. It didn't matter what politics . . . the men went up to the local pub and the women sat at the foot of the stairs . . . that was your life.
>
> Mrs Ruby Clifford

> The social life o' the community . . . was a' done in the back green. You know you would go through the back and you would see these groups o' women, that's where they all congregated, that's where they did all their gossiping. So it was a tight-knit community, and if anything went wrong with anybody there was always somebody that would be daein' something about it
>
> Alex Kitson

> It was like history repeating itself. You just done what your mother done to help one another. It was bred into you.
>
> Mrs Frances Waddell

6   Mary Stirling who worked in Harper's Dairy at 151 Fountainbridge in 1935.
Courtesy of Mrs Isobel Grubb.

My mother went to everybody's help, she was at births and deaths all her life, ye just needed to say to somebody 'My mother was Nell Campbell', and she was an institution . . . Visitors to the house—oh never ending, you see a big family, and then somebody was always looking for my mother.

MRS ANNIE HEPBURN

We stayed on the first landin', and to put it bluntly, we were the only Protestants in the landin', the rest were all Roman Catholics, but then everybody mucked in together. If anybody was ill or wantin' anythin' done, they all mucked in. I always mind when my mother was ill for a week that everybody in the landin' knocked at the door and used to say, 'I made a wee bit extra. Here y'are, seein' your mother cannae cook'. For a whole week we got fed like fightin' cocks!

JOHN WEBSTER

My mother was part of a large family, so the only visitors that would come would be my cousins and aunties and things like that. Because my mother was one that didn't really—she kept herself to herself, she never really had the neighbours running out and in. But the neighbours were there if you needed them, which was good, because we had quite a nice stair there. You knew them all, fae top to bottom . . . I think people got on pretty well. there wasn't any of this, oh Mrs So-

and-So's got this, I'll need to get that, because they didnae have the money . . . we
thought everybody lived like us.

Mrs Annie Kitson

We never really had many visitors to the house apart from the family. I mean we
knew all the neighbours and that but they never sort of came in and out, apart
from one who was my father's aunt . . . I think it was maybe because my mother
didn't belong Edinburgh, she didn't know anybody, she didn't have any friends in
Edinburgh . . . We were quite a decent, respectable stair. We had to be, there was
one woman in the stair, she ruled the stair. She used to check that the stair had
been washed properly by putting crosses in the corners, and if it was your turn to
clean the stair and the cross hadnae disappeared, you hadn't done it right . . . she
was just a wee soul too . . . especially if someone new came into the stair, that's
when all the crosses were put in.

Mrs Alice Burt

7   James Thom outside his parent's shop in East Fountainbridge in 1922. The Thom
family also had shops in Fountainbridge (Grants, opposite the Market Bar), Dalry Road,
Great Junction Street and Dunfermline. Mr Thom retired from his drapery business in
1975. Courtesy of James Thom.

The people in Upper Grove Place thought they were superior to the people in Brandfield Street, who had outside toilets. That's the feeling I was given, that well, we shared a back green with Brandfield Street but we weren't supposed to play with the children from there and I was told never to go up through the pends, Asa Wass Pend and that because the children there were really awful . . . I think all the children that we played with, were told the same by their parents . . . I always remember one family in particular, they were always getting covered with gentian violet and their heads shaved, and we were told to avoid them, I used to feel so sorry for the girl, she always looked so lonely. But if you went and talked to her the other children wouldn't talk to you.

Mrs Margaret McArthur

My brother is mentally handicapped as a result of illness as a baby, and as he became a toddler and was obviously retarded, so people outside found it a bit more difficult to accept him, and in consequence me, so going out to play became quite difficult. Children would shout after us that we were loonies and throw stones, and my mother, I found out later, was often told by neighbours that he should be put away.

Ms Liz Allen

When we got behind with the rent (owing to illness) the factor that came for the money wasn't nice . . . that was the only time you felt different to other people.

Mrs J Plenderleith

I've lived in Lauriston Place for forty seven years . . . in the same stair, though we've moved from the top flat . . . all the young people in the stair are very nice and very kind. The neighbourliness that people talk about from long ago, I haven't seen it diminish—not in this stair. I've seen them come and go, they've always been very friendly. Now there's even a new young man come into the stair, I took in some furniture for him and I got the surprise of my life, he came down with a box of chocolates for me . . . one of them just even put that picture up for me the other day because I couldn't manage it myself—'Now don't do this Mrs Rogers we'll do it for you' and they're all quite ready to help.

Mrs Nellie Rogers

My children loved being brought up here [Drumbrae] because they had plenty o' friends. We never sat in each other's houses or things like that but I do know that there were neighbours I could go to if I needed help, the same as they knew that they could come here. I think you will find that in most schemes.

Mrs Ina Begbie

CHAPTER TWO

At School

Jane Curr

During the twentieth century state education in Scotland has changed dramatically. Secondary education was introduced in 1936, but compulsory schooling, from five to fourteen years, was imposed at the turn of the century. In 1947 the school leaving age was raised to fifteen.

For many, the experience of school before the 1950s consisted of grasping the principle of the three 'R's—reading, writing and arithmetic. Few people from the district aspired to higher education and, if they did, simple economic pressures precluded this possibility, either because there wasn't enough money to buy books, or one was expected to take a job to contribute towards one's keep. Others just did not question it. Only a few achieved a level of academic success and moved on to a more comprehensive education, much of which was denied to pupils of schools like Darroch.

Nursery School

As education progressed, school for some people began at the nursery. Lochrin Nursery was opened by Edinburgh Corporation in 1930 in Ponton Street.

> I was the first pupil in Lochrin Nursery and that was purely by accident because my mother, no matter how hard up she was, always bought the *Evening News*. She read that this new Nursery School was being opened up on a particular day, so she went along to the opening.
>
> It was the official opening and as I was the only child there they used me to let the officials see what a child would look like sitting at the little desks and lying on the camp beds. They had orange and green canvas camp beds that we had our afternoon rest on. Each one had a different motif so that each child knew which was their bed. I suppose that was to prevent the spreading of bed lice!
>
> We got lunches there and the thing I remember best was something we never had at home, fish cooked in egg and I can taste it now. It was lovely.
>
> We stayed there morning into the afternoon. It was run by Edinburgh Corporation. I think it was free to unemployed people, but there was a small fee for those who could afford it.

MB

Five years later an article in the *Evening News* of 26 March 1935 reports that there are fifty children and a waiting list of 150. It also reports:

> A small charge is made to each parent if, after paying the rent and dividing the sum left by the number of dependents, more than 6s. per week remain. The minimum charge is 10d. per week and the maximum 2s.

> I must have went there when I was aboot three . . . I remember the nursery more from taking my own children there, but what I do remember is the aprons you used to wear, you used to get aprons to put over and I can always remember a robin was my picture . . .
>
> But I remember taking my boys to the nursery. I was one of the very lucky ones because once you had one child in you got a chance tae get another one in and at that time it was 2s. 6d. a week . . . We took their things and you got their bags home to wash their stuff at the weekend. It really was a blessing to me because I had my children quite quick . . . I mean we didnae work, well we did housework . . .
>
> Mrs Ina Begbie

All Saints Episcopalian School also boasted a nursery as did other religious establishments such as Freer Street Mission and Methodist Central Hall.

> Before I went to Lochrin Nursery School I went to Central Halls Nursery School. I don't know how long I was there and I don't remember very much about it. I just remember a brown romper suit being handed to us from someone, and I happened to be the member of the family it fitted, so I had this blasted brown romper suit on, and we were playing on the roof of Central Halls, and they had this wire mesh over the cupolas and I tore these blooming brown rompers!
>
> MB

> There were five years between my two sons, you see, so I sent him down to that school at All Saints . . . With him being down there, there was a sort of kindergarten, somebody had a room there, and I got the younger one into the kindergarten which I had to pay for. It wasn't run by the council.
>
> Mrs Nellie Rogers

> I even remember a sort of playgroup thing, and there were sand pits and I'm sure that was in Freer Street at the back of Freer Street Hall . . . where if your mother went tae the sewing class, you were put through in the sand pit, you know.
>
> Mrs Ina Begbie

> I remember going to . . . a playgroup, down in Freer Street in the hall and basically getting expelled from there for creating an unnecessary fuss. It was actually because I was terrified of feathers . . . I didn't tell anyone that was why I was having hysterics and I had to be removed. Oh I'd be about four.
>
> I can remember having to take your own playpiece and think even at that time, obviously, you had to be very careful because I remember one day having taken a chocolate biscuit and going to get it and there were two plain biscuits. I remember going home crying and saying my choccy biscuit had changed into two plain ones!
>
> Mrs Irene Kinder

8   Children at Lochrin Nursery in 1930. A newspaper at the time reported that, 'considerable interest has been taken in the new Nursery Schools of the Edinburgh Education Authority, one of which has recently been opened at Tollcross, Edinburgh.' A Miss Cunningham taught there at the time (Miss Peterkin's aunt) and it is believed that a Miss or Mrs Fenton was in charge. Courtesy of Miss Anne Peterkin.

9   The Methodist Central Halls wartime Nursery. Courtesy of Mrs Mary Cruickshank.

Primary School

But for those who did not manage to achieve a nursery place the first day at school was their first introduction to formal education. The majority of children in the Tollcross area went to Tollcross Primary School.

> I remember my first day at school, my teacher's name was Miss Gray and she had on a floral smock, because they all wore smocks in these days, she had grey hair. And it was a classroom with a big fireplace in it, with grey tiles, but it was in the summer, so there wouldnae be a fire lit. You went in the main gate to the classroom and it was the one right facing you . . . there were about thirty or thirty-five in the class, it was a big class.
>
> Mrs Alice Burt

> We had a coal fire in the school which burned very brightly in the winter time and which was blocked off from the class by the teacher and her desk! We had pipes round the class. There was a furnace in the basement, so there was some heating from pipes. There was an open fire in each classroom if the weather was cold enough. The janitor used to come round with pails of coal, and there was an old-fashioned coal-scuttle at every fire, a black iron coal scuttle, and green tiles round the fireplace.
>
> MB

> In parts of it, you walked up the stairway, it was totally unchanged, but there was something—the balconies had been filled in, maybe that's what it was. Otherwise it's not really changed, even the playgrounds and that . . . they were huge playgrounds in our days, as I remember the little shop at the corner next to the school, I think the premises are still there, we used to buy stuff at the playtime . . . I think at one time we weren't allowed out, you had to do it all through the railings, and I think the shopkeepers, of their own initiative, used to come and stand there and do it for you.
>
> Alexander A Alexander

Tollcross Public School was built in 1912 on the site of the old Slaughter House at the west end of Fountainbridge. It was the successor of Lothian Road Public School which was pulled down to make way for the Usher Hall.

The school had room for about 900 pupils drawn, initially from a catchment area to the east side of Tollcross.

Six years earlier Gilmore Place School had opened to provide educational facilities for the children to the west side of the Tollcross area. It closed to make way for Darroch Intermediate School in 1928.

> We both went to Gilmore Place School, and I left when I was fourteen, that was when you left school. It was a nice school, we had to walk away up the Mill Lane and over the bridge and along Gilmore Place a wee bit. We had our tables and sums and drawing. You had to do your lessons before you went out.
>
> Mrs Chrissie Bothwick

But there were other schools in Tollcross, namely the Episcopalian School of All Saints and the Catholic school of St Ignatius.

Mrs Grace Taylor attended All Saints School in Glen Street and she has recorded her memories of the area in her paintings.

> When I do it [a painting] again I'm going to put myself holding like grim death to those railings—my first day at school—screaming the place down. And Mr Blamire the headmaster, coming down and taking me up. But I was quite happy after that.
>
> Mrs Grace Taylor

Children from Fountainbridge were occasionally moved up to Bruntsfield Public School in a period which saw a great deal of movement between schools for children.

> You see Tollcross School . . . there must have been overcrowding or something so if you were a certain standard you could go up to Bruntsfield School. So we passed, Eddie Mitchell, Cathy Anderson and I. I do remember them saying 'Stand up all those from Tollcross School with more than three errors in their spelling'. But we could spell and we weren't standing up. It didn't matter about the rest of them because they were a wee bit more uppity.
>
> Mrs Nancy Barclay

Bruntsfield School was situated up the hill surrounded by middle class tenement buildings. It even had its own swimming pool! It was definitely a step up from Tollcross and Peggy Weddell was impressed.

> At first I was a wee bit timid because to me these people were awfy posh because they came from Bruntsfield, Hartington and all that kind of thing . . . I'm not going to say they were any better than us because I didnae think there was anybody better than us, I think they just came from a different class.

Some children did stay at the same school for the length of their whole primary schooling but others were moved around either by order of the education authority or because of family or personal reasons.

From the records of Lothian Road School in 1900 and 1910 and Tollcross School in 1940, approximately 25 per cent of all enrolled children came from other schools. In 1920 and 1930 the Tollcross School enrollments from other schools peaked to 50 per cent of the total.

One of the reasons behind the high figure in 1930 was the imminent closure of Torphichen Street School. Many children were transferred to Tollcross and, consequently, some Tollcross children were moved out to Bruntsfield School. Parents were up in arms.

> Now I came under that [catchment area]. So the parents strongly objected and they withdrew the children from the school. And we were on strike for six weeks . . . I think the protest from the parents was the distance we had to go to school . . . I think the main fear was the canal . . .
>
> Mrs Peggy Weddell

10   Children at Torphichen Street School before they were transferred to Tollcross in September 1932.
Courtesy of Bill Lawrie.

11   The St Cuthbert's Circle (Leamington Branch) Country Dancing Team—Festival Trophy winners in 1938. Courtesy of MB.

An extreme example of the transience of the school population is George Ramage. Family problems meant that he and his brothers were shuffled round relatives, even as far afield as Ireland:

> I started school two months before my fifth birthday and left when I turned fourteen. During those nine years I was transferred thirteen times and attended eight different schools. Tollcross was my first, third and fourth school. The register book shows me transferring to Tipperary County, Ireland, each time . . . My brothers did better than I. Ronnie attended ten different schools and Andy had eleven. Can you imagine what the teachers think? 'Oh, he's back.' 'Oh, you were only in school for three months at the last place.' or, 'You only spent a week down here.' What can a teacher do with a student who starts piling up a record like that? They can't waste their time on a student like that when they don't know if I'll be pulled out of school the next day.

> GEORGE RAMAGE

The Curriculum

The Primary School was seen by people as providing a fairly basic education to equip school leavers with skills sufficient to survive in the working world or at home bringing up a family.

Mrs Graham, a Tollcross Primary School teacher during the Second World War, describes the conditions under which she worked.

> I started off with 'second years', and then the following year I had the intake—and there were fifty-four of them, which is really dreadful when you think of it now . . .
>
> I imagine the teaching methods would be different from what goes on today. They learnt the tables by rote, which I think is no bad thing. We taught reading the phonetic way, you know t, h, b, and they seemed to get on very well except the backward ones whom you could not in all honesty give the attention they needed. It was survival of the fittest I'm afraid.
>
> There were some very bright children. They learned their tables, learned their spelling, learned to write . . . there was a lovely little book, I can see it yet, of all the phonetic letters, you know a big apple says 'a' with a picture of an apple with a slice out, so that it looked like an 'a'.
>
> Miss Fraser the infant mistress . . . didn't impose a set pattern—we just knew that they had to learn to count and read and spell and write, and oh, there was story telling and a little bit of nature study thrown in, but it was pretty basic three 'R's.
>
> We went morning and afternoon—I think the infant class, for about a month, just went for the morning only, but then they were in for the afternoon as well. I think they got out about twenty past three.

> MRS I D GRAHAM

> They were pretty strict. They drilled it into us. You recited the tables out loud and it really got it in here. I think the discipline was good, it didn't do us any harm.

> MRS IRIS MUNRO

I don't remember the things like spelling that I can do easily, but things like sewing . . . I remember that every single thing that I had to sew I had to unpick it, oh I hated it. And the knitting was nearly as bad although I could knit before I went to school . . . but the sewing was absolute torture and yet I do all my own dressmaking and that now . . . you went up to the top flat for that (sewing). And I liked the music at the school.

MRS ALICE BURT

We got sums, history, grammar. My first good reading book was *Ivanhoe*, there were 2,000 pages in it. To me that was a treasure beyond anything .,. . and I never remembered a thing aboot it! I just read it. It went in one side and out the other and there was nothing to stop it there.

MRS J PLENDERLEITH

The desks were in twos and twos, and the boys of course were at one side of the classroom and the girls at the other.

MB

And at Gilmore Place Primary School in the 1920s,

It was slates, the old slate and pencil, and of course if you did write on paper everything had to be in ink, you'd no biros then, and I was one of the sloppy ones. It was ink everywhere, you know. Everything was pen and ink and blotter.

TOMMY LANG

Religious instruction was also an important and compulsory part of schooling even outwith the denominational schools.

Every morning you had to go in the hall and sing and have a little lesson frae the headmaster. He used to give, I wouldn't say a sermon, but a little bit religious instruction. It was a low low roof this hall and a balcony above us, and that I found a wee bit depressin' because everyone was packed in so tight . . .
You used tae get poetry, Burns and things like that, but actually it wasn't too elaborate . . . It was just basic, 'This is a noun', and 'This is a verb' and 'What's an adverb?' . . . You'd have to write a composition about your holidays or something like that but you didn't do a lot o' writing. One of the things I really used to like was mental arithmetic.

TOMMY LANG

Discipline

Because of the large class sizes and the teaching methods used, the children could not always build up a close relationship with a teacher. Discipline was usually very strict. However, the experience of children at school varied considerably.

12   Kathleen (7 years) and Barbara Fraser (10 years) outside the boiler house at
      Tollcross Primary School in 1922. Courtesy of Mrs Kathleen Morris.

To me when I was a kid at school, your teacher, you put her on a pedestal. She was
something different, something way, way different. Even her perfume. There was
just a certain perfume and you'd say, 'Oh, she's a schoolteacher!'

                                                                    MRS LEXIE LANG

Miss Lees was my teacher then. I started at Tollcross School when I was five, that
was in 1938. There was about thirty of us. She was a heavy built teacher. She used
to walk with this ruler. If you miscalculated [your tables] she used to whop you. She
used to go up and down the lines. If you mistimed, she used to come up and whack
you with this ruler.

                                                                 MRS BETTY LENNOX

Corporal punishment wasn't bad. You'd only see it about once or twice a week and most parents, if you went home and complained, would say 'If you got the strap, you must have asked for it' . . . And the strap was about eighteen inches long and at the end o' it the sort o' tongs, in two pieces, and of course normally you cut across the tip of your fingers, or they'd say, 'We'll give you a double-hander', and you had to put one hand below the other and bring the other one like that.

TOMMY LANG

Well there was the odd smack on the back of the hand. I think maybe upstairs (juniors and seniors) there was the tawse, but not the small ones, there was just the smack. Actually it was necessary—and sometimes come out and stand behind the blackboard, if you were a naughty boy, because they weren't all little angels by any means.

MRS I D GRAHAM

I remember on several occasions being sent down to get three or four of the belt from the headmaster. Yes, I got quite a few strappings.

ALEXANDER A ALEXANDER

We had nice teachers except one, and that was the last one I ever had, and she was a horrible person. When you went into her class on the first day she opened this drawer on her table and she took out a wee tawse, about twelve inches long, and it was thick and it was split. She had these pinze-nez glasses, and they slipped on her nose on a wee chain. You never knew when she was looking at you, and she says to everyone, she says, 'I'm letting you see this. I never want to open this drawer again for anybody, but if I should, Lord help the one who gets it!' She put the fear of God in ye. She was the only one. The other teachers were lovely.

MRS J PLENDERLEITH

All Saints was a great school. They didn't use the strap unless it was really necessary. They would throw, you know, the duster they used to clean the blackboards with. Well I've seen the teachers throwing that, and different things. But Mr Blamire (the headmaster) was the one who done all the strapping if it was really necessary.

MRS GRACE TAYLOR

I had a very nice teacher (at Tollcross). In Bruntsfield School we had some old bitches! Miss . . . . . . , she always had jet black hair which was out of a bottle and she had this wee [raised] skirt. And she had such a temper, what a bitch! And she'd fly up and doon the rows with her stick.

MRS NANCY BARCLAY

It was a rigid system which left little room for individualism. It was quite common, for example for left-handed children to be forced to write with their right hands. George Ramage was badly scalded when he upset a pot of boiling soup while swinging over the fireplace. He received little sympathy from the teachers at Tollcross.

The teachers would not accept the fact that my arm was so severely injured, and they would not let me use my left hand for writing. They succeeded because I cannot write with my left hand. I eat left-handed, saw boards, hammer nails, everything but write with my left hand.

GEORGE RAMAGE.

At the other end of the scale there was the 'teacher's pet'. Irene Kinder who went to Tollcross School in the 1950s used to make the headmaster his tea.

Oh I was a right pet. When I was in primary seven I used to make the tea for the staff. I used to go along and do that before break time. I was always sent out to get a Kit Kat for my teacher. Every day she used to give me money to go to the shop round the corner . . . that was Miss Cant, a really strict teacher, very, very good.

School Dinners

School dinners were not all they were cooked up to be and the experience for many children was not good. For the fortunate, the opportunity to go home to eat was eagerly taken.

When my mother started work we got school dinners. Sometimes they were all right and other times everything was swimming in gravy. And the tapioca pudding . . . you could stand your spoon up in it!

We used to go to the Parish because my Dad wasn't earning enough money, so at that time you got your school dinners, you got your wee ticket from the Parish. Some days they were cold. After you got your dinner, whether it was snow or sleet, hail, rain or sunshine, you always got bunged outside in the playground. You weren't allowed to stay in the school.

MRS BETTY LENNOX

When I was younger I went home for dinner, but then when my mother was working I went to school dinners and they were vile . . . Irish stew, oh I hated it. You either got a meat and a sweet or soup and a sweet.

If you had the soup you had a roll with a lump of cheese and it was real mouse trap stuff. I don't remember much about the soup so it couldnae have been too bad. And there was never any salt, you couldnae get salt for your meal and if you did manage to, it was the coarse cooking stuff and you got the lumps of salt in it.

Irish stew, stewed sausage . . . tapioca and semolina, . . . I've never been able to eat since. I think the only decent pudding you ever got was one that was made out of chocolate and cornflakes and it was marvellous.

When you were older you got to help in the school dinners and if you were crafty, you got the wee ones' dining hall and if the good pudding was left, you could eat it.

MRS ALICE BURT

When you went tae school, if you had a penny on you, you always got a bowl o' soup and a slice o' bread at half past twelve when you got your break. Nine times oot o' ten you used tae have your bowl o' soup in school an' your slice o' breid and then you run home and had another feed. There was no school milk and nothin' free. You always had tae pay.

John Webster

They got a third of a pint bottle every day, which they drank in the classroom at breaktime and then went out to play, weather permitting. But I think probably quite a lot of them went home for lunch because they were mostly from round about.

Mrs I D Graham

I don't think I ever went to school dinners for any length of time but obviously there would be odd occasions, probably when your mother was in hospital or something of that order. It was considered pretty awful, always the same pudding. I would not liked to have had to go.

Alexander A Alexander

I mostly went home for lunch. School dinners werren't as sophisticated as they are now. It was quite simple. I always remember the school mince was awful—it had a terrible, terrible smell and horrible taste. I don't know what they did with it!

When you were in primary seven, you were in the big ones and you got to help to serve the dinners, and this was a big privilege. The dinners cost tuppence.

Mrs Iris Munro

And even if your mother was working, if she could she'd come back and feed you at lunchtime.

But they went to Tollcross School, you see, and I needed them to be at Tollcross because I could get them for their dinners and take them to the Store at twelve o'clock . . . I took them at dinner time and then they had their tea for me coming in.

Mrs Margaret Downie

School Uniforms

From the evidence, school uniforms did not appear to be compulsory which in such a poor area is not surprising. However many parents seemed to prefer their children to wear as much of the uniform as possible.

You had to wear the uniform, as near as your parents could afford. My mother always made sure I wore a gym slip and a blouse and a wee tie, and the first burberry I got—I was right proud of it—and a wee pair of black shoes, and my hair tied up with a big ribbon.

Mrs Betty Lennox

Well we always had our gym slip for the school and we were made to change that when we came home from school . . .

Mrs Annie Kitson

I don't remember wearing a school tie but I remember wearing a white blouse and a gym slip . . . I had a blazer but I don't remember wearing a badge. We didn't have badges or ties then. It was after the war we got badges.

Mrs Alice Burt

You never had a school uniform. If your mother went to a jumble sale or somebody had something you got cast off, you thought you were the bee's knees. And everybody was the same.

Mrs Annie Hepburn

13   Girls exercising in Boroughmuir School gymnasium, probably in the 1930s. Courtesy of the History of Education Centre, Edinburgh.

Secondary Education

At the beginning of the century there was little provision for secondary education, outside the fee paying establishments. But in 1904 Boroughmuir Higher Grade School was opened on the corner of Whitehouse Loan in Bruntsfield to offer a higher education to more able children from poorer families. Such was the demand that it moved into bigger premises in Viewforth in 1914.

Grades obtained in the qualifying examination decided if the child would go on to higher education. Children in the Tollcross area could go to Boroughmuir, or occasionally Tynecastle and after 1928, Darroch Intermediate School, which provided three year courses in technical and commercial subjects.

The decision to open Darroch seems to have come about because of a drop in school rolls in the Tollcross area and overcrowding in some schools further out of the city. The Education Committee of Edinburgh Corporation were also planning ahead for the imminent raising of the school leaving age to fifteen.

So Gilmore Place Primary was chosen as the site for the school and the existing pupils were moved to other schools in the area.

> I stayed in Gilmore Place till I was about nine or ten. Then they decided to make it a secondary school. The school was split up and so many pupils went to Tollcross and so many went to Bruntsfield and a few even went to Merchiston. And the position we were in, we went to Brutsfield and the rest o' Grove Street and Fountainbridge were transferred to Tollcross School.
>
> TOMMY LANG

The result of the qualifying exam dictated where the children would go. Most went to Darroch while it was only a few of the top achievers who were given the opportunity to go to Boroughnuir.

Darroch Intermediate School was a technical three year school where, on the whole, the classes were vocationally rather than academically based.

> I went in for Commercial so I was supposed to get shorthand and typing. But you didn't get that until your third year and I never achieved my third year because I got this exemption.
>
> I didnae object to any of my subjects at my primary school. It was when I went to my secondary school and got algebra, I couldn't make heid nor tail of it. And I was in my first commercial class, the highest class, but it was an awfy thing but I just couldn't understand algebra.
>
> MRS PEGGY WEDDELL

> I went up to Darroch. I remember I didn't like it when I first started. I think it was the uprooting from one school to the other. Then we were put into Domestic for the cooking. Laundry, I liked . . . but sitting doon doing arithmetic and things like that, that didn't appeal to me.
>
> MRS RUBY CLIFFORD

Then I went to Darroch school—I hated the school—I didnae like it one bit. I was forced to go, of course. My mother was sick to death of me sayin' to the teacher, 'I don't like this lesson', and comin' home. And she was havin' to march me back again. And she says to me, 'You'll have to stop this, because', she says, 'you're never going to learn anything.'

So whether or not I did I don't know.

Mrs Betty McAnna

Teachers in Darroch School, I just remember Mr Ferry, because Mr Ferry would throw the strap at you, and you knew when you took the strap that you were going to get it. I was lucky I never got it, the laddies used to get it.

Mrs Annie Hepburn

And a Mr Innes was the woodwork teacher at that time he gave us a real bad introduction to the school—he gave us a' the belt the first day we were in the playground, because they a' started booing the music teacher . . . it was the people who were leaving, but we a' got the belt and that was our introduction to Darroch School. I got to know him very well later and he turned out to be a nice person.

Stan Player

The step up to Boroughmuir was, perhaps, a more traumatic experience.

I thought Boroughmuir was a terrible place at first because you'd been used to the one school and the one classroom and this having to find your way around—you were only allowed to go round the corridors one way. The school was shaped like a figure of eight sort of style, and you could only go the one way. You could go back one class, but if your next class was two classrooms behind the one you were in, then you had to go halfway round the school to get to it. I remember on the top floor there were murals all round the wall.

Then this having to go to different classes for different subjects . . . I quite liked it because it meant you got a change of teacher and you could concentrate on one subject at a time . . .

I quite enjoyed doing homework although we seemed to get a lot of homework compared to the people who went to Darroch.

Mrs Alice Burt

I hated Boroughmuir as a school, I thought it was too big and I thought the standard of education was far too high. I couldnae keep up with it, you know.

George Robertson

And there were gaping social differences between the children who went to Boroughmuir and those who went to Darroch.

Boroughmuir, up the hill, into Bruntsfield, was of a different class, and on a practical level you were liable to get teased or mocked by your peers.

I never went to the bother o' buying a blazer. They hoped you'd buy it. They liked to see the girls wi' white blouses and green and dark green tie, two contrasting colours, and these black skirts. It was a uniform they asked you to wear but everyone didn't wear it. I might have bought a tie, but if I had gone around Fountainbridge wi' a Boroughmuir blazer on, then I would have got ribbed. Then they would have given me the business. You would stick out, there was no two ways about that. Everyone just wore short trousers and a shirt and a woollen jersey. To come out wi' a tie and a blazer on, you were a wee bit extraordinary.

TOMMY LANG

It was an élite school, Boroughmuir. All the dunderheads like me went to Darroch . . . But I enjoyed Darroch, I thought it was a good school.

STAN PLAYER

And I stayed at Bruntsfield until eleven, and then we had to go through the 'Qualie', the Qualifying Exam. You had to sit it in June, and at that time you had a choice o' three secondary schools. It had to be either Darroch, Boroughmuir or Tynecastle.

To go to Boroughmuir, to the best o' my recollection, you had to get 75 per cent or a little bit better . . . It was a different curriculum at Boroughmuir and there was a little bit snobbery. You had to pay about fifteen shillings a year for your books and this made you a little bit classier.

TOMMY LANG

However not all those who obtained high enough marks in the exam went on to Boroughmuir. You had to pay for books and it was wasted time for families who needed all the wage earners.

We had a qualifying in these days and there were four of us, all about the same age and I think Boroughmuir was a feeing school then, I think it was fifteen shillings a quarter, but you had to have so many marks before you could get there. Anyway out of the four of us I had the highest marks but I couldn't get there because my dad was unemployed and they couldn't afford to pay the fees. Which, too, makes you think that your parents were a wee bit ignorant because there was such a thing as bursary help. They didn't know about it, they just accepted the fact that they couldn't put me to Boroughmuir so I'd to go to Darroch, which I didnae regret either . . .

MRS PEGGY WEDDELL

However some children were given the opportunity of going to Boroughmuir to sit O-Grades and Highers if they did well at Darroch. Irene Kinder attended both schools in the 1950s.

Going to Darroch I was being groomed for technical, commercial type work . . . Everyone who was there (Boroughmuir) had had three years of real academic type education. Having said that perhaps because it was more difficult, I really did work hard and I was one of a few who remained there 'til sixth year.

MRS IRENE KINDER

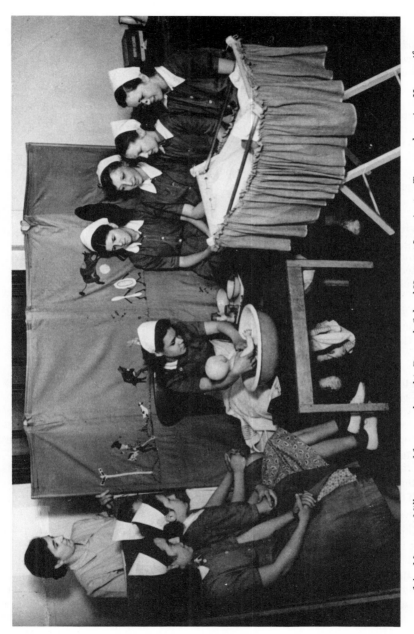

14 Margaret Miller stayed for a week at this Darroch School House at Leamington Terrace, learning Housewifery, in 1949. Courtesy of Mrs Margaret Kennedy.

And whatever your marks sometimes pressure from friends who were going to Darroch forced some to forgo the opprtunity to go to Boroughmuir.

> I went to Darroch because when everybody moved up I wanted to go with my friends, I didn't want to be segregated from them. As it was, in my last year at Darroch I was sent off to Boroughmuir because of the grades I had and the classes I wanted to take we didn't have at Darroch.
>
> MRS BETTY LENNOX

> I went from Tollcross to Boroughmuir School and I quite liked the school but then at night when I came home from the school, my chums were out playing and I was having to do homework and this didnae appeal tae me . . . so I just moaned and moaned and moaned that much that my mother changed me to Darroch—and I was quite happy I was at Darroch beside all my chums. I'm sorry now, I regret it very much now.
>
> MRS INA BEGBIE

Leaving School

For most children in the area formal school education finished at the age of fourteen, although some had the opportunity to continue with night school or day release classes sponsored by the workplace or local societies.

> I always think . . . we were never given any ambition. Nobody said you could be anything you want to be. You left school and you got a job and nobody really said, 'Get your education'. We just did our work.
>
> MRS NANCY BARCLAY

> I left school on my fifteenth birthday, I wanted to stay on but I went from school to college to learn to be a comptometer operator.
>
> MRS ALICE BURT

> I left secondary school when I was fifteen. I suppose I would have liked to have stayed on, but one was required to earn a bit to bring in some money.
>   I wasn't a very academic person and I did struggle at my secondary school. I managed through though. I've just done Higher English and passed it, so perhaps if I'd been able to stay on at school I might have achieved a wee bit more. I wasn't academic at all. I probably larked about too much. I could have done more if I'd paid more attention. Now I've left it to this late stage.
>
> MRS IRIS MURDOCH

Occasionally in special circumstances an exemption was granted allowing the pupil to leave school before they reached the leaving age, normally with a proviso that they attended daytime or evening continuation classes.

> I had to get an exemption . . . I was about thirteen and a half, because my mother

had been left on her own and I had to be there for the nurses. Because you got an exemption, you had to sign a paper to say that you would go to night school, but I couldn't go to that either because the nurses came at night so I had to be there.

MRS PEGGY WEDDELL

But education did not stop for everyone the minute they took a job. Quite often it took the form of continuation classes.

After school I went to night school. The reason I went to night school was to take up Egyptology and History, which I am still very fond of. You didn't get a grant in these days and it was an awful difficult thing for mum and dad to keep me at night school . . . but then again, like everything else, there wasn't opportunities then for us to take further education because it was only the people who could afford it who got up to higher things.

MRS BETTY LENNOX

I used to go to night school from there (St Cuthberts store in Morningside) . . . shorthand and typing . . . it must have been at Boroughmuir School and I got up to fifty words or so.

MRS NANCY BARCLAY

I went from school to college to learn to be a comptometer operator. It was a small college in the basement of Gordon Hotel, Royal Circus—it had just started in Edinburgh and this other girl and I were the last free pupils they took in. The teacher there said to me, forget everything you ever learnt about maths.

I went to night classes for shorthand, typing, English and dressmaking.

MRS ALICE BURT

One form of education outside the formal structure was the classes and exams run by the Co-operative Association.

My mother was a strong member of the Co-operative Association and we were sent to what they called the Circle which was organised by the Co-operative Movement and there we were told how it was started by Lord Shaftesbury and Lord Owen.

Offshoots of this were a choir, which we went to, country dancing, elocution, singing. Then they had an examination annually where we had to write an essay and answer some questions. The best people in each section and each age group were then put forward as Co-operative Queen—we went to Saughton Park and she was crowned there.

But the members of the choir put on Kinderspeil and that was held in the little theatre. That was great fun because you dressed up and most people got something to do . . .

The Circles were attached to the Store Guild and it was the children of the mothers who went to the Guild who took part in these festivals . . . We had choirs, there were vocalists, elocution, country dancing. It was quite a big occasion and they awarded certificates and medals to the top ones. It was quite a thing to get a gold medal. The Poor Man's Mod!

MB

The days of corporal punishment in the classroom and fifty-odd children squeezed into rows having the three 'R's drilled into them are over. The days when a comprehensive secondary education was only for the chosen few have also disappeared. However, the education which people obtained over fifty years ago was perceived by some as better than that of today.

It helped me a great deal. Now there's more computerised stuff. The old way of teaching, you couldn't beat it.

Mrs Betty Lennox

School wasn't a waste of time . . . I think the big difference in schools now is the teachers are too young to take children over, unless they're wee primary kids. We respected our teachers, but when I look at those wee lassies, I don't think the respect's there.

Mrs J Plenderleith

No, I must say I think ours was the best kind of education for the simple reason that the children who come through my office now, all right they're clever and they're more worldly than I was at sixteen, but their writing is simply atrocious and I mean they couldnae sit down and count if they didnae have their calculator there, which tae me, is what helped our brains tae keep going because we've had tae use it.

Mrs Ina Begbie

People

Drew Easton

For many people, particularly in the first half of this century, some of the best known local characters were policemen. Some were known by their full names, such as Willie Blackhall; others also had nicknames. Mrs Weddell recalls Jock McCartney who was called 'Darkie' because of his skin complexion. John Webster remembers 'Basher' Thomson who was a police boxing champion. Even more bizarre is Mrs Lennox's recollection of Gordon, 'the Giant Marshmallow', so called because of his great height and girth.

Nearly all the policemen mentioned were well respected and often well known throughout Edinburgh, as John Webster points out.

> Basher Thomson's funeral stretched frae miles. He was well known in Edinburgh. No matter what religion you were he'd never hold it against ye. I think it was the biggest turnout that was ever known in Edinburgh. Everybody lined the streets as they went on. I think it was Mount Vernon it finished.

Street entertainers too are often remembered with affection. Willie Sives, the spoon player from Newport Street, is mentioned elsewhere, along with Holy Mary the street singer. Many people will recall Mary Capaldi or 'Monkey Mary' as she was also known, who entertained the crowds with ther monkey and her barrel organ, pulled by a Shetland Pony.

Local entrepreneurs were also well known. Asa Wass, whose family scrap merchant business went back to 1858 is remembered for his long fur coat, worn down to his ankles. The Dalton family whose scrap merchant business is still thriving, lived in Fountainbridge from the turn of the century. Mrs Borthwick who was born in 1899, remembers when she was about 8 or 9 years old and was a friend of Maggie Dalton. Maggie's father started the business in a very small way.

> He started with a wee barrie that he wheeled himself, with two long shafts and he used to go round the streets. And on the barrow was a pole with balloons on it. If you took him woollens you got a balloon, but if it were two or three rags, you got two or three sweeties or bits o' rock. Now that man went about with that barrow

for months and months. Then, as he got on, he got a wee float thing wi' a wee pony. Then the next thing, Mr Dalton was in a beautiful car. He worked himself up. He was very well known.

There were many local worthies such as Nell Campbell from Grove Street who was a great organiser and was ready to help everyone in need. Also from Grove Street was the poet William McGonagall (who lived for a while at No. 12 from 1895). He is known to have shopped at Fleming's Stores, as James Fleming's granddaughter, Linna Montieth explains.

> McGonagall used to come into the shop very often and he could never pay his bills. He could never pay for what he wanted, so he used to write poems there and then and give them to my grandfather. My grandfather would take them and thank him very much and grit his teeth, because he'd go away with a hammer or screws or whatever. And he just crumpled them in the waste paper basket—so none of them got handed down.

Perhaps the area's best known character is Sean Connery. He was born in 1930 and lived at 176 Fountainbridge. He was educated at Bruntsfield Primary School and Darroch, and Andrew Laing remembers Tam, as he knew him at school.

> He was always a wee bit o' an actor at school. He was always sort o' mucking about. Bit o' a comedian.

Tommy Lang, who is about twelve years older than Connery, last spoke to him just before he went to London.

> You don't just expect him to be the same now. Its not a matter of saying he's a snob or anything like that. I don't think he is. I think the breaks just went in his favour. The impression I got was he was a very restless person. He never wanted to stick in. He was always on the go but never what I would say ambitious in saying 'I'm going to do this or that'. He was just one of those people that didn't want to hang around.

Indeed the area has seen many hundreds of people over the generations who did not have ambitions in the sense that Tommy Lang means but who were and are remarkable nonetheless. The following miniature family biographies are offered to illustrate this

The McLarens

Dr Alistair C McLaren was born in 1907 at 39 Lauriston Place and was a Medical Practitioner in the area for forty years.

His paternal grandfather, Duncan McLaren, owned an ironmongers shop in Bread Strreet which he kept until his death in 1919. The business continued under the ownership of his eldest daughter, Margaret, until her death in the

1930s. Although the McLaren family no longer have any interest in the shop it is still called McLaren's to this day. Its interior is still reminiscent of a former age and Edinburgh folk will know it better as Ye Olde Key Shoppe.

Dr McLaren's mother, Mary Fairgrieve was born in Lauriston Park in 1876. His maternal grandfather had married into the travelling company of Bostock and Womble's Circus Menagerie and he travelled for several years. In late Victorian times the Menagerie shows were held in the Grassmarket.

His father Dr John McLaren was also a Medical Practitioner.

> My father was born in 1864 and died in 1954. He qualified in 1888 and he worked in the north of England and came into practice in Edinburgh in early 1890s at 126 Lauriston Place. He moved from there up to 39 Lauriston Place in 1902 . . . He was really retired when I took over before the war and then when the war came along I was away with the Territorials and he took over and continued in practice and held the whole thing together until I came back. He was over eighty then.

Dr McLaren has very strong childhood memories of Lauriston.

> We went to bed quite happily with the cable trams running till half past eleven, rattling away. It would start again about 5 or 6, then round about the same time all the dust carts would come up from Kings Stables Road, with the huge Clydesdales with their iron shod hooves and their iron tyres, rattling along the sets. They never disturbed us. And then of course you had the fire engines coming along any time of the day or night.

Lauriston Place was a busy thoroughfare in many different ways. For example, The Royal Infirmary Charities Day was a great family occasion.

> That came along Lauriston past our house. We always had a party on that day and my mother prepared sandwiches and things. My father would go to the bank and get a couple of bags of pennies. And we all stood on the steps and threw these pennies. All great fun.

Weddings, often out of the Rubber Mill in Fountainbridge, were a common sight.

> They used to come marching along Lauriston, a lot of them. You'd hear them in the distance, singing. Then along they would come, with the bride-to-be in the centre, in the front row, with a supporter on either side. They had streamers all over the place and some artificial roses and things like that. But the bride, in the centre, was carrying a chamber pot with salt in it. I have never quite understood why the salt. It was quite a common sight there and they all enjoyed it and had a lovely time of it.

Of the house at 39 Lauriston Place, Dr McLaren recalls it in loving detail.

> Now you went down the area steps to the basement to the back door. There was a

15   Duncan McLaren outside Ye Olde Key Shoppe in Bread Street probably around 1910.
Courtesy of Dr A C McLaren.

stone flagged corridor right through to the back of the house. On the right hand side . . . was a door into a larder . . . stone shelves and a barred window. On the other side of the area (the street side) there were three coal cellars. In the early days of motor cars, one of them was used for storing cans of petrol. I always remember the coal cellar because we would order coal . . . a ton or something at a time . . . and the cart would come along and lift a man-hole in the pavement and pour it down into the cellar.

Then . . . on the left hand side was the kitchen. Quite a big kitchen with a sink in the window. The sink was a stone sink with three taps, hot, cold and main. The heating and cooking was all done on a range and that was on the right hand side facing the window. Down the other side of the kitchen was a long, long dresser with cupboards underneath it. On the end of that was the knife cleaning machine: a big wheel . . . with a handle on it, and you stuck the knives in all round a cawed the handle. Then along the back, above the dresser, a row of lids, ashet lids, the great big one down to the wee one. And a shelf above that with various pots and pans.

Also in the basement was a wine cellar which was not in use, except as extra storage space. There was 'the room we called the Nursery', and also the wash house complete with two sinks and a 'copper' boiler.

There was a door from the wash house into the garden, a narrow back garden. On washing day there were lines and lines all the way down, with sheets and everything.

Up the stone stairs you came to the front hall and the front door on the ground floor.

There was a big door, then a glass door. Inside the glass door, the hall stand with hats and things.

On the right after the stone stair was the dining room cum living room with its two windows sporting venetian blinds, and shutters and lace curtains. One part of the room was shaped in a curve, which included the dining room door and a deep press. Dr McLaren remembers this lovely room with its adjustable length oak table.

The table was always covered with a cloth, a chenille cloth, and in the middle, a pot of flowers or something. Then the electric light coming down from the ceiling was one of those ones you could move up and down—it was great fun. The meals were served and my father served out the meat. Mother would serve the soup from a tureen and the maid would pass it round. Sometimes mother would dish out the vegetables and sometimes the maid would come round with them. Then when we were all served, my father would serve the maids. The same joint, the same food . . . and they took it downstairs.

Again on the ground floor there was the Surgery and the waiting room. Then came the stairs to the first floor.

In my youth the walls of the stair were lined with an enormous collection of stuff my father had collected. All sorts of things. We had Zulu shields, we'd Zulu battle axes, Zulu knobkeries, duelling pistols, horse pistols, flint-lock gun and, of all things, a Tibetan trumpet! Eventually, I regret we kids were allowed to play with them and, I'm afraid, destroyed them.

On the first floor on the left was the spare bedroom.

And of course, in those days a spare bedroom was *the* bedroom ... the best furniture, the new carpet, and all the rest of it! What a lot of nonsense!

Next to this was his mother and father's bedroom and then the bathroom, right in the middle of the house, no window but a ventilator shaft to the roof.

At the end of the landing was the loveliest room in the house. It was actually the drawing room. It wasn't used nearly as much as it ought to have been. It was a beautiful room. L-shaped, and two windows. That [room] also had the best furniture in the house and the main use of that was my mother's 'at home day'. The 'second Wednesday'.

She would retire 'in state' to the drawing room. Her ladies arrived, with their hats on, of course, and they had tea served there: the usual tiered cake stand, sandwiches, little cakes and so on.

The maid who was on duty on this day of the month 'had to distinguish between the patients and the ladies', having to trot up and down the stairs each time the front door bell went!

On the second floor was the children's rooms.

On the left hand side was a boxroom. I loved to get in there and explore it. It had a skylight.

And at the end there was a bathroom ... a bath, a lavatory and a washhand basin. That was pretty well the exclusive use of the maids. We children were somewhat discouraged to use it. That was theirs.

Then there was the maid's room, with two beds.

Educated at George Watson's Boys College in Archibald Place. Dr McLaren won a University bursary to go to Edinburgh University where he studied Medicine. His sister Mary Evelyn, also followed the same career.

She announced quite early on that she was going to go in for medicine and both my father and mother were rather against it, because they hadn't got used to the idea of it, and some of the women doctors at that time were failry aggressive—they had to be—and they didn't like that very much. However, when she eventually said, 'Okay, I'm going for Medicine', my father and mother both accepted it absolutely and after that gave her every encouragement.

His brother, John Fairgrieve, became a mining engineer. He died in 1962.

Dr McLaren started off as a General Practitioner in the area in 1931 with his father and they had many patients in the West Port and Grassmarket areas, as well as further afield in Holyrood, Cannongate, and the Dumbiedykes. Eventually the practice spread, following the patients who wished to remain with the 'doctor they knew', covering every area in Edinburgh, from Corstorphine to Portobello.

> I remember one patient in the West Port—a confinement. I went down and, 'What are you doing here, where's yer faither, I dinnae want you, want your faither'. So I says, 'Well, I'm here so let's get on with it'. And then some years later I remember that same family, her daughter was being confined and the message came and I was at the other side of the town. So my partner was greeted the same way, 'What are you doing here, I dinnae want you, I want McLaren.' There was a lot of that.

The conditions under which people lived, particularly in the West Port, are described from many years of experience.

> There was a lot of poverty. Conditions in some of the places were pretty dreadful, some of it undoubtedly due to the fecklessness of the individual, because I had several families who never ever, no matter what conditions you gave them, they'd never get out of the bit.
>
> The West Port was a rabbit warren. You had Portsburgh Square, which has balconies right round, and I think they were just single ends. I was in a lot of houses in Portsburgh Square and the vast majority of them were as clean and neat as you could find anywhere.
>
> The houses varied so much inside because some of them were spotless others just let themselves go. The sort of thing I came across in one place was a family who drifted. They did midnight flits here, there and everywhere. When you knocked on the door they had to come and lift the door off the hinges because they had broken the lock. They had a great big double bed there and I attended to whoever was in it. Then I heard a noise and asked, 'What on earth's that?' . . . 'Oh, its the dog'. And they pulled a clothes basket out from underneath the bed and there was an Alsatian with thirteen pups. They never paid an account, ever!
>
> Then at the foot of the West Port you had the Vennel, the Salvation Army Hostel. I was Parish Medical Officer and that came into my area. It was the Women's Hostel and I can't tell you how much I respect these Salvation Army people for the work they did. They dealt with these chromic drunks and wanderers, and so on, and they looked after them so well.

Dr McLaren had to move from his surgery in Lauriston Place in 1965 because of a compulsory purchase order. After a long wait he eventually found a house in Brougham Place for the consulting rooms, and lives in the Merchiston area. The site of their Georgian terrace is now occupied by an extension to the Royal Infirmary, fronted by the Blood Donor Centre. He retired in 1973.

Dr McLaren is married to Margaret (*née* Martell) who is a retired physiotherapist, trained at Glasgow Western Infirmary and working in Edinburgh Royal Infirmary. They have one son, Eon Hamish McLaren, who is a Consultant Physician at Stobhill Hospital in Glasgow. His wife, Sue is a Consultant Psychologist, and they have four children, Nicholas (16 years old), Kate (13 years old), and twins John and Robert (9 years old).

Dr McLaren was a founder member of the Scottish Official Board of Highland Dancing, the international authority on Highland Dancing. He was for many years the vice chairman of that body, which he eventually chaired. He is now the Honorary President and still acts as an adjudicator at some competitions.

The Kitsons

Alex Kitson was born in the village of Kirknewton in 1921. He attended the local school, leaving when he was fourteen to an uncertain working career. However Alex discovered, along with others of his age, that there were jobs to be had at St Cuthberts Co-operative in Edinburgh where he began working as a van boy.

> Then of course it was before the war and like everywhere else the employers didnae want to pay full stamps for you, so when you became 16 years old that was you finished. I was there for two years, but I was one of the very, very fortunate ones. I was the only one that came from what we call the country that was given the opportunity to stay on.

Alex graduated—as was the system—from van boy to milk delivery, which was a seven days a week job, delivering to '500 customers every morning' in the Saughtonhall area. It was not without its perks though.

> You built up a relationship with the customers and the customers gave you your breakfast. And if it was bad weather you got cups of tea here, there and everywhere. They would knit you scarfs. There was all that sort o' comradeship went on between the customer and the milk lad.

His first involvement with a Union was that of the Shop Assistants, to which the milk barrow boys belonged.

> If you worked in the Co-operative it was the only place in the country that it was a condition of employment to be a trade union member. When you went in you were told, 'that's the prequisite, if you come and work here you understand you've got to be in the union.' I've never agreed that it should be compulsory, trade unionism. I mean, if the workers want to have a hundred per cent trade unionism that's another story. It's entirely up to them. They'll make it a closed shop, but it's no closed shop in agreement with the employers.

After two years he was promoted to the transport division and joined their union, the Scottish Horse and Motormen Association, later to become part of the Transport and General Workers Union.

Alex describes his experiences of working in general transport as being much more favourable to working in the 'same job every day, six days a week, three hundred and sixty odd days a year'.

> In the job I had . . . you could be working for the meat market, the slaughterhouse, or I could be working for the warehousing in Richmond Place, or I could be working for the undertakers. We used to shift coffins—they made all their own coffins—and we used to shift them from Hamilton Place up to Semple Street. You were meeting practically everybody. You knew everybody that was worth knowing . . . because you moved around the whole o'the Society. You went to the bakeries, you went down to the fishmarket, you went all over the place.

When Alex was eighteen years old he moved into Edinburgh, to McNeill Street, close to the Canal at Fountainbridge. At the age of twenty he married Annie McLeod and they lived with her mother at 149 Fountainbridge until 1943, when they moved to 113 Grove Street.

Annie was born at 149 Fountainbridge in 1921. Her mother had been born in the Dean Village but her grandmother had moved to Chalmers Buildings and then Fountainbridge when her mother was a child. Her father worked as a labourer on the railway and came from Watson Crescent. After leaving school in 1936, Annie also worked in St Cuthberts, in the confectionery department of the bakery at High Riggs, where she stayed until she was married. Annie was then given war work, first painting army trucks and then cleaning submarine parts, until her daughter Irene was born.

By the time Alex was twenty-five he was very well known because of his involvement with the Scottish Horse and Motormen Association. A close friend suggested that he should apply for a job in the union which he did, though unsuccessfully. Soon a second job came up and Alex was taken on.

> It was district collecting in Leith. In the main it was carters. There was not a great deal of motor transport because the war was still on. And the first thing of course was I had to get the Government to agree that I'd be released to go and work for the Union, which was not a problem. I was there nearly eleven years in Leith.

Alex was promoted to the post of National Organiser of the Union based in Glasgow, which he held until 1959. He then became Assistant General Secretary and was promoted to General Secretary later that year.

In 1964 the Union changed its name to the Scottish Commercial Motormen's Union which amalgamated with the Transport and General Workers Union in 1971. Alex was promoted to one of the three Executive Officer posts in the TGWU that year and appointed Deputy General Secretary in 1979 which he remained until his retiral in 1986.

Alex has been a long term member of the Labour Party. He was a member of the National Executive Committee of the Party for twenty years and was Chairman for the year 1981.

Alex and Annie's daughter Irene was born at Simpson's Maternity Hospital.

Irene's sister Joyce is four years younger and lives in Yorkshire. She has a son, Lee.

Irene and Joyce grew up in 113 Grove Street, immediately above the Stores Stables and were educated at Tollcross Primary School, Darroch Junior and Boroughmuir Senior Secondary School. Irene's memories of life in Grove Street are predominated by the sounds and smells of the area.

> Living above the stables, horses were just part of my life. You never thought anything about it. There must have been a dreadful smell but I didn't really smell it at all.
>
> I was always telling people I'd been sleeping with Trigger [Roy Rogers' horse], which I basically was, because they put Trigger on the upstairs ramp, right at the back. My bedroom window looked onto this so I could actually see Trigger's head, a shadow at night on my wall.

The Tattoo was always a great occasion with the excitement of the visiting Canadian Mounted Police, the Horse Guards and the Turkish Horse Guards all using the stables. Close by, the sounds and smells of Dryesdales Coffee Works, McKay's Sweetie Factory and the Rubber Mill are familiar experiences even to earlier generations.

Irene moved from Grove Street when she was thirteen to stay with her grandmother at 149 Fountainbridge when her parents moved to Pennywell. Her school career was flowering and she excelled in several subjects and was offered a place at Boroughmuir School, which was rare for Darroch pupils. Having gained Highers in English, History, French, Typing and Shorthand, Irene was all set to enter Teacher Training College, but as a temporary measure she decided to work at the North British Rubber Mill, in personnel, on which she 'got hooked' and stayed for two years. Irene then went on to work for the Union of Shop, Distributive and Allied Workers, initially carrying out administrative duties, then becoming full time Secretary for West Lothian.

> That was quite strange actually, because when I went for the interview I was quite concerned that I wasn't seen as Alex Kitson's daughter, although it was very difficult with the same name! But I wanted to get the job in my own right really. That kind of plagued me throughout, in that people were saying, 'Oh that's the reason she got the job' . . . I didn't want that to happen.

By the late 1960s Irene had moved on to work at British Leyland in Bathgate, where she went back to personnel work and then on to the American firm Honeywell, where her career in personnel was put to the test.

> They have Appraisal and I'm going to meet with the Personnel Manager to discuss how I was doing and he was saying to me, 'What do you see yourself doing in ten year's time?', and I said, 'Sitting in your chair'. And he said, 'Are you serious?'. I said, 'Yes'. This by the way was before the Sex Discrimination Act. And he said, 'Well I'll give you a piece of advice, if you are really interested in this job you'd be far better looking for work in either Chunky Chicks or Ladybird', because women were

employed mainly, whereas in engineering you were talking about it being mainly male oriented. I was quite shocked.

It was at this point that Irene decided to go into teaching. She taught English, Economics and Modern Studies and latterly Trade Union Studies, when again she found that male domination of the trade union movement presented problems for her, simply because she was a woman. Undeterred Irene became heavily involved with the Women's Movement and helped to set up women's courses on a national basis for the TUC, which she enjoyed greatly.

In 1984 Irene became a trade union officer with the Educational Institute of Scotland and was active throughout the protracted industrial action affecting the whole country at that time.

> It just seemed to go on and on. And at that time teachers had fallen so far behind in their pay. They were really forced into action. I was quite surprised at the numbers of people who took part and the commitment they had to it.
>
> It wasn't just the money; the class sizes, all the new developments that the government were trying to introduce without any extra time being given to do this. Teachers were working hours and hours at home.

Irene points out that assaults are a common occurrence in schools, not only children assaulting teachers, but also, unfortunately teachers assaulting children. Tempers are often frayed because of working conditions, reduced budgets and limited resources.

During her college career Irene joined the Labour Party.

> It was at that time that I thought there's no point in just scratching about here. Much better actually getting and doing something. I had no ambitions politically at all. It just seemed a natural progression.

As time passed Irene was asked on several occasions to put her name forward and hopefully be elected as a local councillor, which she felt unable to do as she was bringing up two young children. Irene has been married twice and was for a number of years a single parent. Later, as her children grew up, she agreed to be put forward for selection as a potential Regional Councillor but when the District Councillor for Haymarket resigned in 1989 she decided that this would be of more interest to her.

> I have to say sentimentality took over and, because of my upbringing here, because of the affinity I feel here in this particular area, I decided that I would actually like to become a District Councillor.
>
> I remember telling people within the Labour Party that I didn't think it was a very good reason to stand; it was a sentimental one. They felt it was one of the best reasons there could be insofar as, if you care about an area, then that has to be very, very important.

When Irene was electioneering, the main issue facing the local residents was the consequences of the Poll Tax. This was a particular concern to elderly people who constituted about a third of the population of her Ward. Local environmental concerns were also common, particularly dogs fouling the pavements. Jobs were seen to be scarce in the area and it had one of the highest youth unemployment rates in Edinburgh.

> This was once a thriving community. There doesn't seem any longer to be a core to it. People tend to be tucked away in their little boxes, and that was seen by a lot of older people as an issue. I think it is very important.

Irene was elected as District Councillor for the Haymarket Ward and she describes some of the problems which people bring to her.

> People come to the surgery with *any* kind of problem. In fact people sometimes come to the surgery with ailments because it is called a surgery!
> Sometimes I've got to say it really has nothing whatsoever to do with the District or Regional Council, but hopefully I can help to put people in the right direction. It can be quite distressing when people come to you for help and you know that really their chances of having their problem solved are quite remote.

Irene has dealt mostly with problems with housing especially older people who are living up a stair and 'feel trapped', not fully able to go up and down stairs but not willing to move away from an area in which they have spent much, if not all of their lives.

Irene's children have now grown up. Nicola is 20 years old and works for an insurance company and Jonathon is 18 years old and works for a firm of stockbrokers. Although neither have strong affinity to the area they are both interested in their mother's work and in their heritage.

> Both like to listen to my father telling stories. He's got some wonderful stories.

The Andersons

Olwen Anderson was born in Toronto, Canada in the year 1919. In 1986 she visited Edinburgh to celebrate the publication of her father's Journal, written between 1903 and 1906, entitled 'No Ordinary Man'. Her father, William, had written his journal in the last few years before he emigrated to Canada and it is clear that he was far from ordinary, although he lived an ostensibly ordinary life.

William was born in 1875 at 1 Newport Street, now a barely discernible cobbled road in the middle of waste ground off Morrison Street. In later childhood his family moved to 1 Freer Street Terrace. William makes an amusing reference to an incident when he stayed there.

> March 3, 1903. I remember a good many years ago—perhaps fourteen years when I would be about fourteen years of age. A friend of mine and I were hunting all over town for rubber with which to make catapults. After an unsuccessful evening and

we were home again to Freer Street, it struck me we might try a little shop at the head of the street. We did and we got what we wanted there. Then we got outside and were near kicking ourselves.

William attended the Vennel School founded in 1843 by the Free Church. His later interest in reading and writing is perhaps echoed by his comments on his former schoolmaster.

> April 23, 1904 I went to Panmure Place and saw the funeral of my late schoolmaster, Mr Patrick Corbett. He was something like forty years in the Vennel School. His career has been a most useful one.

William's father, James, like his grandfather, Alexander, was a plasterer, and his mother, Jane Sessford was the daughter of Joseph Peel Sessford, a carpet manufacturer. William carried out a more humble occupation at the time of his writing. He was a coalman with St Cuthberts Co-operative, a job which he obviously detested.

> February 2, 1904. February has started badly. Yesterday morning when I went out I was surprised to see a dirty, wet morning. The night before was splendid. It has rained continually since. We who are carrying coal in dirty, wet bags are having a rather bad time.

His understatement is the next day turned into a reflection on the world in which he lives.

> February 3, 1904. Still dirty weather. How comfortable everybody is. We are all prospering and happy and yet we are slaving and working in a place that a pig would think twice and not go into. The people who talk about wealth and welfare of the nation are generally those that have a very big share of it.

At the age of twenty-seven, William was married at St Cuthberts Church to Elizabeth Ann Cook who was born in Ysleferra, Wales. Reflecting upon the year 1903 he states:

> This is the first full year of our married life. It has been happy indeed.

However his married life was not without friction, principally because William had many interests which he pursued on his own, while his wife, Liz was at home looking after their first child Margaret, born in May 1903.

> October 7, 1903. I intended going out this evening but alas! 'The best laid schemes etc'. My wife declared otherwise. Our home is like unto a ship of which she is the captain, the baby is the first mate and I am the crew. I am under the stern rule of a stern feminine hand.

From his writing we know very little of Liz other than her reaction to his absences. No doubt hers was a hard life too. However his frustration did not appear to be of a selfish nature. He was an energetic and thoughtful man, deeply interested in the ways of the world.

16   Liz and William Anderson at the turn of the century, probably taken on their engagement. Courtesy of Olwen Anderson.

At the time of their marriage the Anderson's were living at 69 High Riggs but, as the need for more space grew, they moved in 1903 to 105 Dundee Street and to 49 Fountainbridge in May 1905.

They certainly weren't well off, but William rarely mentions money in the context of his own life.

December 1903. 'Early to bed, early to rise, makes a man healthy, wealthy and wise'. I learned that old saw when I was very young but have never yet seen much wisdom in it. I have been an early bedder and an early riser all my life. I believe I am healthy, I think I am wise, but wealthy I am not.

Poverty was not very far away. He records many incidents of begging and, on one occasion, he put himself out to help a man who had been in the Poorhouse.

July 20, 1904. This afternoon an old man was rapping at the door of one of our neighbours. I went out to speak to him. He had left Craighouse Poorhouse that morn at 9 o'clock and had taken until now—5 pm—to come here, during which time he had not had anything to eat. He had come in search of his son who, however, had left that house eighteen months ago. He was downhearted on hearing this but was glad to come into my house where I got him some spirits and gave him some tea. I then went and found his son and took the old man to him.

July 21, 1904. 'Oh, man, it's an awfu' job when a body has tae gang tae the Puirhoose at ma time o' life,' so said the old man to me last evening. Poor old soul! He does not know that it is more than a pity—it is a swindle.

Death too was also a frequent visitor to the area. William records the untimely deaths of friends and relatives in these hard times, but he stands back from emotion and prefers to give his intellectual view even when death occurs in his own family.

October 18, 1903. This morning I went up and saw my sister's dead child. How sweetly it was laid out . . . what a beautiful thing is death in a child, yet how hard it is to console a mother to such a fact. They say it is better away than suffering. But I say it is better away whether suffering or no. What is there in this world for offspring of working people to grow up for? Nothing but misery and hard knocks, and hard working for a living, or rather a starving. Man's life in the working classes is not enviable. The child that dies young is the luckiest child born.

There's not much between death and mirth after all. Last night, while my little nephew was drawing his last few breaths, the people next door were laughing and singing. Truly I cannot think of a thin wall separating two such scenes.

William was a Socialist and attended meetings of the Social Democratic Federation. He was an active member of the St Cuthbert's Young Men's Guild, the Sons of Temperance Friendly Society and the Ancient Order of Free Gardeners. In addition he was a prolific writer of essays and poetry and an avid reader of the Classics. He also attended evening classes at Lothian Road School and Heriot-Watt College.

His active life was not, however, without frustrations. William recalls the great efforts put into promoting political consciousness amongst the labouring classes.

November 30, 1903. On November 12th I took my first active part in the Guild, seconding a debate. The result was disastrous, the principal and I being the only voters on our side while there were ten on the other side. This evening I went up to

50 South Bridge and got five bills for the 'Town Crier' which I distributed in the various newsagents. What a thankless task it is working on behalf of the working classes. This little monthly Labour paper is struggling for an existence, and the people spurning it are those it was started to help, the working classes. I remember seeing Queen, the editor, trying to sell a copy to a would-be swell on Calton Hill one Sunday evening. He refused, as one above such a paper. Yet he is a sweated brewery employee with hands on him like 'baps'.

William's life in Edinburgh was to close with a determined decision to emigrate to Canada, which he did alone in 1906. He was followed in 1907 by his wife, daughter and his son, William, who was born in 1905. He wrote the following poem on board ship.

AN EMIGRANT'S ADDRESS TO HIS CHILDREN

Good-bye, my child, I see your little hand
Waving to me that tender sweet farewell.
Ah! it is good, you do not understand
That I'm about to cross the ocean's swell.
Nor can you on the uncertain period dwell
Of how long your daddy will be gone from thee,
Ah! my wee darling, Peggy, it is well
You do not feel the pain that dwells in me.

Here as I write this message from my heart
I see your dear delightful little face.
I face again the kiss ere we deaprt
The little handshake, all again takes place.
But I my spirits upward try, and brace
As I reflect on when we'll meet once more.
Ah! what a theme a poet's mind to grace
The landing of you on Toronto's shore.

And you, my babe, thy prattle I still hear,
Here on this watery desert, called the foam,
I wonder will you miss your daddy dear
Or think it near my time for coming home?
Nay, I have further yet afield to roam
Ere I return, or bring you out to me.
But, children, be it you or I to come
'Twill do me good each dear wee face to see.

Rouse ye, my dormant muses, rouse ye up
And make my effort worthy of my theme.
Recall their faces that my bitter cup
May after all not quite so bitter seem.
Oh, that I had you here, my little dream,
To tease you with my pencil or my watch,
Or see you try to get the big sunbeam,
Or throw you up and as you come down, catch.

But as I'm robbed of that sweet part
That follows close the first year of your life,
The growing sense, the toddling, 'Willie's smart,
See how he comes to me with laughter rife'.
And thy wee fingers seldom out of strife
Pulling things out from where they ought to be
And happiest with a fork or a sharp knife.
All these things for a time I shall not see.

And you, my Lizzie, who their mother is
With confidence, I think of you, my queen.
And though your faces all I sadly miss
Again we'll have the happy homeside scene.
There to renew the joys that come between,
To live and share our love again, my wife,
And never let a parting intervene,
Till death, the reaper, cuts away our life.

> William Anderson,
> Steam Ship 'Sicilian'
> June 1906

In her Canadian Epilogue to her father's journal, Olwen outlines the jobs which he took and the houses they stayed in. The first was described as a 'shack' costing $30. In a later house there was no water or electricity, and her mother had to walk up to the next block to get water from a well.

William continued to read and write and was interested in the formation of the Co-operative Commonwealth Federation (now the New Democratic Party), a socialist party in Canada. He continued to study and gained a certificate to become a Stationary Engineer. He died of a heart attack in 1942. Liz lived until 1959. In her lifetime she had brought up eight children, although young William died at the age of four and a half years.

Olwen's brother George was a salesman and 'could have sold igloos to Eskimos'. Latterly he worked for a textile manufacturers but died the day after his mother in 1959. Her brother Jim began his working life at fourteen years working for a Toronto newspaper and ended his career as a general manager in a daily newspaper. Jim died in 1986.

Olwen's two sisters Rheta and Peggy were both married with children but Peggy died in 1987. Fred, like his father was a Stationary Engineer, but he too died in 1987. Olwen's surviving brother Llewellyn was a chartered accountant and during the Second World War was 'on loan' to Britain helping with the war effort. Olwen, Rheta and Llew live in Toronto.

Olwen is proud to inform us that the Anderson clan comprises

> about a dozen nieces and nephews, some great-nieces and one great-great nephew. One grandson is called William and one great-grandson the same. One great-grandson also has the Christian name Anderson. There are a number of teachers in the midst, one chartered accountant and a fireman. Several grandchildren are attending university.

17   In 1986 with the permission of his family in Canada, Edinburgh City Libraries published William Anderson's Journal under the title *No Ordinary Man*. The family were so delighted with the publication that they made a bequest to the City Libraries from which Denis Mann (the engraver of the Mastermind bowl) was commissioned to engrave a Caithness bowl depicting incidents in William Anderson's life. The bowl is awarded annually to the winner of the William Anderson Memorial Local History Project, for a study to be carried out by pupils of Lothian Region Schools. The first year of the award was 1989. Courtesy of Edinburgh City Libraries.

Olwen has carried on her father's interest in writing and has a keen interest in the local history of Cabbagetown and South Riverdale in Toronto. During her working life she carried out office clerical work but retired from her full-time occupation in 1972, and has since been working on a part-time basis. She regularly attends conferences, readings and writing classes and she corresponds regularly with Tollcross Local History Project, keen to know more about her family's roots.

The Borthwicks

Mrs Chrissie Borthwick (*née* Benson) was born in Wardlaw Place in 1899 and her brother William fifteen months later. Soon after the family moved to 7 Murdoch Terrace.

> But we werenae very long there because my mother didnae like it, and she went to a lawyer, a Mr Boag up in Causewayside, and she got this kitchen and bed closet in No. 6 Freer Street, top flat. We were up there for a number of years, then she got this bigger house, two rooms and a kitchen down in the first flat in No. 6 Freer Street. Well, I was married out o'there.

Mrs Borthwick lost her father, William Benson, at a very young age and remembers only a little of him.

> My dad was a mason and I just have a faint recollection of him. My dad was an Englishman; he belonged to Carlisle. And I just have a faint recollection that he was a bonny man. I always mind he had lovely auburn hair and an auburn moustache.

She recalls that her mother 'was a bonny woman too', hard working and proud, unafraid of bringing up two children in hard times.

> We had a mother in a million. She did without to give us. She used to always say, 'If you havnae got the money, do without'. You see my mother's people were well off. They had a great big fresh fish shop down where 199 Fountainbridge is, and there was her and my auntie Chris, her sister and two brothers, Jock and Dan. And I mind my mother saying to me one time, 'You know I never knew what want was until I got married'.
>   But, one time, she was hard up and I mind she cleaned my brother and I up, and we were a' decked up and she took us down to the 'Parish' in Castle Terrace. Now you went in, and I always mind, it was a terrible looking place wi' terrible looking people in it, and as we went in, my mother was asked her name, and then you went and sat on this wooden form.
>   Now my mother was sitting and she had my hand and she had Willie's hand . . . and I looked up at my mother, and there was two tears running down my mother's face. She said, 'Come on', and she up and pulled us out . . . 'No, there's never anybody will point a finger at you and your brother and say you were brought up off the Parish'!

So I just looked at her. I said, 'Well, we're a' dressed up and ye're getting nothing fir it'!

Mrs Borthwick's mother worked in the Rubber Mill in Fountainbridge from seven till five whilst bringing up her children. She recalls her mother was the head machinist during the First World War, making rubber helmets for the soldiers. She worked in the Mill until she was seventy-five. Even into old age she was a determined woman.

She had a mind of her own, and ye werenae allowed to dictate to her.

Mrs Borthwick remembers an amusing story which seems to sum up her mother's personality.

And after ma Betty got married, she was takin' us a' to the Kings Theatre and it came tae 'The Queen'. And ma mother was still sitting. And I says tae her, 'Ma, will ye get up'. 'I'm no getting up . . . she's nae better than me . . . would she stand for me? I'd send her tae Ponton Street Washhouse wi' a bag o' claes! Don't you dare ever tell me tae stand fir the Queen!' And she was in dead earnest.

Mrs Benson died in her ninetieth year in 1966.

Mrs Borthwick attended Gilmore Place School until she was fourteen. Her first job was working in a fresh fish shop in William Street, but she left after falling down the stairs in the shop. She got a start at the Rubber Mill, at first as a message girl, but went on to make rubber shoes. Mrs Borthwick remained at the Mill for about nine years and married her husband Johnny whilst working there. He had just started work as a butcher when the First World War broke out and he was away in the trenches before he was eighteen.

By the Second World War Johnny was working in McEwan's Brewery after working for some time for an American company out at East Calder who were digging for oil, very unsuccessfully.

He got started in the Brewery, for his uncle was a foreman there, for the Coopers. He was there for thirty-nine and a half years. When he first went he worked in what they called 'the cellars', but he worked himself up to a foreman.

Unfortunately Johnny took chronic bronchitis, but he kept going to his work. He died in 1962 at the age of sixty-four.

Before her husband died, Mrs Borthwick was back out to work, first doing housework and later becoming head cleaner at Aitken and Niven for thirty-three years. 'Well they gave me a lovely pension; they were very, very good to me.'

Mrs Borthwick's daughter was christened Jean but became known as Betty after a nickname which her grandmother was called because of her jet black hair—'Black Bess'. Betty was born in 1922 at 6 Freer Street, where Mrs Borthwick lived for the first two years of her marriage, before moving to 149 Fountainbridge. Six years later Betty's brother Ian was born.

But Betty stayed with my mother because with it being a big single end, I couldnae have her up there. My mother has the three places still down there to herself in 6 Freer Street. It was a lovely street, with lovely neighbours.

Betty remembers her early childhood with some trepidation. On her third birthday she was on a trip with her family to the foreshore at Cramond. They had an open fire and Betty slipped and fell on the fire. She couldn't sit down for a long while!

When she was four Betty remembers an incident during the General Strike in 1926.

> We were in the High Street. I can remember seeing the horses running down The High Street and my grandmother took . . . and pushed me into a pub! The strikers had been on the march. Whether it had got out of hand or not I can't remember, but they were trying to disband them. It was mounted police on horses. And my grandmother shouting, 'Oh my God, the bairn'!

When she was five she remembers going to Gilmore Place School for the first time. She started at the same time as Katie White and, 'the tears were tripping us'! In September 1989 Betty was to wave Katie goodbye when her old friend emigrated to Australia after retiring.

Betty's first job was in a laundry in Gorgie, which she hated. Soon she moved to the Waverley Rubber Mill at Roseburn, where she started as a message girl. She worked there until her first marriage in 1940. Betty was then put into 'war work' at Scott Morton's off Gorgie where she made bunks for ships and war office furniture. But soon she had to leave to have her first son John, who now lives in London.

After his birth Betty spent seven years working in the Palais cloakroom from afternoon to early morning. Over these seven years Betty saw a lot of life. On one occasion things really got out of hand.

> One night a Canadian chap had been in. There had been a fight and he had got badly hurt, and he had been taken to the hospital. After that about two or three weeks after, a Friday night, a whole group of Canadians came in, vowing vengeance on what had happened to their friend. So we were locked in that cloakroom for hours. When we did get out I think four of them had been taken away to the hospital. The Canadians were just tossing people over the balcony onto the dance floor. It was really awful!

Betty was married again in 1947 to Frank McAnna and had two daughters. Christine was born in 1949 and has three daughters, Carolyn, Lyndsey and Joanna. Linda was born in 1951 and has a daughter Janine, two sons, Danny and Scott, and a grandson also Scott. They all live in Edinburgh.

During the 1950s she became interested in the Labour Movement through Annie Kitson and was active in her local Labour Party branch. In 1964 Harold Wilson visited Edinburgh to highlight the city's slums as part of an electioneering campaign. Betty recalls going to see him talk at the Usher Hall.

I remember going to that meeting because my mother and my grandmother came with us. And the queue was fantastic outside.

I came away feeling disappointed because it was worldy events he was talking about. He hadnae actually touched on things that were happening in Edinburgh, the things that I actually thought he should have been talking about that were happening in wir own district.

Undeterred, Betty is still a Labour Party member.

18   Betty McAnna (standing), with her daughter Linda, grandson Scott Dow (on the left), and (seated) her mother. Mrs Chrissie Borthwick with great-grandson, baby Scott.
Courtesy of Betty McAnna.

Betty's working life continued after the Palais when she worked as a home help with a family at Merchiston for twenty-five years until 1972. During this time she had moved to Broomhouse in 1961. She retired in 1986 after working in school kitchens, finally at St Giles School in Broomhouse.

Apart from being a campaigner Betty is also an organiser. In 1981, after visiting Margaret Kennedy and Annie Kitson, who remembered all those who lived in Fountainbridge, Freer Street and surrounding streets, it was decided to hold a reunion. The first gathering was arranged for 11 December 1981 and fifteen people turned up. Soon a small hall in Maitland Street became inadequate to contain the numbers attending and eventually the reunion meetings settled on Slateford Bowling Club, which holds 120 people in its function room. It meets four times a year, thrice for women only and once for the 'younger element' and their partners at Christmas. A charge is made and any money that is left over is put to the 'flower fund'.

> If any of the group has anybody who gets into hospital, or they have a bereavement, we send flowers or fruit.
>
> It makes an awful difference. We get so many 'thank you' cards and letters from people who said it was nice.

Betty's feelings about the area in which she was brought up can be seen in her poem about Freer Street.

> I took a walk the other day
> And found myself by Freer Street way
> Oh what a change, I had to stare
> For Freer Street was no longer there.
>
> And as I stood there all forlorn,
> I thought of the street into which I'd been born.
> Memories of long gone Childhood days
> The things we did, the games we played.
> The Mission teachers, who taught us how,
> The friends we made, where are they now?
> We all grew up, we moved away.
>
> But what I'd give, if I could say—
> 'Freer Street, Fountainbridge, that's where I stay'!

In November 1989 the Fountainbridge Reunion raised enough money from donations to buy a commemorative seat to mark the site of Freer Street (until now seemingly forgotten by Edinburgh since its demolition in 1967), Fountainbridge, parts of Brandfield Street and Grove Street and all the Pends, in this once close knit community.

Betty's hope is that younger people will realise that a community like Fountainbridge will always be remembered. After all there were many children born in the late 1950s who will one day seek out their old friends in the way Betty and all her friends have done.

19   In February 1990 a bench was placed near to where Freer Street stood, to remember the people who lived in the Fountainbridge area. Betty McAnna is seated on the right of Councillor Irene Kinder, Neil Ballantyne (representative of Scottish and Newcastle Breweries), Margaret Mowat and Annie McCafferty, and surrounded by some of the many members of the Fountainbridge Reunion. Photograph by John Porteous.

The Linns

Nancy Barclay lives in Glendale, New South Wales. She emigrated with her husband Lawrence in 1952, but will never forget her roots in Scotland.

Nancy was christened Jane Agnes Fulton Linn and was born at the Elsie Inglis Hospital in 1926. Her mother Jane Fulton, came from Lochwinnoch, near Glasgow, and her father, Thomas Linn, came from the Gorbals. Her grandfather and his brother had escaped the fighting in County Armagh to find refuge in Scotland.

An only child, Nancy was later told the story of her birth by her father.

> It was terrible weather, freezing cold, and snowing heavily. On the morning I was born he was cycling along Slateford Road when his bike got caught in the tram lines which were obscured by the snow and he fell off and hurt his head. He came to the maternity to see my mother with his head bandaged. My mother was forty-two. She'd lost three babies before I was born, so you can imagine how the man felt. He was fair anxious, and this old bitch of a nursing sister wouldn't let him in. So he just barged his way into the labour ward. Isn't it funny how narrow minded they were in these days . . .

Thomas Linn worked at the LMS Railway Laundry where he stoked the boiler. The work was hard and he was subjected to extremes of temperature between the boiler and elements outside where he would shovel coal to feed the fire. On three occasions he had pneumonia, which affected his heart. When Nancy was later working at Alexanders in Semple Street she recalls that:

> Mrs Buchan, who worked beside me in the Munitions Department where 25lb of shells were manufactured, must have told Mr Mack, my boss about my father having pneumonia, because he came to me one day and asked, 'Do you think your dad would like a wee job here sweeping up the shavings?' He took it and that was the best and easiest job he ever had. He was just getting on fine when he died. He sat up at the kitchen table for two nights. I didn't think he was going to die. I was only 17.

Growing up in 176 Fountainbridge, Nancy first attended Tollcross School, but was transferred to Bruntsfield School. She left Darroch School at the age of fourteen and applied for two jobs, one for McVittie and Price to learn cake decorating and the other working at the head office of St Cuthberts Co-operative. After sitting entrance exams at St Cuthberts Nancy started work in the store.

> Anyway, you sat up there in the ticket office and you got one of thon rubber things on your finger. There must have been 40 of us sitting putting the cheques in order. An old bitch sat at a desk on a platform, she had a bell which she rang. 'Ding/ding'— and one half of the girls got up and went to the toilet—'ding/ding'—they came back.
>   Another 'ding/ding'—your bladder had to go by the bell! This is supposed to be great, working in an office!

Some months later a job came up in the Store grocers shop in Morningside Road, because the young grocers were called into the Armed Forces. This wasn't so handy, but was a little more entertaining.

> So I went up on the Monday morning to start. I wore my hat and coat set and had my wee handbag and my piece. I crossed the road to where the men were standing waiting on the shop opening. As I walked down the road I dropped my piece. I always remember this man, George Ballantyne, a real comedian saying 'As soon as I saw you dropping your piece, I knew you were for us.' He was good with all the women customers. He would shout out, 'Mrs DUNG . . . CAN!' He kidded them on. We remembered all the store numbers of the customers.
>
> They used to have a cellar for the potatoes. They must have loaded them from the top and there was this wee door at the bottom and you shovelled them out. We had a cat as well, and sometimes when you put your hand in to get another tattie—it was cat dirt!
>
> We used to cut and wrap our own margarine from bulk. We had 'standard' margarine and 'special' margarine. 'Special' had a more yellow colour to it. It was softer. 'Standard' was half the price. You know we used to have a special man who cut it, and we had to wrap that cheap stuff in the dear paper! When we had a roll of meat that wasn't selling and it was going all sort of slimey it was cut to a square shape and sold as 'Angel Food'! That's just what that George Ballantyne christened it.

A man who worked in the shop was concerned that Nancy should find a better job and asked his daughter to help Nancy compose letters.

> I always remember she ended the letter with 'thanking you in anticipation' and I thought that was a good word, which I still use today.

After a short time working at the North British Rubber Mill, in the shoe ticket office, Nancy moved to Alexanders in Semple Street, working in the wages office of the munitions department which she greatly enjoyed. She also worked later at the Ethicon Company, Fountainbridge.

In 1946 Nancy married Lawrence Barclay, an ex-miner from East Lothian. It was quite an occasion. Her husband was one of a family of ten and she says, 'they had a big stack on their side'. Nancy had several second cousins, but not as many relatives as Lawrie.

> So everybody in my stair, ages wi' me and older, all came to my wedding. They had a ball!
>
> Of course, the Guildry girls all came. Miss Herdman asked, 'Can we have a Guard of Honour?' . . . 'Oh yes, Miss'. Because I kept in it[the Guildry] right up to when I was twenty. They were all standing outside St Cuthberts Church and Lawrie was astonished when he saw them.

At this time Lawrie was in the Royal Navy. A stoker.

20 The wedding of Agnes Linn and Lawrence Barclay in 1946, with a Girls Guildry Guard of Honour. Miss Herdman stands on the extreme left of the picture and Miss Brown on the extreme right. Courtesy of Mrs Nancy Barclay.

He had a couple of trips to Australia on the aircraft carrier, *Formidable* returning Australian prisoners of war back home. He liked the country. He went riding about on horses and on the beach, and all that, which we never do.

Later he came back and worked in the Dumfriesshire Dairy for a while, worked in the SMT battery shop and also returned to mining. He always wanted to go to Australia, so Nancy filled in the forms. She had hoped her mother would also come but she was advised not to travel because of ill health and later died before the couple finally made the move.

They had joined the Emigrants' Club where they were shown films about Australia and told of the wonderful opportunities to be had there. Unfortunately when they arrived it was the end of the financial year and no work was available in Sydney. They joined the long queue of unemployed at the labour exchange. 'This—after all the bullshit we were given!'

Lawrie eventually found work on a huge sheep station.

> There was a job in Katoomba for me in a guesthouse if I wanted it, while the 'house' was 'being prepared'. I took the job.

Lawrie then came back to meet Nancy in Katoomba and, after a long slow railway journey inland, they arrived at the house.

> The ground was solid hard, all cracked. The house was wooden with an iron roof. You could see where the bales of hay had been piled up the walls. It had only been a storage place. The rats were still in the ceiling. You had a brush and when you swept the floor . . . you didn't need a shovel because all the dirt fell through the floorboards! The door was about two inches off the ground so was no deterrent to flies or blow flies. We had a parrafin lamp. A basin for bathing. The only butcher meat we had was mutton which was usually fly-blown with maggots.

To someone, who had come from a Fountainbridge tenement this experience was quite alien. Spiders came up through the floorboards and cockroaches came out at night, 'big whopper cockroaches'. And Nancy endured this all day on her own while her husband was at work. Flies pestered all day and mosquitoes at night and there were venemous tiger snakes. The heat was scorching!

> We had tankwater which was warm and it was all lousey with mosquito larvae— so you had to boil it all. We had an auld grate in which we burned wood. That's where I did my cooking. I did my washing in a petrol can. I used to iron with a flat iron, but I gave up on it. Who could dee me? Naebody! You could have run about naked!

During this period Lawrie worked for the owner-farmer (Cocky) putting up fences, miles and miles of them, building silos and driving wheat trucks, six days a week. Nancy who was pregnant, spent her days in solitude. Luckily for both Nancy and Lawrie they were only to stay there for seven months.

I gave up Fountainbridge to go there! Not having known any other life than in Fountainbridge I was quite happy. I had the best of friends and the best of neighbours and everything I wanted. What else can anybody have from life than just three meals and friends with good health? But oot there I was going mad, and I didn't want a vet to deliver my baby. It would have taken him a couple of hours to reach us anyway.

They went back to Sydney and eventually Lawrie found work in Newcastle through a second cousin of his at Broken Hill Propriety Company, a steel works.

We bought a piece of ground. We didn't have much money. I didn't even know where I was when I was driving round with the estate agent. I'm happy there now because its central and we have great neighbours.

Our plot of land was about 130ft long and 118ft wide. We built a garage there, 24ft by 12ft and lived in it for an awful long time.

I helped to build my house, except for the roof—we had a tiler in for that and a tradesman for the plumbing and electricity. Other than that we did it all ourselves.

Nancy didn't work whilst her children were young. As soon as they were at school, she found work, first selling cleaning brushes, and then demonstrating hand massage equipment for arthritis and other complaints. However, she didn't make much money out of this and a friend managed to find her cleaning work at the nurses home at Newcastle Hospital.

Her cleaning career brought her into contact with books in the nurses home library which she found fascinating. Nancy was forty-seven years old and had not had a chance to know what opportunitites may have been open to her in nursing but she showed great interest and enthusiasm.

A nursing sister told one of my friends, 'when she [Nancy] comes back from her holiday, tell her to just put her name in'. I did.

She had to go and see the matron but received only discouragement, probably because she was seen to be just a cleaner and was far older than most who take up nursing. Nancy asked for a Vocational Guidance Test which proved she would be a suitable person for the nursing profession.

When I did my nursing final examination I got a distinction in marks. I loved working with the patients. I wish I'd started nursing in the beginning. I was there about ten years.

Nancy completed her nursing career at the William Lyne Hospital where she helped rehabilitate stroke patients and amputees to return to normal life.

Nancy looks back to her last days cleaning with pride. 'And so one up for the Cleaners!'

In 1989 Nancy returned to Edinburgh for a holiday in which she renewed old friendships. She said.

Now I'm really happy, although I wish I could take Edinburgh with me, because I love it.

I've got fantastic friends in Australia. You could say I'm Australian now. I go about in my bare feet quite often, and swim every morning at 6 am. My old friends, in Scotland are always in my thoughts. I love them.

Nancy and Lawrie have three children, Lawrence Linn was born in 1953 and is a conveyancer in Sydney. He has two children, Aidrian James and Erin Linn. Jane Fulton was born in 1961, lives in Glendale and works in a pipeline supplies company. Dianne Margaret was born in 1966 and now lives in Sydney. Dianne is an art graduate and works for Wills, the cigarette company.

Before Nancy returned to Australia she confided that she felt like crying at the changes in Fountainbridge. It was to her 'the rape of a community' that so many tenements were demolished and never replaced.

I've read things about being brought up in the slums. It's a lot of rubbish. It was the slums but people had the wrong impression. Everybody in that stair was like my family, very special to me.

But Nancy knows that, even if you take away the buildings, you do not remove the spirit of the people who lived there. The distance to Australia is only a step away from her roots.

The Langs

Tommy Lang was born in 1917 and now lives in Penicuik with his wife Lexie. Tommy was born in Colchester, Essex, where his father Tammy was stationed with the Second Scottish Rifles. His sister was also born there in 1918 but the family returned to Edinburgh in 1919 where his brother was born a year later.

Tommy recalls that his grandmother Catherine Buchanan came from a reasonably well-to-do family.

Her father used to own one of the biggest hansom cab businesses in Edinburgh . . . Anyway, the father married again and the second wife took over the business and the business drifted out of my grandmother's control. (I think someone told me someone like Croalls bought them out. This must have been in the 1890s).

This woman he married was a bit of a mistress and my grandmother left home and went up to Dundee to work in the jute mills. She worked up there for oh, just a pittance in those days, I would presume.

On her return to Edinburgh she married James Lang, who was a carter, and their son Tammy was born in Semple Street in the 1890s. At an early age he joined the Army in 1912 as a regular and, up till the outbreak of the First World War was stationed in Malta. During the war he served in France and was twice wounded.

After the war my father just worked generally as a labourer. Work, as far as I can remember, was very hard to get, there wasn't a lot of skilled work around. I can remember him working as a labourer somewhere down by Cramond. I've no idea what he was working on but . . . he wasn't accustomed to the physical work as a labourer. He was a fit man, being an ex-Army boxer, but the physical labour wi' a pick and shovel—he used tae come home at night and he was really exhausted.

Times were harsh in the post war years but Tammy was luckier than most when his mother gave him money to buy a shop at 158 Fountainbridge. Tammy's father had died in 1917.

It was a very, very tiny shop. A window about 6 feet wide, 6 by 6. If you got more than six people in it you were crowded. You were standing on top of each other.

Tammy was also a determined man.

I think if he hadn't died so young we would have moved from there into far better things.

He wasn't a man who wanted to stand still. He was a man with ambition; different from myself. He was prepared to go on, you couldn't shout him down. If he wanted something and you said no, he'd keep going and keep going, and he'd check all corners to try and advance himself.

21 Outside Tommy Lang's Ice Cream shop at 176 Fountainbridge stands Duncan Moncur (on left), John Edwards and Andrew Edwards, who were all in the Navy during the Second World War. A caption at the side of the shop doorway read: 'Try Lang's Ices—Oh Boy they're hot stuff'. Courtesy of Mrs Chrissie Allan.

The shop sold ice-cream, confectioneries and cigarettes and was run by Tammy and his wife Violet. However, Tammy was not content with this.

> He used to have an ice-cream stall in Harrison Park. At that time the Corporation were beginning to lease these little stalls, like one of these huts you'd get to keep your garden tools. He got a hut like that and he used to transport the ice-cream out in his freezers with the ice all packed round, and candies and cigarettes. And he was beginning to look for concessions in these other parks, plus he was trying to negotiate at the time for the concession to sell chocolate and that at Tynecastle and in those days it was a very big thing. There were forty-odd thousand people and there was nobody else selling there.

And he wasn't idle in his spare time. Although he boxed in the Army and won championship titles he did not compete professionally as we would know now. He subsequently used his skills to motivate others.

> He'd taught these youngsters up Fountainbridge at the Freer Street Mission. It's funny I was at a reunion recently and a guy came over to me and says 'You're Tammy Lang's son?' and I says, 'Right, Ye-es?'. 'Well I remember' he says, 'your father made me what I was. I wouldn't do anything and I went down to the boxing club and he taught me boxing and I went out to Canada and I held my own with them out there, just with what he taught me. I've got an awful lot to thank him for.'
>
> He [Tammy] just couldn't stand still. He got into things. He was prepared to try his hand at anything. He was a very dominant person, but for all that, he'd do anything to help you.

Tammy was also an ardent Hearts fan. However he was a small man and often, within the crowd, he could only see the ball when it was in the air. He was also very frustrated at times with Hearts' performance on the field. One day he let go and shouted at the top of his voice 'COME AWAY HEARTS'! *The Sunday Post* on 20 January in 1935 took up his story:

> The result dazed him. The referee dropped his whistle. Players stopped in their tracks. Night-shift workers, sound asleep in the neighbouring tenements, tumbled out of bed and scrambled into their dungarees. Corner flags were jerked to a rakish angle. But, best of all for Tammy, the space in front of him was as vacant as a dance band crooner's stare!
>
> He's wee—but game. Visiting fans to Tynecastle have often thought they were on an easy thing when they tried to curb his enthusiasm by vocal and physical means. They know better now. Tammy Lang was a big-time feather-weight boxer in his youth. He beat two champions in the one night—Harry Smith, Dunfermline, and Bob Baxter of Musselburgh.
>
> But Tammy has a sense of humour. One day an elderly lady behind him reprimanded him. 'Please be quiet!' she rapped out. Tammy turned round pleadingly. 'Oh, lady, give me a chance,' he begged, 'I can't get saying a word at home. Now you won't let me speak out in the open.'
>
> The lady relented. 'Oh, is that the way of it, sonny? Then just carry on as long as you like.'

22   Tammy Lang at Tynecastle Park in the early 1930s. The photograph is signed by
the Hearts Football Club Manager, Trainers and Players. Courtesy of Tommy Lang.

His son adds to the story:

> In the area everyone knew each other and being a personality down at Tynecastle
> at the Hearts football ground, he wasn't just known in the Fountainbridge area by
> this time. People from away out by Gorgie and all around the surrounding area: sort
> of, 'Oh aye, that's the man that shouts at Tynecastle'.

It's hard to imagine how one man can be heard over the whole ground, but you see you didn't have the PA announcements like you have now. Everything was just shouted around. And he'd just wait till there was a sort of lull and he would suddenly bellow out this 'Come Away Hearts'! And everyone in the ground could hear him.

He wasn't a loud speaker. He didn't talk very loud. But when he bellowed, it was like those sergeant-majors in the army. And you've got forty-odd thousand people going to this match every week, or every second week when they played at home. He got known.

Sadly not for long, as Tammy was to die at a young age in 1935. He was buried at Merchiston Cemetery after a military funeral.

And the floral tributes: there was a big one actually frae the Hearts theirsel, a big maroon and white heart. I still remember it, frae the directors and players of the Tynecastle club. That's how he was well known, basically between having the shop and being known there. He'd lived there all his days.

Tommy's mother kept the shop on and sometimes had to work seven days a week from 9 am to 9.30 pm. Tommy remembers the hard work making the ice-cream.

She had to make the ice-cream herself, and it wasn't an easy job. The milkman used to deliver milk in two or three gallon cans and she used to have a double boiler, and you filled it with water. Then this other inset went in and you put the milk in this. She used to boil thee or four gallons of milk herself on this little ring till it was boiling hot. Then she added the ingredients: sugar, ice-cream powder, . . . to the right consistency. Then she had to let it cool off, and then she poured it into these big white enamel pails . . . covered . . . wi' a muslin cloth. Then she had to lift it up on shelves to allow it to cool off. It was boiling hot. At one time she knocked one over on her leg and badly burned it.

It used to lie on the shelf till the following day. Then you'd a big freezer, we used to pack it with ice and salt and . . . we used to turn it by hand. It was a killer, especially when the ice-cream got really thick.

I used to have to go round to the ice factory . . . round at Lochrin, where Arnold Clark's the motor dealer's are—right next to there and get two big blocks o' ice.

His mother died when she was 55-years-old , in March 1945. Tommy was still in a prisoner-of-war camp.

She had the business right up to the end. And then when she died my sister tried to keep it running. We kept it running for another couple of years, right up to something like 1947.

Tommy met his future wife Lexie in 1936 and they were married in 1941 at St Cuthberts Church. He had left Boroughmuir School at the age of sixteen. A school teacher had asked his class before he left, 'Now anyone wantin' tae be an apprentice tae the printing trade?'.

Now, I had no notion. I just couldn't have cared less. But I went home and I happened tae mention it at home, and my father says, 'Oh, now that's what ye want tae get intae. So and so along the street, he's a reader at T and A Constable's and he gets a lot more money than anybody else around here. He's got a good paid job. They're well paid. Put your name down for it'.

So I went ahead and put my name down and got called up for an interview by the Master Printers' Guild. They sent us tae the University and we had a test o' wir capabilities, reflexes, and a little examination in English and mental arithmetic, and agility tests.

I can still remember one o' them quite plain. There was two metal bars, and they were quite wide at the top, and they tapers as they went down. It was graduated. They gave you a metal pin and you had to drag it down the middle, and go down as far as you could until you touched one side. The minute you touched one side you made contact and the bell rang.

And of course they took down how far you'd gone sayin, 'steady hand', or whatever the test was for. So they said, 'Fine, we'll call you'.

His first job was as an apprentice with Nelson's printers at the top of Dalkeith Road, which has since closed down business in Edinburgh. However, six years later he was registering for the 'call-up' in October 1939.

During his long and eventful period abroad during the war, Lexie worked in a chemical factory in Wheatfield Road where she made medicinal tablets and saccharine. In 1954 the Langs emigrated to the United States where Tommy continued his work in the printing trade and Lexie worked in a chemical laboratory. They retuned to Edinburgh in 1956 but went back out to Chicago again in 1964, finally returning to Edinburgh in 1980.

Tommy and Lexie have a daughter, Margaret who was born in 1946. Margaret is married and has two children, Susan who is 23-years-old and Julia who is 19-years-old. In 1990 Tommy and Lexie celebrated the birth of their first great grandchild, Danielle.

Tommy retired in 1982 from Pillan and Wilson, Printers. The Langs now live in Penicuik.

CHAPTER FOUR

To Earn Their Daily Bread

George Brown

The teeming tenements around Fountainbridge were primarily barracks for workers needed by the large factories in the area. Their construction dates coincided with the expansion of the larger industrial concerns in the district in the latter half of the nineteenth century, for example, the North British Rubber Mill and McEwan's Brewery. In those days and well into the twentieth century, all forms of production were labour-intensive.

Female workers were required in many of the manufacturing processes, to such an extent that the traditional stay-at-home housewife was the exception rather than the rule. Unless a woman was housebound caring for young children, she would be out earning a living. Everyday economic necessity provided the spur.

Local people, both male and female, were educated from childhood by family and school to expect no other future than finding their place in the labour market, usually to do manual work. The 'Protestant work ethic' was deeply ingrained on the population of Fountainbridge.

> But then again, like everything else, there wasn't opportunities then for us to take further education, because it was only the people who could afford it who got up to higher things. I had to give up [school] and take a job.
>
> Mrs Betty Lennox

> I was fourteen when I left school. Nae option. No I didn't find my schooling useful.
>
> Mrs Annie Hepburn

> I left secondary school when I was fifteen. I suppose I would have liked to stay on, but one was required to earn a bit, to bring in some money.
>
> Mrs Iris Munro

> . . . because I went to Darroch I was able to leave when I was fourteen, so I was really only two years at secondary, you could leave in March or summer, and my birthday was January so I left in March.
>
> Mrs Ina Begbie

23   Girls from the Bottling Hall of McEwan's Brewery Fountainbridge in 1916.
Courtesy of Mr William McKay.

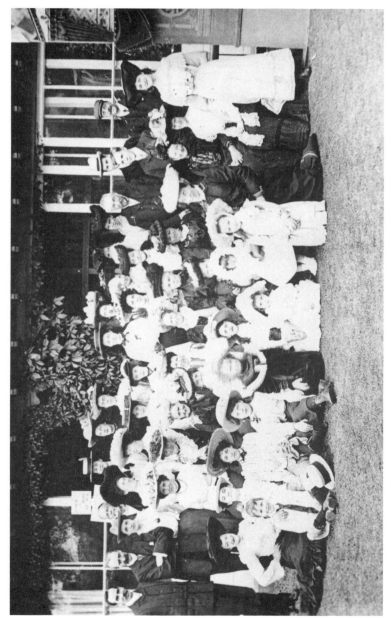

24   Employees and their families, from Flemings Stores sometime between 1909, when the Earl Grey Street shop was opened, and 1912 when James Fleming (standing on the extreme left) died. There were also Fleming's Stores at Home Street and later in St John's Road, and in the 1960s at Lochrin Place where they sold white wood furniture, popular at that time. Courtesy of Mrs Linna Monteath.

Annie Kitson's regrets are even more forcefully expressed.

> I left school in March 1936 and I went to the High Riggs. I can remember finishing school on the Friday, I was fourteen in September and this was March. I was about fourteen and a half, and I didnae want to leave school, I liked school. I cried when I left school. I would have stayed on. But we never got the opportunity. And it was a case o' it wasn't what you wanted, it was what job was available.

The men felt the same pressures as John Webster recalls.

> I left Darroch when I was sixteen. I'd done the Higher School Certificate. It was then 1936 and jobs were hard to get, and the biggest majority o' the lads leavin' school then joined up, and I joined up masel.

Their prospects were patently limited.

Locals were likely to have experienced the joys of work at an early age, as Annie Hepburn recounts.

> I did paid work as a child frae I was ten years old. I went papers in the morning and papers at night. Then when I got a bit older I worked in the dairy, and then I had a wee job at night up at Bruntsfield delivering—it was what they called the Umbrella shop. You starched the stiff collars and then you were sent to the houses. For that you got about 2s. 6d. a week, and for the papers much about the same.

> I used to do the milk in the morning before I went to school . . . on the milk floats at five o'clock, away across to the dairies at Gardners Crescent, and help deliver milk in my own area . . . Fountainbridge Gardners Crescent and Freer Street. At the end of the week I think I got about 2s. 6d. which I thought was marvellous. But my mother used to take it off me and give me sixpence.
>
> MRS BETTY LENNOX

> Before I left school, my mother . . . had a friend who was the manageress in the Buttercup Dairy at the top of Temple Park, so she thought I should go into the Buttercup Dairy. So after school I had to go there and do my two-hour stint delivering messages, making up butter, and that was when you patted the butter and you weighed the sugar and what have you, but you also had to wash this floor. The Buttercup Dairies were all black and white checked linoleum and I mean they were spotless . . . I remember I had to go up to Spylaw Road, wi' these orders, so you went in the tram car away up to Spylaw and then came back and it was snowing out and it was cold an' oh, I was awfie sore fur masel. So when I came back intae the shop it would be maybe a quarter to five, well you worked till six. So she says, 'Hurry and make yourself a cup o' tea because you've got the floor to wash'. Well, you can imagine what the floor was like, it was filthy wi' the snow from outside . . . so I'm sitting having this cup o' tea and feeling sorry for maself, I was freezin' and I was miserable and she comes through and says, 'Are you going to get started?' I says, 'I cannie wash that floor its too dirty', and I remember cryin' you know. I had tae wash the floor, there was no way . . . but I never ever went back and that was

the finish of the Buttercup Dairy. But I always worked . . . I mean I delivered early morning milk: we just a' done these things, it was automatic and it never done me any harm, least I don't think it has, unless it's worn my body oot quicker than it should have been!

Mrs Ina Begbie

Mr A Alexander remembers working on his own account.

I also remember selling firewood, sticks, you know round the doors to make money, getting empty boxes from the fruiterers, they used to throw them outside and you used to take them. You didn't pay for them, and just chopped them up. My brother was the organiser, he had two or three of us all going round doors, he'd get the money and give us so much back. He was a real business man, sort o' style, with the firewood. Yes he had all his good customers and the good districts, he'd go to the posh districts.

When eventually they were looking for their first adult job, how was it achieved?
There were variations.

My first job as an adult was actually working in St Cuthbert's Laundry at Chesser Avenue. Somebody that my mother knew that worked in there said that they were looking for young lassies from the school, and my mother happened to say, 'Oh well, my lassie's looking for a job'. So I was sent along and I started.

Mrs Betty Lennox

My first job would be a junior in an office, an office girl. I did evening classes at McAdam Secretarial College in order to qualify in shorthand and typing. My job was advertised in Boroughmuir School, up on the board. I did all the running about, making the tea, the post and all that.

Mrs Iris Munro

Then Peggy Weddell had a different approach.

I sat the 'Store' exam. You had to go up to 92 [Fountainbridge] and sit the Store exam before you could ever work in the Store. And I passed the Store exam, so I didn't feel my schooling was altogether wasted. I think, at thirteen and a half folk might laugh at it now, but I achieved the Store exam.

Tommy Lang obviously had the potential to achieve a better life.

How I got intae the printin' trade was, they come round the school once, at Boroughmuir, when I was about 15 or 16, and they said, 'Now, anyone wantin' tae be an apprentice tae the printin' trade?' Now I had no notion. I just couldn't have cared less. But I went home and I happened to mention it at home, and my father says, 'Oh, now that's what ye want tae get intae. So and so along the street, he's a reader at T and A Constable's an he gets a lot more money than anybody else round here. He's got a good paid job. They're well paid. Put your name doon fir it'. So I went ahead and put ma name doon an got called up for an interview by the Master Printers' Guild.

So I got word to start as an apprentice in Nelson's at the top o' Dalkeith Road. At that time, I think, Nelson's was the top notch printers in Edinburgh. There was a lot o' big firms, Morrison and Gibbs, T and A Constables, which are all gone out o' business completely. There's none o' them are there now.

In comparison Annie Kitson comments.

It was somebody that my auntie knew . . . her husband or a friend of his, said that my mother should take me up here. So I remember going up there and there was a job in what they called the icing room at that time, learning to decorate cakes, which was a trade, which was very good. But I'd never thought of doing anything like that, it was just the job was there and you were put into it.

Then again Mrs Thompson's experience was different.

I went to the Women's Employment Bureau in Rose Street—I think we all had to, and I got it there. There was another job in an ironmongers at Goldenacre but I didn't get that.

Alex Kitson was even obliged to move from his home to Fountainbridge.

I was born in a little village, Kirknewton, about 15 miles from here and I was brought up in the village, educated in the village, and left school at fourteen and I came to Edinburgh. I came into Edinburgh and I got a job with St Cuthbert's Co-operative, in Fountainbridge. I think about that time there were about three courses, you could either get a job in the pits, you could get a job on the railway or you could get a job in the local authority. And well, they were all taken up, it was like the old dockers tradition, you know, if your grandfather worked there, and your father worked there then you had the best chance to work there. So I never had that possibility. And it was the younger element, we suddenly discovered we could get a job with St Cuthberts. So there was quite a crowd of us that started our working life in St Cuthberts Co-op.

Alternatively there was the direct approach utilised by Robert Stuart who was determined to get a job with Alexanders in Semple Street. When the foreman interviewing him asked, 'Why do you want to be a coachbuilder?'. 'I like wood', was his short, direct and successful answer.

Or it could happen coincidentally.

Ah met one o' the chaps ah went tae school wi'. Ah said, 'What're you workin' at?' 'Oh ah'm workin' wi' the lorries, ah'm workin' wi' Mackays, (the sweetie works)'. He said he wis gettin' 17 shillings a week an ah wis jist gettin' 16 shillings. So ah went tae Mackays. Ma muther was gonni murder me!

ANDREW LYNCH

The Mill

'People swear by
(and sometimes on winter mornings at)
the sound of the hooter from the
North British Rubber Company's
Castle Mills at Fountainbridge, Edinburgh.
It regulates their lives.
They get up in the morning,
and they know to stop work, when it sounds.
They set their watches by it;
They eat by it; some have depended
on it for more than 50 years'

'It blows six times a day—at 6.55 am,
7 am, noon, 12.55 pm, 1 pm and 5 pm.'
Evening Dispatch, Monday 22 May 1950.

As the largest factory in Edinburgh, the 'Mill' was easily the main employer for locals. Women, especially, could expect to find employment there.

My first job was down in a fish shop in William Street, delivering fish and with the result one time I was delivering fish and I fell down the stair in the shop. Well I left. Then I got started in Castle Mills. I was a message girl there first then I started making shoes. I was there for I think nine years and I was married out of Castle Mills. It was rubber shoes. It was a Miss Stevenson that was our foreman. I always mind because she was a gem. There was like four at one side of the table. Of course it was tables right up and down, and you had seven wee lasts and you sat, and you had this thing for holding it in your lap and you put the rubber of the shoe over the shoe frame. You could make as many as you liked, and you were there from 7 to 5. But if you were finished early you could go and ask for 5 paid extra, and that was extra money. You were paid according to the number you made. When I first started as a message girl I think my wage was five shillings a week. You had to be a message girl for, I think it was oh, well over a year, but you could go and sit, if you had no messages to do. You could sit beside a woman who was making the shoes and sort of learn a wee bit.

You see when you made the rubber shoes, you had your last and then you had this thing that you pit between your knees, and you worked the top of the rubber shoe over your last. Then you put your insole in, and then you took the top of the shoe and you worked it over and it stuck. Then you had whit you cried a roller and then you rolled it. Then you had your rubber insole and you put some cement on your rubber insole, then you put the shoe in your hand like that, and you took the rubber insole and placed it on the toe, and then you just worked it right down until you came to the heel. Then you took the roller and just rolled it up and down. Then you put it back on the last and when you, I think it was either five or seven you had on a row, you shouted on this Mr Handyside and he would come and lift it and take them away tae the back.

MRS CHRISSIE BORTHWICK

25   William Brown moved to Fountainbridge in 1948 and was the last bargee on the
Union Canal, responsible for the maintenance of its water, banks, towpath and bridges,
from the canal basin at Lochrin to Ratho in Midlothian.
    At that time the canal was still used as a water supply for the local factories such as
the Rubber Mill, and it supported a wide variety of wildlife—fish, insects and wild-fowl.
His son, George, recalls as a child:

> seeing a shoal of roach, numbered in hundreds, swim beneath the iron bridge
> at the Mill Lane. We caught them by fashioning harpoons from garden canes
> and darning needles.

    George's father died suddenly on the canal bank in 1962. From that time the canal
went into decline and has only been kept clean through voluntary effort. Courtesy of
George Brown.

26   Certificate awarded to Isabella Handyside for her service with the North British Rubber Mill. Her father worked there when Mrs Chrissie Borthwick worked in the Mill. Courtesy of Mrs Edith May.

In those days we got employed from the big gate at the door where the department sent down who they needed and that was how you started. You didn't go through all the rigmarole that they go through now. I carried on working off and on—during my babies I worked always—got a job back again in the Mill whenever I wanted. I did several jobs. The very first one I did was rubbering, putting the rubber round cycle tyres. Then the tyres went off like a bang. More motor cars were beginning to come into use then. Then the cycle tyres went off, so for a lot of us that part of the work was finished. So many folk were kept for motor tyres.

The First World War was still on at that time . . . it was a department that made lots of little things that had to do with something in the War. I got in there for a while and then we were paid off from that.

Mrs Henrietta Johnstone

I finished up in the rubber works. I was in the office under Miss Gammie and Mrs Campbell. I took everybody—the female employees—to the room where they were going to work, to be interviewed by the foremen of the different departments. Well gradually I thought I would like to go into a department myself. I realise now how foolish I was. Miss Gammie wanted me to go into the big office but I didn't want that. I wanted to mix with the girls. That's what I did, and I was there for ten years.

When we were busy in the winter time with the hotwater bottles, I can remember us going in at seven o'clock in the morning and it was seven o'clock at night before I came out, with a break for dinner, twelve to one, and a tea break of half an hour. My wages when I left the rubber works was twenty-four shillings a week.

You were paid piece work, you had to make so many bottles—I was a bottle maker and a football bladder maker and various things—actually I worked in sundries. Then the Bedeau System was introduced. That was the name of a Frenchman who was friendly with the Prince of Wales. They introduced this system to get more work out of the girls. We were already on piece work but they were trying out a new system. There was no union.

AHR

I was a coat maker. And the woman that taught me was the best coat maker in the Rubber Mill. We worked seven to five and sometimes seven to seven, on Saturday seven to twelve. As a lass you only got eight bob and tuppence off for your insurance, but my first full wage was thirty-seven bob.

In the Rubber Mill the women and men didnae do the same jobs—no really. In my department the women made the coats, anything heavy the men took away.

Mrs Annie Hepburn

When I started I was in the stock room as a message lassie. The stock, that was the materials that we used for making the boots and shoes. The stuff was cut . . . it was like layers of crepe paper. So when the lassies were making the boots and the shoes, that paper was torn off and that landed on the floor and, see by four o'clock in the afternoon, you could be up to your knees in this paper. It was stretched and it could cause accidents . . . your boots got stuck in them.

In the stockroom it was the men who were the cutters. It was all hand cut then. It was all the lassies that made boots and shoes and the men were there to lift them, and the boots went away to the varnishing. I went on to be a bootmaker. Paid 17s. 6d. Of course I was quite young then. You done ten pairs a day, that was your 'ticket'. Then you worked like hell and tried to do extras, you know to get extra money. I can mind o' coming out with nearly four pounds. I think I just about had the strength tae bring it hame!

Mrs Peggy Weddell

Mrs Downie worked on and off in the 'Mill' for years and witnessed many technological changes and conflicts.

First I did what you cry canvas, that's like tennis shoes. You worked on a rate, so many in a rate, like four dozen shoes, you know, and after you did that, that was you finished, and if you got any more that was extra. I think . . . six shillings a week . . . it was piece work. You could get extra. If you were getting two pounds it was a lot of money. It wisnae like good pay, but you were glad to get the job, glad to be working I suppose. You didn't get what you get nowadays. But then after I worked in that bit I got a shift and I worked all the time in the car part, it was a good bit, good money that was there.

Yes I saw big changes in the Mill when I was there. You see one time they did everything by hand. Then after that they had a machine and it did four people's work. We used to thingmy the rubber, we just pressed a button and that was all done. Oh aye, we were all afraid for our jobs, and that's how we got shifted. But I was no sae bad, I was in the tyres. You see I came from the shoe place, a lot of the shoe ones went to Dumfries, then the workmen got paid off. I know a woman Effie who was thirty years and she was what you cry a 'boots', she did the boots, she was thirty years and got paid off after all these years.

Mrs Margaret Downie

Seventy-seven year old Miss Agnes Bennet retires at the end of this month after $59\frac{1}{2}$ years service in Castle Mills. She is the oldest woman employee in the Mill.
Evening Dispatch, Saturday 25 February 1950.

Mrs Downie continues.

Oh aye, there was a problem about the women's pay. You see . . . the women were doing more jobs than the men were doing. There was a kind of a thing against that.

We hadnae a Union at first, I mind that . . . everyone was out, you went to your work right enough but you were stopped, you couldnae get in. I don't know where the man is now, but we got ourselves a Union . . . They made a steward in each department, and he used to come every Friday when we got our wages and we paid the Union. Oh aye, the Union definitely helped . . . I'm sure I was there when we had that other strike. But that was the big strike that was in, I would say roughly 1930 or 1931. It was for money. We had a huge thing, we all went in a crowd. We all went to the Meadows and I always mind the woman's name who was saying it all, Mary Munro, standing up and fighting for the money, the rates that we were getting.

But to be honest with you, it was the Yanks that came in and spoilt it. That must have been 1955, something like that . . . it went to Newbridge. But when it was a real Mill, you worked and that was you finished, but in that kind you slogged, you had to work hard to get your money. That was when it came to US Royal. Before that it was North Castle Mills. Then you didnae slog . . . you just did your work and, when you did your rate, that was you. I know the money was bigger, but you had to work to get it. No skiving and nothing like that. I was eight years in the Mill, in US Royal.

What are these ladies lasting memories of the Mill?

We were all friends at work and had a happy time. It was a good place to be in.

MRS HENRIETTA JOHNSTONE

I was quite happy in the Rubber Works but I would have been better if I had done what Miss Gammie wanted me to do, stayed in the big office.

AHR

The conditions were quite happy. The place was kept quite clean. Equal pay for women never came up. We were quite happy.

MRS ANNIE HEPBURN

I dinnae think it was altogether a bad place to work. I think it was a place for its time, lets put it that way, fumes and all that. But there was a lot of harmony because there was people who came from all walks of life.

MRS PEGGY WEDDELL

When you were getting married at Castle Mills, it was marvellous, they used to have the table all decorated and when you went in the next morning of course you knew nothing about it, you went in and they all had their roses in their hair. They had sandwiches and everything and they used to carry you home. It really was good, I mean I enjoyed every minute of it.

MRS CHRISSIE BORTHWICK

As a place to work in I wouldnae say the shoe place was very great. It was more cramped, but the tyre place was really airy, it was good, airy with a stone floor, but over in the shoe place you were more all together at benches. The social life—oh aye, you had like menages.

MRS MARGARET DOWNIE

'I found a happy team of 17 workers gathered round the conveyor adding their individual pieces. Many of the girls were singing or humming the chorus of a popular tune. "Music While You Work" was on: it is very popular and served twice daily'.

Evening Dispatch, Saturday 25 February 1950.

In 1951 Castle Mills employed 3,664 people.

The Store

Another important employer in the area was St Cuthbert's Co-operative, now Scotmid. During its heyday in the 1940s and 1950s the 'Store', as it was affectionately called, was an institution to the local people. Most women were members and 'divi' day was a major social event. All kinds of skills, craftsmen, drivers, van-boys, shop assistants, office workers, bakers, and so on, were required by the numerous departments specialising in their particular product. The 'Store' could supply all the needs of the local population from babies nappies to funeral arrangements. If the relationship between the Co-op and its customers was special, its relations with its employees were equally so.

I started as a van boy. And in St Cuthbert's, well, you could apply yourself to anything, because they did everything, laundry to bakery, to grocery. You mention it and St Cuthbert's done it. So it was just your luck, which one you got. I was one of these, I think, fortunate anyway that I wasn't stable in one sort of a job. I wandered around. I was in the laundry for a while, and I was in the milk for a while . . . I was there for two years, but I was one of the very, very fortunate ones that was given the opportunity to stay on, provided I took a share number . . . Well I had to take a personal share number, and I started on the milk. And that was a seven-day-a-week job. . . . That was the system, you graduated from being a van boy, onto the milk. Or if you were lucky enough . . . you may have graduated into one of the St Cuthbert's warehouses. Or they had a meat factory, you might have been lucky enough to get a job there. But in the main you went from being a van boy to the milk delivery.

In these days it was a door-to-door delivery. I mean people ordered their stuff oot the shop and then the van delivered it to them maybe twice a week, or three times a week in some cases. So that's the kind o' work you done if you were on the grocery vans, well grocery-cum-bread vans. In the main it was the van man and a couple o' lads . . . there was more horse transport in these days than there was motor. You were sort of a privileged guy if you got a van boy's job on a motor, in the main they were horse-drawn.

When I started on the milk, I started in the depot. It was a shop actually, they had it in Stenhouse . . . at the bottom of Chesser Avenue. And then I shifted to Saughtonhall, which is still there. So the manager in that shop was responsible for you, though you were not employed by him, he didnae pay your wages, your wages were paid centrally. 92 Fountainbridge was the core, and the Dairy was there, that was where all the milk was processed and produced. There was quite a big staff of transport lads there, on—it was barrows they called them, milk barrows, They had . . . about half a ton of milk. And that was the central point. From time to time you got shifted in there and you worked out o' there or you might get shifted to another branch.

You got your perks on the Friday and Saturday deliveries. I mean you had maybe been delivering on Monday and Wednesday, and you had the good customers that dropped you thruppence or tuppence or something like that on the Friday or Saturday. And then if you did the odd jobs for them, you know, if you had a bit of spare time waiting for the van coming, and they wanted something shifted in the

27   A St Cuthbert's Bakery van in 1909. The driver on the left is Andrew Haggard. He began working at the Bakery in the High Riggs and eventually became chauffeur to Mr Young, Manager of the Head Office, for thirteen years. Mr Haggard retired in 1954. Courtesy of Mrs Margaret Mowat.

28   St Cuthbert's Cooperative Check Office at 92 Fountainbridge in 1952. Courtesy of Scotmid Ltd.

garage or something, well that was another perk for you. And then at Christmas time of course it was a bonanza, you could make anything up to ten quid.

ALEX KITSON

Alex's wife Annie was working in a different department.

I started to work in the High Riggs, in the bakery, in the confectionary. I was about 14 and a half . . . starting on the Saturday morning at 6 o'clock, because they done cream cookies on a Saturday morning. That was their speciality on a Saturday. They put *loads* out and they had a machine that you pushed them in and they got cut. I was at the other end, and all these cream cookies were coming running oot at me and I didnae know what to do with them! You had to place them on trays and then they went into the room and got filled with cream. That was my first day. However, I got used to it, quite liked it and I learned to decorate cakes. I went to night-school. For that I was getting more than Alex was getting, shoving a barrie wi' milk. I was getting 12s, 6d. a week. That was my first wage. At night-school you learned to decorate cakes and you could take another course. So I took dress-making. I learned to make skirts and things. But they paid for that.

George McMillan who is now Chief Executive Officer with Scotmid recalls how he started.

I started as a junior clerk on the 8th of March 1943. At that time the wage for a junior clerk was 12s. 6d. a week which in terms of todays money is about 63 pence. It was 12s. 6d. then and there was a small war bonus, I remember, of a few shillings, because at that stage, during the war years, a bonus was added each year to try to keep pace with the increased cost of living. And eventually, after the war finished, the war bonuses were consolidated into the basic wage. But pre-war the basic wage for a full-time fully-fledged clerk was £3. 4s. per week and that was even higher than, for instance, a shop assistant, who would have a few shillings less than that. The clerical staff always had the benefit of a few shillings more. At that time of course, even a tradesman was only earning you know, maybe something between £3. 10s. and £4 a week.

As a junior clerk, basically you were almost a message boy, opening mail, delivering mail round the various departments It is a big office here. I've always worked in this actual building at Head Office—92 Fountainbridge.

At that time we employed more people in the office than we do now because obviously with mechanisation, and latterly computerisation, the staff have diminished tremendously. But at that time even in one department, in the check office there was something like 150 girls working in that one department alone. Their sole job was to rearrange the copies of the check slips the members got when they made a purchase, and these had all to be arranged into share number order and then added up so as, at the end of the half year, to arrive at the total of each members purchases on which the dividend was based at that time.

George continues to relate his progress through St Cuthbert's.

Gradually you graduated from that to doing more senior clerical work and I did go round every department in the office in the early years.

But in the meantime in doing that I had realised that if I was going to progress to any level of seniority then I had to do something about some further education.

So I started to study for the examinations of the Association of Certified Accountants and by the time I was 22 I'd qualified as a Certified Accountant, which meant that obviously I was recognised by the Managers of the Society here. Gradually, as openings became available, I became second in charge of a department and then I was made Assistant to the Chief Accountant. Eventually when he retired I became Chief Accountant and I was in that position for 13 years in the old St Cuthbert's Society.

What was George's opinion of the relationship between St Cuthbert's management and their workforce?

In general I do think we have a reputation of being a fairly good employer. We don't suffer a tremendously rapid turnover of staff. We have a fairly stable staff and I think that probably speaks for itself.

Being a Co-op of course, we've always been associated with the trade union movement and, at one time, although it's no longer legally possible, it was a condition of employment that you joined a trade union, whichever it might be, the most common one was USDAW. I was a member of that when I started. But the Society was involved with virtually every union that there was because we had all the tradesmen. We had our own Works Department (at Upper Grove Place) for doing repairs and maintenance of property—joiners, electricians, plumbers, engineers, you know we had all the unions involved. And obviously as union employers we always tried to cooperate with the unions' demands, conditions, wage rates and so on.

We had to work much longer hours than we do now. The office hours were 8.00 in the morning to 6.00 at night and we had two half days: eight till one on a Wednesday and eight till one on a Saturday. And even Christmas Day you got away early but you didn't get a holiday. The only holidays at that time—the 1st and 2nd of January. The basic holiday entitlement in those days was two weeks.

The only strike I can recall—and I can only remember it vaguely was in my early days when I wasn't really directly involved at management level so I didn't have to deal with it as such—was with the milk delivery people. I can remember on one occasion [they] went on strike.

Eventually it was resolved because it would be done in close consultation with the unions involved . . . you get some local agreement with the local trade unions even if it is not a national agreement.

What 'extras' could an employee expect?

We have in the past given concessions in certain departments . . . We recently introduced the 10 per cent discount on non-food purchases.

We had a very good rapport amongst the staff. There was always, if not exactly a club, a gathering of staff. We'd go on outings, even if it was only to have a dominoes or darts competition.

And there was an Employees Welfare Association formed. That was just shortly after the war and it still operates to this day.

Who better than Alex Kitson to explain the trade unions' position.

First I was involved in the Shop Assistants Union, that's now USDAW. There was USDAW and NUDAW that was the two unions in the Co-op. And the Transport Union was the Scottish Horse and Motormen. When I started on the milk I wisnae driving, I wis on the barrow, so all the barrow lads were in the Shop Assistants Union. We had a very active organiser (Annie Davidson). Oh, she was a real dictator.

I started at £2. 13s. 4d. a week, for a 44-hour week. But once you got elevated to the Transport you had the kind o' things that you didnae have when you were on the barrows, the overtime, and that kind of thing then. So that enhanced your wages, and during the war, well, there was no restrictions on driving hours or anything, and you worked all sorts o' hours. You could start at 5 o'clock in the morning and still be messing about at 8 o'clock at night—and Saturdays and Sundays. If you went home with about four and a half quid, you had a good wage.

What were these former employees' opinions of working for the 'Store'?

St Cuthbert's were a good employer. And then we were superannuated you see. It was a steady job, it was quite good. It was a big bakery that, and the biscuit factory was there as well, so there was a lot of activity going on round about there . . . That's where I started, and I was there till I got married . . . I think by the time I left I was getting about 35 shillings. I think that was my wage when I left the Co-op.

MRS ANNIE KITSON

I was lucky there in the laundry if I got 35 shillings a week. You handed over your money every week. Your mother got the pay packet. You daren't open that pay packet.

The toilets were inspected every day. You had a spot check every so often in the canteen by the environmental people.

We were asked to join the union. Then it was compulsory to join the union. A closed shop. Complaints were taken to a higher authority through your line management. You weren't allowed to strike. You couldn't walk out of the job then, it just wasn't the done thing. Equal pay for women was unheard of. The man was keeping the house; he was the breadwinner.

MRS BETTY LENNOX

If you compare the employment now, you look back, and say, well we used to complain about one thing or another, but the Co-op was like the local authority, like the railways. They were the ideal employer. When I started in full-time work, we had holidays with pay, we had sickness pay. That was the only place you would get these things. But the unfortunate thing about the Co-op was they never improved upon them. They were still doing the same things after the war that they were doing before the war, and of course other people were catching up with them, other industries were catching up with them. So it wisnae just as lucrative to be employed by the Co-op as it was before the war.

The workforce and the management, there was never any real dispute. No I wouldnae say they were closer, but I think the conditions were such that the Co-op blokes could look outside and say, well, we're a hell of a lot better off in here than we would be across the road.

ALEX KITSON

Working Women

Before the Second World War the role of working women was strictly defined, they were expected to pursue traditional female occupations. Although the North British Rubber Mill did provide a ready opportunity for women and girls to gain employment, not every local woman regarded that route as the only one open to them. However restricted, women and girls had alternatives.

I got a job with what they called 'coupons', that was when Strang ran the football coupons. We went in on a Saturday. You emptied the envelopes, put all the postal orders up. You went back on a Sunday and you filled the coupons for getting posted. But for these two days you could only get 21 shillings. There were some adults. It was a temporary job, only while the football season was on. On the Saturday night there was a guy used to walk round. There was a woman at the top table, who was the boss, he'd give her a nod to say, 'give her an extra day'. If she didnae like you, if she didnae see you working, you were out. The result was, I finished up doing sort of full time, and I was making as much wages as my dad. Really! Some days you got as much as £3. I handed over. Oh aye, it was a big help to my mother.

MRS ANNIE HEPBURN

My first job was as junior clerkess at a plumbers and electricians with James M Wall. I think it was . . . in Lauriston Street. I didn't fancy it terribly much, not because of the work but because of the person who owned it. I did enjoy working in the plumbers with the Walls'. It was a nice cheery job. My duties were typing, answering the phone, taking the orders, helping to make up the wages, checking the workmen's timesheets and going out to try and collect some of the overdue accounts. There was a shop and a workshop at the back of it. . . . I was usually in the front shop, in the actual office bit. There was a partition, then a space to go through to the counter where you saw to the customers.

My pay was 8 shillings per week and then it went up, and when I reached the 12 shillings a week they said, 'I think you should try and find another job which will pay more because we can't afford to pay anymore'. So right enough I did. I'd already had my name down for McVitie and Price (Robertson Avenue) for the office, and I got word to go for an interview and I got the job there and that was much better. When I left Walls I was getting 15 shillings a week, at the other place it went up to 19 shillings a week. By the time I left I was at the top of the scale for what I did. I was in the invoice department . . . I think I ended up with about 35 shillings, the top rate . . . I liked it, although you weren't supposed to speak, just like you were at school. But of course we did, every chance we got.

MRS J D THOMSON

First of all I was in service. I think I was about a year in service, with an old couple that lived in Parkside Terrace. The wages were too small of course. I think it was 2s. 6d., it came to 2s. 6d. a week. A pound a month . . . and my food. That was the wages, and of course my mother needed more money and I went into the Mill.

MRS HENRIETTA JOHNSTONE

I got a job working in a shoe shop, in Carr's shoe shop. I did my trade in there. A vacancy came up in the GPO for a telephonist and I did my training there. I was in the GPO for three and a half years when I went into nursing. I started in the Royal Infirmary for a year and then I went to the Royal Victoria at Comley Bank for six months, then to Bangour for six months and then I came to Simpsons. Then I got married.

MRS BETTY LENNOX

I worked in Harris's the hosier at the top of Lady Lawson Street for a time. Very high class hosiery, didn't do any rubbish. It was all for shops like Forsyth in Princes Street—kilt hose and things like that. I was an examiner there. I can't remember my pay, I was always hard up and broke so I couldn't have been well paid.

I kept Mr Hogg's shop for a while, down in the Cowgatehead, right next to a lodging house, a pend. It was a little Johnie a' Thing—vegetables, everything.

I went nursing at the beginning of the war. I saw the first air raid over the Castle. I was in the shop at the time, and shortly afterwards I took up nursing which I had always wanted to be. I went to Bruntsfield. Well at that time you weren't allowed to marry and train. If you were trained and married you could go back, but you weren't allowed to finish your training if you married. And then my wage there was £2. 10s. a month, and you had your stockings and your collars and everything to buy. I couldn't have done it if it hadn't been for my people, they got my books and things like that.

MRS GRACE TAYLOR

Mackay's sweetie works was a fair size employer of female labour. Here an ex-van driver with the company recalls the ladies who worked there just before the Second World War.

I remember a' the girls that worked there, wi' their sack aprons and clogs. A right rough lot they were. A lot o' them came fae the country, Livingston and a' that way. A lot o' the girls came from the Southside. I cannie remember them a' but Maggie, she was the woman in charge, ruled them wi' a rod o' iron. But it wis great times, a' covered in glucose, You'd see them there during the day wi' a' their curlers in.

At that time the Palais used to give oot free tickets tae a' the firms and we would get a ticket and go tae the Palais. They'd say 'gaun tae the Palais the night Andy?'

29   Staff from Mackay's Sweetie Works in Fountainbridge, and their children, around 1956.
Courtesy of Mrs Mary Cruickshank.

And you'd go tae the Palais and you'd see a' these dolly birds and you'd realise that these were a' the girls you'd been working wi'!' In the morning they'd say, 'enjoy that dance last night?'. And you'd say tae yerself, 'I never danced wi' her!'.

I reckon it was mostly a' women. I think the workforce might have been about three hundred . . . The women were employed in the sugar hall and they used tae twist the toffee on these hooks and things. And also for packing and working on the machines. And they were mixing too. They a' wore clogs and sacks roond their middle. There was a warehouse side where they made up a' the orders. There was never any security. I remember the girls used tae come oot wi' bars o' chocolate, toffee, things like that, but they never got searched. What was going on was, they used tae wear long drawers an' that, an' stuff the toffee down there. I think that was a well known fact. But then came a time—there was a big widden stair that went up tae where they a' worked and at 5 o'clock at night they a' used tae gather at the top o' this stair. I'm talkin aboot maybe, a hundred and fifty o' them. And the yard man used tae walk across the yard. It was a big bell then, and he used tae look at this clock an' when it came tae five he used tae gie this bell a ding, an' they a' used tae rush doon this stair. Anyway, on one occasion, it did happen. One o' them slipped an' the whole lot went, a' on top o' each other, legs in the air an' everything, toffee all over the place! Then from that time onwards they had a plain clothes woman in the gate office. She used tae stand there and just indiscriminately pick out one o' them. So that put the wind up them. They never knew when they were going to get stopped.

ANDREW LYNCH

One girl, a former employee of Mackay's in the 1950s remembers (laughing).

The gaffer used tae say goodnight tae ye and give ye a pat on the head.

MRS MARGARET SMITH

All the girls wore turbans in the works and it was just possible that a snowball or two might have found its way under there.

Even before the Second World War there were some independently minded women determined to challenge the *status quo* over womens' role.

My sister Jessie was a bit o' a Tomboy, she wanted tae be a motor mechanic, an' she started round where the wash-hoose used tae be at the back o' Tollcross School. She started there as an apprentice mechanic—at Lochrin. She worked there, she never completed it, but she worked there for quite a few years, but a' the lads wi' their dirty overalls . . . (she changed her mind). She didnae want tae be a mechanic. She worked in the Mill for a long time too, that was after that, then she got married.

But Jessie was a bit unique, then again, she'd come home at night, get all washed up then half an'oor later she'd be dancin' at the Palais. After the war they were more self reliant, weren't they?

ANDREW LYNCH

Directly across the road from Mackay Sweet Works the famous firm of Asa Wass employed a number of local women. It was another institution to the people of Fountainbridge. This was a scrap merchants occupying the premises which had previously been a silk mill. The yard was to be found through three pends on Fountainbridge. One gate for rags, one for scrap metal, the other permanently closed.

He was a real character. He wore a long fur coat. He was the only person I knew who had a car when we were at school [1920s]. If you were lucky he took you to the Store. He used to put three in, and you got a halfpenny biscuit each, oot the Store. He took ye up the length of the Store and turned at the Coliseum and brought ye back.

MRS MARY CRUICKSHANK

There used tae be Asa Wass's Pend, the big Asa Wass pend. Then there was the iron pend, that was a different one. Then there was the next one, right facing Grove Street.

MRS INA BEGBIE

You could go into Asa Wass's pend—there were seven or eight women worked under him, but they were a happy crowd o' women, they nearly a' stayed in Freer Street. They never went to their work wi' coats and hats on—just shawls.

MRS CHRISSIE BORTHWICK

You used to take your rags when you were a kid and get thruppence for a big bag of rags or woollens. He used to weigh it on the scale. They used to have the woollens separate from the rags. You could have a big huge bag of rags and, as a youngster, you didn't realise, you'd take a big bag, your mum sent you along with it, collected over the months, maybe two or three times a year and you might only get fourpence. Then you'd see somebody else with a little tiny bag and they'd get ninepence and you couldn't fathom it out that this was woollens with a higher price. You got a ticket. It was all official. And then other people took heavy stuff like metal, scrap. Further down you took the heavy stuff.

ALEXANDER A ALEXANDER

One o' my uncles lived in Asa Wass's pend. There was Mrs . . . . . she worked in Asa Wass's. She always had this big long black dress on an' string roond her waist. I remember, I always felt there was something sinister about her. But then ye looked in, ye saw these bales o' rags an' a' these skins hingin' up. It was a creepy sort o' place. But ye would always go tae yer ma and say 'ye goat any rags Ma!'.

ANDREW LYNCH

> Asa Wass being the rag and bone pend,
> where everybody brought their rags to blend,
> bones and skins were up for sale,
> guts and everything in a pail..
>
> extract from *The Auld Dames of Edinburgh*
> [popular song]

Working Men

The male population of the area had a choice from the wider scope of employment opportunities, depending upon their ability and ambition. From ordinary labourer through tradesman to craftsman—unskilled, semi-skilled and skilled. The building trade absorbed many of these men.

> My dad worked on the building of the Regal. It was at the canal basin. He started on it, roughly I would say about 1934 or 1935.
>
> They worked on it for quite a good while, because the canal basin had to be drained and everything, and got ready for building on it, the foundations and everything. So it took quite a while. The war started in 1939, and by that time it was pretty well through. I can't remember what company he worked with. He was just a builder. Previous to that he had been a miner, but then he came out o' the mines and he got a job labouring. Then he started picking up. He had two or three tests and went as a builder. It was bricklaying he did. Oh dear God! my dad would be out of the house at six in the morning, and no back till maybe seven or eight o'clock at night. They had to carry a piece for their lunch. They had it in a bothy and they made a cup of tea; they carry'd what you would term a flask, but it was a jug. It was matal wi' a spout on it, and it had a lid. You filled that with tea in the morning and carry'd it with you, then you put it on the fire to heat up. I think he had about £2.10s. a week, and that was for all these hours. They worked Saturday mornings. That was his week's work—Monday to Friday full time and Saturday morning. He didn't have protective clothing; there wasn't such a thing. He went to work in a jacket and trousers and that was it. The most protective thing he ever had was a scarf round his neck for the cold. The toilet on the site was a wooden hut with a bar across to balance theirself, so it was a dry outside toilet. Nowadays they widnae do it, I mean they wouldnae work under these conditions now. They had to build it—you know, dig the pit, erect the wooden hut, and put the bar across.
>
> He got hit with a stone, a big one. It fell and hit my Dad on the shoulder. He wouldnae stay off his work. He often used tae say that he had a pain there, but he never went to the doctor. There was no report of the accident. It was your own fault, you just shouldnae have been there where that stane was falling.
>
> When he came in my dad would tell us some laughs that had happened. He would say, 'How's your day been Bell?'. Then he would go on and tell her what he'd been doing, how his day had gone. He liked the work that he was doing. He didn't complain.
>
> MRS JANET DOW

> My dad was a stonemason, and he had hard times because, years ago, they hadnae all these things for cement where they can do without, like beating it up. Years ago they could be off for weeks and weeks with what they called 'black frost', and my Mother hardly got a penny.
>
> MRS ANNIE HEPBURN

> My Dad was one of these men—you see, he was a stone mason, when my Dad came in frae his work he didnae want tae be bothered by anybody, as they did in those

days. He had his dinner, read his paper, washed his face and hands and was in bed by eight o'clock at night.

Mrs Ina Begbie

Some found it hard to settle in a job.

It was my first job, but I left there and I went to become a motor mechanic. The wages there were 11s. 4d. a week. But I always wanted tae be a jiner, so I left there and I got a job as an apprentice joiner, but I had a row wi' the boss and I telt him to stick his job. I went wi' the Store milk after that. This is all within about 18 months. Then I left the Store and I went back tae the Brewery and I was in the Brewery ever since. It was quite easy to find a job then.

Hard work! Pilin' boxes o' beer, things like that, what you call box-tippers, emptying the boxes and all that. I think my first wage was 24s. It was quite good compared to being an apprentice.

It was a full day's work. At that time everything was manhandled, you put them on a barrie and you hurled them doon tae the warehouse, piled them up eight high. Well you take a box o' screwtaps it wis then, they were pretty heavy, and they went six high. It was a high as masel', and you're shovin' them up. It was hard work. It took a lot of getting used to. I used to start at half-past six in the morning and finish at five o'clock at night..

After that I got a job as a machine assistant. And then I got a job as what you call a machine man yourself, as a charge hand, wi' say about sixteen people under ye, men and women alike. Then I got a job as foreman. Then I finished up as a shift supervisor.

Andrew Laing

Others were not so lucky keeping one.

My father was a baker in Simon Hendersons. 170 Fountainbridge was always called Simon Henderson's stair. The bakers was through the backgreen and the shop was at the front of the foot of the stair, the big double fronted shop. To begin with, when I was very young, I would say my mother was quite well off, because she had what you called the tradesman's wage. Then Simon Hendersons, like everyone else, was caught up in the slump. So the bakers and everybody went on half days. Half time they called it. And then eventually it closed down, which really hit 170 and 176 Fountainbridge quite hard because there were bakers in 170 and vanmen in 176. They lost their jobs. And then it was the case that everyone was on the dole and eventually they went on the means test.

Mrs Peggy Weddell

Some jobs were held in high regard by local people, jobs where there was security and a decent wage.

My father was an engine driver in the LMS in the old Dalry Road engine shed. My father was about the best paid man in the stair. My father's income then was intae two figures, I know that, but I couldn't tell you the actual rate he got because my father's wages varied. It depended on what run he was on. He was on different shifts . . . the further ye went the more ye got paid. When he went tae Aberdeen he wid bring back a box o' kippers and we got fed on kippers for a week. Also then, if ye worked on the railway, ye either got a free pass tae take the family anywhere in Britain or ye got a privileged ticket where ye paid one-third o' the fare.

JOHN WEBSTER

And there were those who went on their own, in the true spirit of private enterprise.

My husband had a window cleaning business. He bought it off somebody in Freer Street—Willie Dickson, he had built up the window cleaning and he wanted to sell it. So my husband was working for Thomas Graham at the time and thought, 'maybe I'd be better working on my own'. Because one of his mates had had a fall. So he says, 'Well I think I'll just start up on my own', and I says, 'Well that's up to you, I'll back you if that's what you want to do'. It took a bit building up because before he had sold him that business, he was still interfering and trying to take the business back again. It was all people like lawyers and that. He never looked back after that, being his own boss. I think everybody knew him along there. He was well liked by all the auld yins because he helped them all. He wasn't just doing windaes for them, he'd go up to see if they weren't well, light their fire and put a kettle on for them, and make them a cup of tea. It was all in his day's work, it didn't matter who they were, if they needed help, he would have done it.

He did Mackays on his own. He could have had the Brewery. He did so much of the Brewery. But he done a lot of business. All the banks, Fountainbridge, up Polwarth, all the TSB banks. When he started on his own he thought it would be better because of his health, the way it was, he'd be better on the ground. So he took all the shops, contracts and that. It was better for him. He was never, ever off in all these years. He never had a holiday, all these years. But he bought his wee car. And after he bought his wee car, he got around a bit. We never had a holiday together. If you didnae work, you didnae eat, that was his attitude.

MRS RUBY CLIFFORD

Although not necessarily being well remunerated, the aristocrat of the manual skills class was the craftsman.

My father (Richard Steedman) was a grainer and marbler. He was the champion of Great Britain, and any painter who knows his work will not paint it out. They refuse to paint it out. When he was retired, before that he had marbled pillars for the Royal Bank of Scotland in St Andrews Square, and they got another pillar, later on . . . nobody else but him was to come and marble it. If you go up there you can't tell the difference between the real marble counter and these pillars.

Then he was a teacher at the College of Art, night classes, for years and years. He served his time with Sinclair in George Street and then he was with Bonar for years. He went to Heriot-Watt night classes when he was just an apprentice. He got medals and a certificate from them. One of his certificates was signed by the first Principal of Heriot-Watt University and they are now in the Museum of Heriot-Watt's.

He used to practice a lot, even when we were teenagers. We wouldn't dare go in the room if my father was painting, or practising.

MRS GRACE TAYLOR

A similar skill is recalled by Tommy Lang.

I didn't start my apprenticeship right away. I had to work on the big printin' machines when they were finished wi' the work. Ye had tae clean all the plates wi' naphtha—Oh, terrible smell!—and tidy up things, clear all the waste paper away. You had to wear an overall when you were workin' on the machines, because it was too dirty with ink and all that. I'm sure we had to buy wir own overalls. I did that for a year, then I got an apprenticeship as a compositor. That was quite interestin'. They taught you quite well. The apprenticeship was seven years. In those days they were long apprenticeships and the printers were the longest of all. The others, like electricians an' the plumbers an' that, were four tae five years. But the printers were supposed tae be the élite, the gentlemen o' the unions. It was 1933 when I started, an' 1934 when I got my apprenticeship, so that meant it was till 1941. You had tae go tae Heriot-Watt College from your second year onwards, one day a week for three years, and also spend a couple o' hours at the Art College in Lauriston Place, handwritin' and artwork, an' things like that, an' this went on up till the start o' the war in September 1939. We used tae work from 8 till 6, wi' an hour off for lunch, an 8 till 12 on a Saturday. That's 57-odd hours we worked then. My first week's pay was 10 shillings.

Andrew Lynch describes a skill exercised in Mackays Sweetie Works which probably no longer exists.

Then ye had yer sugar boilers, it was a trade then, a sugar boiler—he done a' the mixture and what-not. Of course Mackays were famous for their snowballs an' there was a German, a Mr Herman. He must have been an expert on the snowballs, an' he had a hooked hand, ye know, like Capt'n Hook—so he must have had the recipe for the snowballs because he was the only one that ever done them.

Then there were the men who broke away from the 'wage slave' mentality altogether.

I came to Ponton House in 1958 from the Home in Bridge of Weir. I served three years as an apprentice draughtsman but I discovered I could make more money playing snooker. I played every day in Pearsons in Fountainbridge sometimes from ten in the morning to ten at night. I was only earning £2. 7s. 6d. as a draughtsman and realised I could make £20 on some days as a player. At one time I had £800 in the bank, good clothes, and a nice flat, all earned from playing snooker

WILLIE THOMPSON

Alexanders Garage and Coachworks in Semple Street were the number one dealer for Ford in Scotland. They were renowned for the craftsmanship and service they provided. They employed first class tradesmen in all the

30   Semple Street in 1959 showing the cars of the Ford Anglia 105E Club run by staff
      at Alexanders, Edinburgh Limited. Courtesy of Jack Gillett.

coachbuilding skills; seven woodmillers, seven blacksmiths, twenty-two metal workers in the bodyshop, four trimmers, twenty-five painters and thirty-one labourers: Alexanders employed approximately 125 operatives.

> I remember Mr Weinstock of Craighouse Cabinet Works in Morningside ordered a ranch wagon [a precursor of the station wagon]. I worked on it, cutting all the timber parts. I saw it again twenty-five years later and it looked just as good as the day it was built.
>
> ROBERT STUART

> A customer could come in at 5 o'clock and we would say, 'would you care to go to the ABC for a couple of hours sir?', and he would come back and his car was ready with a reconditioned engine fitted.
>
> JACK GILLETT

> A coal-lorry might come in, in the afternoon, we'd work late so the chap could carry on with his business in the morning.
>
> ROBERT STUART

They seemed to take great pride in their craftsmanship and service.

Team Spirit

Some of the smaller firms of the past seem to have fostered a team spirit between the boss and their workers. Acts of friendship were also commonplace.

> On a Saturday auld Mackay himself—used tae wear an auld warehouse coat and a bowler hat. I'd come in about ten o'clock in the morning, he was gettin' on a bit ye know, I think I must have been his favourite van boy at the time, and he'd say, 'there's some sweeties for ye, dae ye want tae work this afternoon?' an' I'd say, 'Oh yeah!'. An' then when we loaded up the van, auld Mackay wid come over an' say— 'Thanks for workin' Andy', and he'd gie ye a bar o' toffee and thruppence.
> In Mackays ye had your wages, I think it was a Friday night—ye a' queued up wi' yer syrup tins and jars, ye had your name on it, and ye got yer boilings, pound o' boilings. One o' ma mates said, 'yer workin' for sweeties!', and so we were right enough!
>
> ANDREW LYNCH

> If we had tae work late on a job Alfie Alexander (the boss) might go over to the Marble Arch and buy us a fish supper.
>
> ROBERT STUART

Two excellent examples of team spirit are provided by the management and staff of Ethicon and Alexanders.

During a gale in 1974 the roof was blown off Ethicon's main factory in Fountainbridge. This disaster could have led to up to one hundred workers being laid off. However, the employees volunteered to 'pitch in' and try to retrieve the situation. They worked over the weekend, and their temporary repairs were so successful that the works was able to resume normal working on Monday morning.

JIM ALEXANDER

When in the fifties the staff wanted a social club it was agreed with the firm that they would supply all the materials if we would provide the labour. It was a great success and we opened the Social Club at Gardners Crescent with Ronald Alexander. It had everything—bar, skittles, dance-hall, snooker room, it was great!

JACK GILLETT

CHAPTER FIVE

Everyday Health Care

Margaret McArthur

There have been so many advances in health care this century that it would be impossible to cover them all. It was, therefore, decided to ask our interviewees very general health questions and find out what were their strongest memories and concerns about health. Naturally, having to pay for health care before the National Health Service, featured in the memories of many, but the dramatic changes in medicine, surgery and radiography were hardly mentioned and it was the everyday conditions of childbirth, infectious diseases and skin conditions which people seemed to remember most clearly. Two local general practitioners—Dr A C McLaren who retired in 1973 after working for 40 years in the area and Dr W Grant McIntosh who has been working in the area for the last 25 years—have also given us their memories and will add their experiences to the picture of health changes in the area.

Childbirth

The major area of change here has been taking women out of the home and into maternity hospitals for the delivery of their babies.

> I think most babies were born at home when I was small (1930s).
> I mean anybody that I remember, neighbours and that, nobody seemed to come back with a baby from the hospital, they all just seemed to come out of their house with a baby with them. All of a sudden the rest of the family were put out to play and neighbours took the odd one in to give them their tea and kept them for a wee while and the next thing the nurse disappeared and they all went in to see the new baby.
>
> MRS ALICE BURT

In the 1920s nearly 80 per cent of babies were delivered at home, by the 1930s this figure had dropped to 70 per cent, and by the 1940s to nearly 40 per cent.
Nowadays, it is difficult to picture how babies could be delivered in the cramped, overcrowded conditions that existed in the Tollcross area, but it does not appear to have caused too many problems.

111

We did a lot of home confinements in all sorts of conditions, I have confined a patient in a big double bed in the alcove with the patient at one end and two or three children sleeping at the other end, and they never moved.

Dr A C McLaren

Neighbours could be relied on to help in all sorts of ways.

My mother—Nell Campbell was her name—was a great woman for working for charity and she delivered more women in that area of Grove Street and Brandfield Street than will ever be known. I don't think she had any training, she was just that kind of woman. It's no the first time we've had to jump oot our bed when she's come up and wakened us, and this was her going into her big kist to get some white sheets for somebody who'd just had a baby. I mean we got them back again, they took them to the wash house and brought them back again, but they needed clean ones then.

Mrs Ina Begbie

If big Aggie along the road was having a baby, they used to come round and shout 'Come on Fanny, you'll have to come and help us' and my mother used to down tools and away she would go and help Aggie to have her baby. And she used to wash and do the nappies for Aggie or whoever was having her baby.

Mrs Frances Waddell

There was an old woman along the landing from us who—Mrs Hogg—and my mother would say 'Oh, for God's sake, run for Granny Hogg!' and you knew there was something happening.

Mrs J Plenderleith

These untrained neighbours who helped with confinements and other ailments were known as Howdies. Although in the main, they had had no formal training, they appeared to be extremely resourceful and had learnt much from the experience of being with numerous women during their confinements. Dr McLaren's father delivered 'many, many babies' with only a Howdie helping.

By the time I really started (1930s) the nurses were coming into it . . . people would say, 'Oh well, I've got the Howdie', and I would very often say, 'Okay, right, I would like you to have a nurse there, go down to Castle Terrace, the Queen's Nurses, and fix it up'. We woud do the antenatal if they would come along, but many of them didn't and some of them didn't even warn you that they were pregnant. I well remember one patient in Upper Grove Place and I got a message to go as soon as I could, so I went along and went in and put my hat down on the end of the bed and said 'What's wrong?' and she says 'Oohhh!!' and produced a baby into my hands and that was the first I knew of it. This did happen, but we did get them trained to come and make some arrangement, and as I said we did the antenatal and if we had any doubts we referred them to the Simpsons for an opinion.

Dr A C McLaren

When I had the bairns, a doctor and nurse came in, and a sister. You must have a doctor, and then the sister, and then the nurse comes in every day.

Mrs Margaret Downie

When my mother was going to have a baby, I had to go up to Simpson's and get a nurse to come down. She would help and a neighbour would come in, the doctor would probably pay a visit and from then on I took over. I was only ten when my sister was born—I washed her nappies and had to make soup and do anything that was to be done in the house to help my mother.

AHR

Even when the arrival of the baby was not as straighforward as could be desired, the general practitioners were able to cope.

I must say we did all sorts of things which we wouldn't dream of doing nowadays. You'd go in and eventually you might have to say, 'Well, I think we'll have to give you some help'. So you produced your forceps and—it sounds awful now when I think about it—and you sterilised the blades more or less in a pan of hot water, the blades, but the handles were sticking out, and boiled them for a bit and, of course, that made them red hot, so you had to wait for them to cool. But my father put on forceps many a time and as soon as I was able to get around with him, even before I qualified, he would make me put them on, so I had good practice and training there and we never ever had a fatality or sepsis or anything, not once and I never remember him having any either.

The nurses, the Queen's Nurses were super, absolutely super. We did our confinements and when it came to a question of putting on forceps or when it actually came to the last bit when they were actually beginning to stretch and produce the baby, we often gave them chloroform. We always used chloroform, these other sophisticated things hadn't arrived, so we just used chloroform most successfully. Very often what would happen would be the patient lying in the bed, on her side—I'd give the nurse the bottle of chloroform and put her up at the top end and tell her to pour on a bit every now and again, and you got a Howdie if she was there or a relative to get on the bed too and they would kneel there and hold up a leg while you delivered the baby . . . it all sounds most appallingly primitive, we didn't even have rubber gloves in those days but, I can only repeat, I never knew of any trouble any time. We had these confinements in all places, the Grassmarket, the Pleasance, the West Port, Tollcross, all over the place—in single ends and so on and as I said children would be sleeping there and pay no attention—at other times they were sent out to a neighbour.

Dr A C McLaren

Occasionally, however, there were problems which made a lasting impression on the mother concerned.

When I had my son I was in a nursing home. My mother-in-law had a breech birth and she never forgot that, she had only two children. She booked me into the nursing home just solely on account of her having the breech—she never forgot it.

AHR

Edinburgh was supplied with a large number of small nursing homes, usually ex-private houses, with perhaps two single rooms, a double room and a four-bedded room. There was also a small labour ward and a staff of a trained midwife and two or three nurses. However, the cost of having a baby in one of these homes was often outwith the means of many in the Tollcross/Fountainbridge area.

There also appears to have been some confusion as to the cost or otherwise of having a baby in hospital.

> You see with the insurance . . . with my stamps and my husband's, I could get three or four pounds to go into hospital for my first, but I didnae like the hospital, so I had them in the house and paid 30 shillings—fifteen shillings for the doctor and that and fifteen shillings for a woman to look after you. There were other ones that it didnae cost them anything because they had their mothers, but it did cost me.
>
> Mrs Margaret Downie

> Probably my mother couldn't have afforded to have her babies in hospital. Now as far as I understand it, the old Simpson's Maternity—I've heard people say they were confined in there and I think I heard somebody once say they had to pay 10 shillings, but I don't know whether it was for the full lying in period or a week or two weeks. Well, my mother wouldn't be able to afford ten shillings so she had her babies at home and then she lay in.
>
> As I say the neighbour maybe came in periodically, but I did most of the work.
>
> AHR

> It didn't cost anything for them to go into Simpson's . . . I think if they went into Simpsons they handed over their maternity benefit or something like that, when there was a maternity benefit, but prior to that before the war, I don't think it cost them anything, just the same as it didn't cost them anything to go into the Infirmary.
>
> Dr A C McLaren

But even in hospital things could go wrong.

> My mother lost her first baby in Simpson's, not Simpson's now but the old Simpson's up at Lauriston. The baby was premature and she was only about 4 or 5 pounds. Mum got out of hospital but she used to have to go up every day to feed the baby. Then she was told she could get the baby home, and she was all ready and going out the door to collect her when the policeman came to the door to tell her the baby was dead. Mum always blamed the hospital for it.
>
> Mrs Alice Burt

> In actual fact going into hospital to have a baby was more dangerous then, than having it at home . . . and I think it still holds good. There's still controversy going on about that—having a baby at home or in hospital—and in many ways having a baby in hospital is much easier and safer because they've got everything there—more or less skilled people all the time—but the snag is that there are more infections

going around in hospitals although they try, of course, to prevent it. Whereas in a house, having a baby at home by the time you've reached that stage you are virtually immune to the infections in the house.

Dr A C McLaren

And quite apart from the safety point of view, some mothers found having the baby at home more pleasant in other respects.

My mother had a' the kids in the house, but I was in hospital with the oldest one, but Peter was born in the house I was born in . . . and I preferred the house to the hospital. You could get a cup o' tea when you needed one and you get visitors at a' times.

Mrs Mary Cruickshank

Some, however, neither went into hospital or sought medical help for a home delivery possibly because of attitudes of that time.

They were very narrow minded . . . they were terrified to tell their mothers they were pregnant . . . they just werenae accepted.

Mrs Ina Begbie

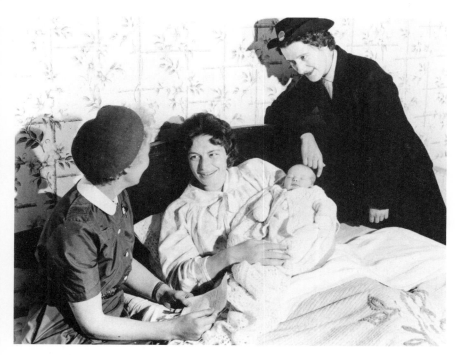

31   Mother and baby with (on the left) the Midwife handing over care to the Health Visitor at four days after birth. Taken in the 1960s. Courtesy of Lothian Health Board.

And the consequences of these attitudes and fears were often most unfortunate.

> I'm quite sure that there were people, in fact I know there were people who didn't
> have anybody, and most of the time it came off all right. You had, of course, the odd
> one who was concealing a pregnancy and produced it at home. I do remember one
> case that I was sent for and this young woman told me that she'd had a baby the
> day before and I looked round and said 'Where is it?' and she says, 'Oh, it's in the
> drawer'. And she had actually strangled it, so there was nothing I could do except
> report the case.
>
> Dr A C McLaren

By the mid 1950s, nearly 85 per cent of babies born in Lothian Health Board
District were delivered in hospital, and by the mid 1980s this figure was up to
99 per cent. This steady change from home to hospital deliveries was mainly
due to Lothian Health Board policy, but there was also a change of attitude in
general practitioners and patients.

> When I came back here, I came back from Africa where I had a pretty vast
> experience of obstetrics and I was involved in the consequences of confinements
> taking place under relatively primitive conditions outside hospital and then coming
> into hospital in a desperate situation. Having seen how quickly things can go wrong
> in obstetrics, my attitude was that the Edinburgh obstetricians' policy of having as
> many confinements in hospital as possible, for the benefit of the mother and the
> baby, was confirmed. I, therefore, did not book anyone personally for a home
> confinement.
>
> All along being geographically close to the Simpson's and knowing the Simpson
> obstetricians personally just because we're so near, I therefore worked from the
> beginning on a shared care basis. I asked the Simpson's to book my patients and they
> sent them back to me for most of their antenatal care and then they went in for their
> confinement. Then quite early on, the Simpson asked me to do their postnatal check
> at 6 weeks as opposed to the majority of people who were told to go back to hospital.
>
> Dr W Grant McIntosh

Today most young mothers expect to go into hospital to have their baby and
often take for granted the many technological advances that have occurred in
the field of obstetrics . . . but what would great-grandmother have made of it
all?

The Spread of Infection

In the annual report of the Edinburgh Medical Officer of Health in 1935, the
population of Edinburgh was given as 460,877 with a density per acre of 14.2.
The population of St Giles Ward, which included Fountainbridge, Tollcross and
West Port, was 18,213 with a density per acre of 68.5. In such over-crowded
conditions, it is not surprising that infections of all kinds were rife and feature
clearly in people's memories.

Skin infections and the use of gentian violet were spoken of by many, although strangely enough scabies, one of the most common skin infections according to the statistics, was not mentioned.

> We used to get quite a lot of impetigo and things like that. In poor homes where there was a lack of cleanliness and people crowded together, then you'd get impetigo spreading all round. It was a nuisance to treat, because we hadn't anything very powerful to treat them with. Likewise with ringworm, there were so many children with ringworm of the scalp that they had to be segregated and put to a special school.
>
> DR A C McLaren

> I remember I got impetigo once and my mother wouldn't let me go out because she was horrified. It was only a wee, wee bit on the side of my mouth, but I had to have that gentian violet on it . . . oh, it was terrible. I mean a lot of the kids at school had it, but she thought it was only dirty kids, and she was a fanatic about anything like that, I mean she used to scrub us from top to bottom.
>
> MRS ALICE BURT

> I don't know who it was from school that had impetigo and she had to go to High School Yards and I remember going with her. And it was just one big room with big sinks all round it and when she came oot, I couldnae believe it, she didnae get gentian violet but they covered her in this paste stuff and bandages all the way up her arms and on her fingers. And whit a shame, I remember we cried all the way home, because she had all this stuff and a mask on her face wi' just her eyes showing. I don't know why, being brought up in such close proximities, people didnae understand about these diseases, because nobody wanted to speak to them if they had gentian violet or that . . . instinct used tae say 'Oh dinnae go near them'.
>
> MRS INA BEGBIE

> All three of us boys had impetigo. The school was the one who sent us, I think it was down the West Port or the Grassmarket. We had to go down there to some Board of Health type of thing. They had big sulphur baths and they used to soak us in there for an hour at a time. I don't know if it did any good or not, but we got over the impetigo. Of course, we had lots of lice. We used to get our heads shaved every once and a while. Teachers would check us in the school. And after you got your head shaved, they used to scrub it with kerosene. We had that two or three times.
>
> GEORGE RAMAGE

Head lice were a problem and not only for the children concerned. Mrs I D Graham, a teacher at Tollcross School, from 1941–43 gives her recollections.

> We had a nurse who came round occasionally to examine heads. As far as I know the nurse just came round the classroom at very infrequent intervals and I think it was mostly heads she was examining—there might have been more, I might be doing the system an injustice, but I don't remember any more in the way of medical inspection We had one very irate mother furious because the nurse said her son had nits in his hair, and she wouldn't have this, but he did. And there was a bit of impetigo and things like that, but I think on the whole they were pretty healthy, I don't remember any sickly children.

Lice were treated at the Depot at Infirmary Street, where they sterilised the sheets and things, one of the treatments was to wrap them up with cloths soaked in paraffin—stank to high heaven. I don't remember lice ever being an epidemic, you did come across it but you got it off and on, but funnily enough not as much in the poorest homes as you might expect. If you got scabies in, it went round and round and the other thing that spread round and round were threadworms.

I must admit that, as children at home, mother used to go over our heads with a small tooth comb as a routine, but she never found anything—but I think this was a sort of normal routine.

Dr A C McLaren

Then you had people with infection of the hair and they used to get their hair cut out. I used to think it was unfair . . . there were three girls in our class who had poker straight hair, and they had their hair shaved, and when it came in they ended up with beautiful heads of curly hair. They always had to go around with these scarves on until the hair grew. I think it was a real cruel thing to do to anybody. I mean surely they could have given them something to wash their hair with, there was never any need to cut all their hair off.

Mrs Alice Burt

In Lauriston Place, there was a school for children with ringworm of the scalp. It had been a private house and it was extended by taking in the adjoining house. Dr McLaren recalls.

The noise from these children playing in the backgreen which was their playground was terrific. It wasn't a residential school and you would see them—they were all bald. Sometimes this was done by giving drugs, Thalium, and sometimes it was done by X-ray along at the Infirmary, so you would see them marching along to the Infirmary and back. Then their heads were painted with gentian violet and it was quite an astonishing sight to see these children, both boys and girls all with their bald heads—the only way you could distinguish them was that the girls wore skirts or dresses and the boys shorts. But that died out and I'm not going to say whether it was due to general cleanliness or better treatment or what. Certainly you can treat it now and the same with ringworm of the skin. Eventually—by the time I retired I don't think I'd seen ringworm for years, and certainly not ringworm of the scalp, not for years and years.

In 1945 over 600 children attended the skin clinics with ringworm, 13,892 attended with scabies and a further 3,936 with impetigo. In 1965 there were no cases of ringworm, 532 cases of scabies and 21 cases of impetigo. However a new 'epidemic' has raised its head.

The new epidemic in skin problems is 'ladies' hands'. Now I've been in the game long enough to remember the day when eczema of the hands was confined to people working with diesel oil and such irritating materials. But nowadays one may see perhaps even two ladies in the surgery with dermatitis of their hands. And going into it, one finds that it is either due to a biological detergent or washing up liquid

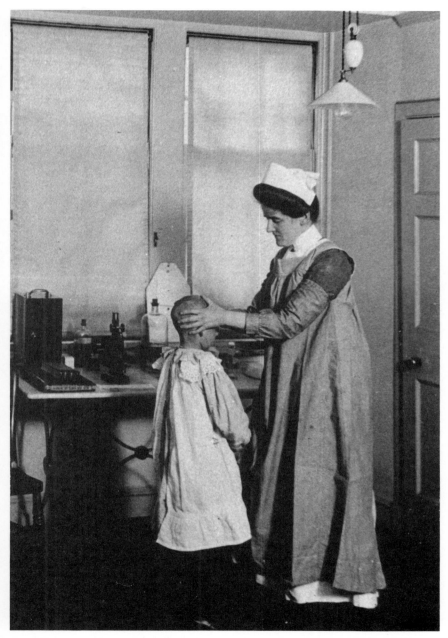

32   Nurse examining a child's head at Lauriston Special School at 41 Lauriston Place,
      around 1912. Courtesy of The History of Education Centre, Edinburgh.

33   Children attending Lauriston Special School at 41 Lauriston Place, probably soon after it was opened in 1912. Courtesy of The History of Education Centre, Edinburgh.

or because they are using some potent kind of soap or they've been using some paint stripper or something like that. And I would say that one of the new epidemics is dermatitis of ladies' hands. You see a young doctor wouldn't know that because he just assumes that ladies have troubles with their hands.

Dr W Grant McIntosh

Infectious diseases were something else that thrived in the cramped overcrowded conditions and at the beginning of the century nearly all cases were sent into the City Hospital. At that time each disease was treated in a separate ward and most of the wards were full and overflowing. No visiting was allowed due to the risk of infection. Each patient was given a number and these numbers were published in the *Evening News* under 'seriously ill, contact' and 'improving' and so on. These numbers were also posted on a big notice in the window of the Public Health Chambers at Johnston Terrace—and this was how relatives were able to find out how their children were. However children were often in hospital for several weeks and this long separation from parents made quite an impression on some.

I had pneumonia when I was just over two, and I can vaguely remember all the neighbours being in. One wee kitchen, that was all we had. I can just see the steam coming under a blanket that was over the cot, and this was evidently the thing they did then to loosen the lungs.

That was my first recollection of Scott's Close. We were there I think until I was five, and at that time scarlet fever was rampant, and it seemed that everyone had someone with scarlet fever or diphtheria or something like that. We got off lightly.

I took scarlet fever, and one night I was taken away, it was like in a Black Maria, no windows in it, just twelve of us, laddies and lassies altogether in this van. And we were looking at the top—there was a sort of opaque thing at the top, and we could see the leerie as we called it . . . the gaslight. We were all crying, of course, we had just a blanket round us. We were sitting on seats, bar seats. Now I was away eighteen weeks and my sister went away the next day and she was twenty-two weeks in. Up in Colinton.

I remember every night the *News* had the numbers in of the patients. I don't know if they had it in then, but I do know when I was able to read and write in Freer Street that we looked at those numbers every night. We knew everybody's numbers that were in, in the Street, and we looked to see if they were all right. It was the only way people could find out without 'phones. Everybody had to walk from where they were—no conveyance of any kind—no trams, cars, nothing. We walked every foot of the way. And of course when they walked they weren't allowed in, and they just stood at the door, and we screamed and cried and we wanted home. They were telling us to be quiet, to behave a wee while, but it didnae dae much for us, I'll tell ye.

Mrs J Plenderleith

I remember my mother telling me I spent my first birthday in the City Hospital with diphtheria and I think these days you were away of about two months.

Mrs Peggy Weddell

34   One of the two pavilions for the treatment of Non-Pulmonary Tuberculosis, Ward 12 at the City Hospital, around 1930. Courtesy of Edinburgh City Libraries.

Infectious diseases were more serious conditions then as Dr McLaren explains.

Scarlet fever to begin with was quite a serious thing, but the most serious of all was diphtheria and sometimes the patient left it too late to send for you and you would find perhaps a child with diphtheria with obvious signs of complications, but you just sent them in, you couldn't cope with that at home. You sent them in, but I had several deaths from diphtheria. I don't remember any deaths with measles or scarlet fever, but of course, with whooping cough in babies, you could have quite a lot of trouble.

Once more neighbours often provided first aid and help until the doctor arrived.

About the community life in Glen Street—where I was young there was a good feeling. Everybody knew each other and everybody helped, like young Chris, she took very ill when she was a baby with diphtheria. We ran down to the woman in the first flat, because the baby started to take croup and my mother had never had to deal with that, but Mrs Kennedy, who stayed in the first flat, came running up and plotted her, hot baths, cold baths, until the doctor came, didn't dry her, wrapped her up in a blanket, then refilled the bath and—she saved her, we may say. The doctor came and she was whipped away—my sister was whipped away too, for she happened to say she had a sore throat—to the City Hospital.

Mrs Grace Taylor

However Edinburgh was very far advanced in the treatment of infectious diseases and things began to change.

Very early on, we started treating our infectious diseases mostly at home. We did not treat diphtheria at home because it was one of the most infectious. But very early on we were treating scarlet fever at home and measles, unless they started getting the complications of bronchitis and bronchial pneumonia and so on; the same with whooping cough. I was treating all these at home before the war, except diphtheria. Then, of course, you had the polio epidemics and so on, those you sent into hospital as soon as you had diagnosed it.

That has all changed a great deal, you see they used to have whole wards at the City set aside for each individual infectious diseases. They're not so acute or so serious as they used to be. There's very little diphtheria because of the immunisation and Edinburgh I think was one of the first to really go to town about that.

Dr A C McLaren

I remember there was a lot of diphtheria and whooping cough—a few of my friends had that . . . then they were always giving you injections. I don't know whether it had something to do with the war or what, but you seemed to be forever getting jags for this or that. We had to go down to Torphichen Street School, it used to be a health centre sort of thing then.

Mrs Alice Burt

And, of course, when I was at Darroch that was when we were all getting inoculations for the war time diseases and you had this big thing on your arm to tell people you had your inoculations and I remember we were playing this day and I got pushed and I fell on this arm—well, I ended up in hospital with that because the thing erupted . . . but I had a very sore arm oot o' it and I wisnae the only one, quite a few people had sore arms wi' these inoculations.

Mrs Ina Begbie

And Dr McIntosh brings us right up to date

Apart from minor infectious diseases the incidence of them is very low now. In my practice I started off advising mothers—if I found that any mother had not had her child immunised against diphtheria and tetanus and polio—I advised her to get it done and get the course completed.

Early on, when the measles vaccine became available I thought that was a good idea, because once again I had seen children dying of complications of measles and children who are deaf as a complication of measles and I therefore started using the measles vaccine. As a result, I have seen very little measles and, of course, I haven't seen a case of diphtheria, tetanus or polio. I haven't seen a florid case of scarlet fever since I came here. I've seen very minor cases of scarletina, but because the mothers in the practice here tend to bring their children along on suspicion—any child coming in with tonsilitis, I would tend to treat them, if it were of a significant degree, with Penicillin or some suitable antibiotic at the beginning, so one doesn't get to the florid scarletina stage.

I've seen one case of whooping cough in my practice in twenty-five years and it was simply because that mother, in spite of all the chasing up she got, just would not get that baby along to be immunised, and the baby had had the first triple antigen, and then developed whooping cough and she had to suffer a child that coughed at night for weeks as a result.

But there was another infectious disease in which overcrowding and insanitary conditions were thought to be an important factor. A disease which people were loath to talk about.

The other infectious disease we had to deal with was, of course, tuberculosis. It was a big problem and people concealed the thought of it by talking about consumption, going into a decline and phthisis and things like that. Edinburgh again was very far advanced. Robert Philip was one of the pioneers and made a big difference to tuberculosis. But it was a very nasty thing to have around the place and people were rather ashamed. Why I don't know but they were ashamed and yet you had it in all sorts and all stages. There again, treatment was up at the City or the Victoria or up at Liberton, but treatment went on for years, years, so they would be away for years and sometimes they recovered and sometimes they didn't. There was no real treatment in those days except fresh air, good food and general nursing care.

Dr A C McLaren

I remember my mother and her great old friend Mrs Fairley were talking about somebody this night and ma dad was sitting on the open fender stool reading his paper, and they were talking aboot somebody and ma dad suddenly pipes up, 'Don't you dare talk aboot that in front o' the bairn'. Now he wasnae even in the conversation and I was aboot fourteen then, certainly no' a bairn . . . but it turned oot that they'd been talking aboot some woman with consumption and ma dad thought it was terrible they should mention that in front o' me.

Mrs Ina Begbie

TABLE I

Cases of Certain Specified Infectious Diseases notified in Edinburgh during the last 30 Years

YEAR	TYPHOID FEVERS		DIPHTHERIA		SCARLET FEVER		CEREBRO-SPINAL FEVER		*MEASLES		*WHOOPING COUGH	
	Cases	Deaths	Cases	Deaths	Cases	Deaths	Cases	Deaths	Cases	Deaths	Cases	Deaths
1923	29	2	770	69	1,897	93	12	8	Not notifiable	79	Not notifiable	89
1924	27	1	720	73	1,761	68	15	11	Not notifiable	120	Not notifiable	85
1925	30	1	870	82	2,351	62	12	10	2,252	85	2,043	188
1926	33	7	552	43	1,852	32	25	20	3,346	42	280	17
1927	78	2	599	44	1,848	19	30	25	2,803	71	850	43
1928	19	2	629	30	1,046	6	25	21	4,340	77	1,390	80
1929	76	2	1,171	55	1,154	3	63	48	338	—	863	39
1930	35	2	1,102	71	1,278	8	52	37	7,182	106	1,638	72
1931	14	1	901	28	647	4	48	36	811	4	839	19
1932	26	4	662	27	1,080	8	54	39	8,786	89	1,205	56
1933	50	3	606	21	4,516	21	41	25	178	2	984	65
1934	13	—	546	27	2,419	17	34	22	3,200	67	189	6
1935	32	3	308	16	1,511	7	19	13	854	11	877	37
1936	25	5	374	26	1,083	5	19	13	2,491	41	804	25
1937	16	—	622	43	1,680	10	19	15	1,508	16	1,425	67
1938	35	1	600	44	1,430	5	20	14	2,248	36	253	4
1939	25	2	361	29	734	1	23	2	678	2	1,521	41
1940	32	2	749	61	652	1	326	45	2,818	13	255	8
1941	68	4	446	28	1,070	3	194	36	1,123	7	1,365	44
1942	14	2	480	31	2,023	5	84	14	2,307	10	135	2
1943	7	—	422	15	1,598	4	37	7	1,723	7	775	19
1944	8	1	306	12	1,222	3	37	1	1,124	—	409	10
1945	3	—	362	13	1,029	1	55	4	2,920	16	494	17
1946	5	—	172	10	434	—	73	10	2,064	4	483	7
1947	6	—	50	2	310	—	57	8	1,403	10	790	20
1948	4	—	14	1	1,051	—	17	1	2,240	8	402	5
1949	8	—	7	—	1,183	—	27	3	1,392	1	760	6
1950	4	—	2	—	1,004	—	22	2	2,489	—	1,768	3
1951	7	—	—	—	451	—	23	6	2,009	—	2,385	9
1952	2	—	2	—	752	—	22	5	3,136	2	782	—

* From 1925 only first case in household notifiable.   From 1933, only first case (under 5 years) in household notifiable. From 1950, notification of whooping cough extended to include all cases. (*Source* for this and Table II: MOH Report. 1952)

My brother Jimmy was in the hospital with tuberculosis of the spine and he was in Colinton for a long time and then he landed up at a hospital in Haddington. He would have been a hunchback if he hadnae have went in. And he was in one of the big . . . what dae ye call them . . . trolleys that ye used tae wheel them about. He had tae lie straight, well he was strapped in. When he got off of that, he got this wee straight jacket and it was hard and belted at the front to keep his back straight. And he eventually got . . . well, he was in the Air Force during the war and he was in the Territorial Army . . . really he was a marvel after what he had gone through as a kid.

Mrs Mary Cruickshank

My mother's older sister died of TB, she was nursed at home I gather and my mother used to tell me, that she was very fond of this sister and she was very intrigued because the sister had to wear a mask over her face and my mother used to play with that mask and put it on to see what it felt like—which shows the ignorance of TB because hers was not a medical household. I had a cousin who died of TB in Bread Street, he died at the age of twelve . . . he was the grandson of the Key Shop.

Dr A C McLaren

In 1947 a new antibiotic streptomycin and the drug para amino salicylic acid (PAS) began to be used, and by 1952 actual deaths from pulmonary tuberculosis were declining, but the actual number of people suffering from the disease were constantly rising as Table II shows.

TABLE II

Pulmonary tuberculosis—Edinburgh Register
Number on Register at 31st December each year

Year	Male	Female	Total
1938	981	788	1,769
1939	880	746	1,626
1940	919	720	1,639
1941	880	789	1,669
1942	906	847	1,753
1943	913	873	1,786
1944	910	883	1,793
1945	948	1,012	1,960
1946	993	1,065	2,058
1947	1,299	1,043	2,342
1948	1,484	1,206	2,690
1949	1,610	1,312	2,922
1950	1,723	1,451	3,174
1951	1,876	1,521	3,397
1952	1,882	1,642	3,524

Medical concern over this gave rise to the mass X-ray campaigns and contact tracing of the 1950s, which proved to be so effective that Dr McIntosh is able to say:

I have probably only seen a couple of new cases of tuberculosis, but they were both in ex-miners who had a degree of silicosis to predispose them. And I have seen a few people who had been previously infected whose lesions had lit up as a result of some other illness. And I've seen one or two primary lesions spotted very early on in contact by the Dispensary at Spittal Street, who have referred them to me and I've put them on perhaps a year's medication. None of them have required to go to hospital with it.

The Cost of Health

Many people recalled the problems of paying for health care prior to the introduction of the National Health Service in 1948.

> You paid to go to your doctor and for the doctor to come out. My mother had to pay him 7s. 6d. one time . . . it would be for my brother, because she never paid for me because I was never ill . . . and I thought it was an awful lot of money just for him.
> MRS ALICE BURT

> When I was at Tollcross School, I developed this abscess and instead of coming oot it went in and I was bandaged with just a place for my eyes, my nose and my mouth for a long time and then I had an operation. I went down to the dispensary in Torphichen Street and he drew a chart on my face and this was where I was to be cut. And I remember my mother saying, 'You're no marking my bairn like that', and he said, 'That's all we can do unless you go to Bruntsfield Hospital'—which was a feeing hospital—'to see Professor Herzfeld'. So I was taken up there and that's the mark—*nil*. Now, how my mother and father paid for that I just don't know. Before I had the operation I had to get hot fomentations. My dad took me up there every morning and every night at 5 o'clock to get this boiling hot lint slapped on my face . . . it must have been an awful sacrifice for them
> MRS PEGGY WEDDELL

Having to charge for their professional services caused problems for the general practitioners as well.

> There's been an awful lot in the paper about how dreadful things were and how the doctors wouldn't visit until the patients had the money in their hands—well, I never experienced that, nor did my father. He attended them knowing perfectly well he wasn't going to be paid but he didn't ask for it. I always remember I used to help him with his accounts when I was a bit older, and he made them up in a most haphazard way. He had a record of visits, you see and he reckoned so much per visit, I think it was something like 3s. 6d. a visit and I know a confinement was 3 guineas—a lot of money—and he reckoned out the accounts and he would look at it and say, 'Oh that's too much', and chop it down a bit. Sometimes if an account had been rendered several times, each one went out with, 'Please pay something towards this'.
> He still went on attending these people and they still sent for him although they knew they owed him money and he never worried about that. And when he got to

the other side of the practice, he would make out the account there and add a little more because they could afford it and I think that was done in general. I do know there were people who wouldn't go and see a patient unless they had the money ready, but that wasn't common in Edinburgh.

Dr A C McLaren

There were a variety of ways of coping with this cost.

Then, of course, in those days you had the National Health Insurance—about 1913 I think that came in—and that meant that the manual worker was insured and he went on the Panel, so he got his treatment and medicines free, but not his family, they had to pay.

And undoubtedly, there's no question about it, a lot of the times they didn't send for the doctor. In many cases it didn't matter, because often it was the minor illnesses which got better of themselves, but sometimes it could be bad . . . although I never heard very much word of anything like that happening in our area.

Dr A C McLaren

My dad had to pay . . . I think it was half a crown a week . . . to an insurance, Foresters I think it was called. He paid money into that. And when ma mum had the kids, he got money to help him with these things. And when the bill came in for the doctor's visits and things like that, she just gave the bill to Foresters and they paid it.

Mrs Mary Cruickshank

There was the Parish Medical Service where the 'pauper poor' got their medicines free. And often people who felt they could not afford a doctor went directly to the Royal Infirmary.

My father was in the Deaconess Hospital for 8 months with an ulcer. So there was no rent paid, so when he came out again he had to work twice as hard, so it all broke out again. The landlord was Waddell, he was a nice man. The factor that came for the money wasn't nice, he had no sympathy for anyone. That was the only time you felt different from other people.

Mrs J Plenderleith

But even in these early days people sometimes looked for 'alternative health care'.

Oh aye, it was difficult paying for the doctor sometimes—but there again I must come back on that. Now you could go to a chemist, it was in Fountainbridge, and you could say, 'Oh, I'm no awfully great', and the chemist man would give you something—you had to pay something but you never needed to go to the doctor.

Mrs Margaret Downie

But there was a herbalist in Bristo called Napier's. Now ye used to go up to Napier and explain what was wrong and Napier never turned ye away. He always gave you something tae take and nine times out o' ten he cured ye.

John Webster

If I had a cough, we got a wee pinch of sulphur with cream of tartar—stopped the cough. Or they rubbed our nose with a bit of butter—that cleared your nose. I remember we had neighbours who were interested in you—in your health.

J WALKER BLANCH

Health Care was some of the old fashioned cures which was handed down in families. If you had whooping cough, or anything like that, if your mother came across a tar boiler, where they used to boil the tar in the street, you got held over the tar boiler, which cured the whooping cough. You didn't have no inoculations. The only inoculation ye got was your vaccination when you were a baby. When my mother had a serious illness she was looked after at home by the people in the stair. Ye paid for everything. I think it was about two half crowns for a doctor's visit. Medicines ye had to pay for as well.

JOHN WEBSTER

And the doctors often found home cures being used when they were called in, and sometimes the simple advice they gave had somewhat unexpected results.

Time and time again you went and found people with a sweaty sock round their throat for a sore throat, always a used sock. Another thing was a hot onion for earache or hot salt and gargling with all sorts of curious things.

I remember one place I went to—this was later of course—and this poor woman was really in a dreadful state. She'd had a dose of 'flu or something like that, and the neighbours were all hovering round and one of them said, 'I don't know what's happened, doctor. We've given her everything we saw advertised on TV' . . . Anadin, Aspirin, Codiene . . . they'd poured the lot into her!

I used to go in and find children with poultices, stinking poultices, bread poultices on their chest and fingers. Fresh butter poultices which had gone rancid, then there was linseed poultices.

One home remedy that was used by quite a lot of people for a sore back was heat. I used to recommend it too. And I'd say, 'The best thing to do is lie on your face and cover your back with some brown paper and get your wife to run over it with a hot iron'. And I went in to see one man one time and he was up and out of bed and sort of very coy about it. And I said, 'Let's have a look at your back', and here's the shape of an iron in the middle of his back, because his wife had been treating him when the bell rang, and she'd put it down in the middle of his back . . . cured his back!

Toothache—clove oil or aspirin rubbed into it—which ulcerated the gum.

And of course the number of laxatives that were poured into people—cascara, senna. You had all these advertisements in the paper, 'Mother, is your child constipated? California Syrup of Figs'. And people latched on to it.

DR A C MCLAREN

But I dinnae mind o' any o' ma pals having coughs or colds or that, for the simple reason that the food you got kept them away and your mother . . . ma mother made sure ye got your Syrup of Figs and your castor oil. I used to have to go into the cupboard to take mine—Syrup of Figs I didnae mind, but castor oil I just detested.

She used tae put it on the orange, squeeze an orange . . . and a wee drop orange juice
wi' this castor oil, and I couldnae look at it, so she used to shut me in the cupboard
for tae drink this castor oil.

Mrs Ina Begbie

An article headed 'Family Doctor Service' in the *Scotsman* of 15 December 1934
reported on a new scheme to care for the non-insured.

A significant step in connection with the medical services of the city has
recently been taken by the inauguration of a public medical service . . . a
service organised by the medical profession in an area for the purpose of
providing medical attendance on a voluntary insurance principle for persons . . .
who frequently have difficulty in paying for medical attendance in the ordinary
way.

One of the limitations of the existing National Health Insurance system is
that its benefits are not available to the dependants of insured persons. It is
being increasingly recognised that if it is necessary for the wage earner to have
the services of a family doctor made available to him through a system of
insurance, it is at least equally so in the case of those dependent on him. It is
to meet this situation that such medical services have been organised.

The contribution for subscribers to the service are so arranged as to present
no difficulty for the classes for whom it is designed. The rates vary from 4*d.* per
week in cases where there is only one dependent to 1*s.* in the case of a family
however large. Medicines are also covered by this payment.

You had to pay for every child, I paid for all mine. You paid for that and you paid
for medicine. The Panel, aye, that's what you got when—like I burned my leg when
I worked in the mill, and you got Panel money, twelve shillings it was. Not just for
accidents at work, I burned my leg at my sister's house, and you must have a doctor,
and you did it through the insurance man. That came off your wages, your health
stamp and your unemployment stamp, but when your health stamp was filled you
gave that to your insurance man and the unemployment stamp was for what we
cried the buroo.

My husband didnae work in the Mill, he was more of a barman . . . he was in the
insurance scheme too . . . everybody had to be, it was a thing that came out of your
wages. Every time the doctor came in . . . same with the ambulance, St Andrew's
ambulance then—you had to pay 7*s.* 6*d.* for my man was never out of hospital. I
must say the hospital is a thousand times better to what it was then. I mean in 1936,
it wasn't lovely wards like what you've got now, it's lovely but—well, maybe I
shouldnae say it, but I do think there was better nursing, the nurses was nurses at
that time, and even when I had my bairns, oh aye, dedicated.

Mrs Margaret Downie

There were also dispensaries at Riego Street, Marshall Street, West Richmond
Street and the Cowgate, where medicines and attention were often given free
or for a very nominal charge.

But looking back further to my student days—I worked for a time in the Marshall
Street Dispensary. During the war, the dispensary system was that there was a
doctor in charge of each dispensary—as it was called for the sick poor, for people

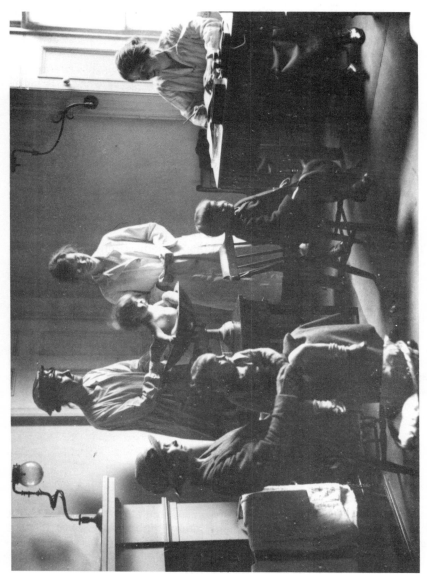

35   Grove Street Dispensary, around 1920. Courtesy of Lothian Health Board.

who did not have National Health Insurance. The system was that some of the dispensaries had a GP in charge and other dispensaries had an Honorary Physician from the Royal Infirmary in charge. What happened was that the medical consultation at the dispensary was free and each dispensary had a pharmacist, and we as students would write a prescription but then they were checked by the pharmacist and if proper and reasonable they were dispensed for a very nominal figure.

The sort of thing was, one would go to the dispensary on one's official afternoon, one would accompany the Consultant, or Honorary as we called him, as he did his consulting and then there would be some home visits to do and if they sounded serious, the doctor would go and do them himself. If they sounded ones that the student could cope with, we were sent out perhaps to do two visits. But during holidays, most of the students were away but those of us whose homes were local took on the job of practising as a sort of assistant GP to the Honorary and if one could cope with the thing without his further help, one did. If one couldn't cope one had to contact him at his ward in the Infirmary or wherever and he would come and visit the patient and make the decision. It was marvellous experience which I'm afraid medical students today don't get.

DR W GRANT MCINTOSH

The Second World War brought about many changes in health care in this country. A survey of hospitals had been carried out in 1938 and it was found that, not only were there an insufficient number to cope with the number of casualties expected, but the fact that some were run by the voluntary organisations and others by local authorities, made the central adminstration of them extremely difficult. An Emergency Medical Service was created which imposed a regional organisation of the hospitals. It also created a general laboratory service and a blood transfusion and ambulance service. New hospitals were built, medical staff were sent to the areas most in need and set wages and conditions were laid down. Gradually free treatment was dispensed, firstly to civilian and military war casualties, then to war workers, evacuees and so on, all of which laid down the foundations of the National Health Service. People's attitudes were also changing.

We considered the Health Service part of our right.

J WALKER BLANCH

Nobody should have to pay to be healthy.

MRS MARY CRUICKSHANK

So the National Health Service came into being and a booklet entitled YOUR HEALTH SERVICE—How it will work in Scotland, published in 1948, laid out the services that the NHS would provide.

Every man, woman and child in Scotland comes within the new National Health Service, and is able to get, without medical fees, whatever help, care and attention are needed for health. There is no question of having to pay insurance contributions to qualify. The service is available to everyone from 5th July, 1948.

Here in more detail is what the Service offers:
A family doctor . . .
Medicines drugs and medical aids on doctor's prescription . . .
Dental services, including dentures . . .
Full treatment in general and specialist hospitals . . .
A comprehensive maternity service . . .
Health visitors . . .
Home nursing service . . .
Eye tests and spectacles free . . .
Hearing tests and hearing aids free . . .
Ambulance service . . .
Vaccinations.

Naturally the introduction of the NHS increased the work load of those employed in the Service.

> I think the NHS made an enormous difference to people's general health. People really took hold of it and in some cases virtually went to town. We were flooded with requests for eye tests and things like that. I don't really think people took unnecessary advantage of the National Health, I'm inclined to think that they take more advantage now than they used to. We carried on exactly the same and we tried to make no difference at all and I think we succeeded quite well.
>
> Dr A C McLaren

> At the start of the NHS in 1948, women and children who created, because of their tendency to need medical care, far more work, became eligible for the free prescription system as did people with disability, and so it was then said that the road to the chemist shop went through the doctor's waiting room. This was true, of course, because prior to that day, one in seven of the people going to the pharmacy had come via the doctor's surgery, and after the start of the NHS, seven out of seven came. So there was a tremendous increase of traffic through the doctor's surgery just to get a bit of paper to get medicine. I'm not saying it was a bad idea, I'm just saying it happened and that's what overwhelmed the GPs, and led to queues of fifty or a hundred outside the surgery, when previously there'd be a queue of ten or twelve or something.
>
> I think the NHS helped to vastly improve the health of people, I'm a firm believer in the NHS.
>
> Dr W Grant McIntosh

And the patients agree.

> I think the National Health Service was a marvellous thing—ye could go and get your teeth out and things like that whereas yer mother had tae pay half a crown, but the National Health Service cleared a' that, that's why the children nowadays have better teeth.

But other modern factors have increased the General Practitioner's load.

> Another thing too, in the old days people if people were in difficulties very often they would go and see their minister, they would go and see the priest and get help there.

They don't do that now, they come to the doctor and much more now than it used to be, the doctor is a social worker. Lots and lots of people who come to surgeries are more social problems, psychiatric problems and things like that rather than physical illness.

DR A C MCLAREN

But many of the general public still consult the chemist before 'troubling the doctor' and some also seek other sources of help.

I think probably that the old apothecary/pharmacist was in a better position to give suitable advice than many of the younger people today. Therefore, I think it's common experience that many of the younger generation of retail pharmacists deal with the things that they feel confident in dealing with and then they quite rightly refuse to sell things to certain people and say, 'You'll have to go and see your doctor'. And they won't sell them anything for their complaint. I'm talking about the local pharmacists here, the ones I've had experience of, they're very good.

People do go and buy simple things like a bottle of cough mixture or a treatment for diarrhoea or something like that, they do go. And they do buy things for skin rashes, if they show it to the pharmacist and the pharmacist thinks it's something he can cope with.

More of my patients are asking me if I mind if they go and get acupuncture or hypnosis for things such as smoking and overeating and things which I find a bit irrational. I think there's an increase in that kind of thing.

DR W GRANT MCINTOSH

Social and building changes in the Tollcross area have affected doctors' practices and work life style.

I've been affected as regards patient list by the demolition in the Fountainbridge, Morrison Street area. Quite a lot of patients were moved out beyond the Lothian Health Board boundaries that arrange my practice. Since we are paid on a capitation basis partly, we either have to keep ourselves within a reasonable geographic area and have time to spend on the patients, or looking at one's list size and therefore one's profit at the end of the year, spend more time in one's car going out to places like Sighthill . . . I chose to do the former.

Another thing that affects me, of course, is the vast increase in traffic in Tollcross/ Lauriston and the need to double park, when one is visiting patients at times, because the yellow line is frequently fully parked up.

And one of the other sad things as regards being a GP here is that young married people who come to live here, once the baby arrives, or certainly once the second child arrives, they move to a house with a garden, and because I don't follow people to the suburbs, I lose them. So I might say that I lose most of my young families. There are, of course, some families who stay but the majority of them move out. So it is the younger population that moves through Tollcross and Lauriston, but the older people are a very static population. Some of the young ones do come back again. In actual fact I have people who have gone out to live at Penicuik and East Lothian and so on, and who come back to this area, perhaps having sold the car and decided it's better to live in Tollcross/Lauriston and walk to work and hire a car for a holiday.

I think there's a lot of support from the various agencies in the community and there's never any problem in getting support for someone who needs it. There's a first class social work department in Victoria Street in my opinion. If there's any problems of a social nature, one can ring up there and they're on the ball and get on with it.

DR W GRANT MCINTOSH

These building changes combined with social and medical advances, have done much to improve the health of the area.

I think a big advance was made during the war when we learnt more about diet than we knew before. Before the war you undoubtedly got people who were living on tea and toast and things like that, tea and buns, but I saw poverty. I've no recollection quite frankly of ever being in a house where people were completely starving; they were destitute, they were dressed more or less in rags, some of the houses were filthy dirty, but the children, taken by and large, were healthy. You did, of course, if anything like scabies came, it spread all round, and things like impetigo or ringworm. But we had patients in what I think were some of the poorest quarters of Edinburgh.

We have, of course, since then learnt a great deal and we have learnt to treat so many more diseases, because I was in practice before the war, before the days of penicillin. In those days, quite frankly, you could treat very, very little—it was all mainly chance, selling your own personality and so on, because the medicines that you used, we knew they weren't any good. The main thing a bottle did was improve the morale of the patient, they felt they were getting something. Since then there's been such a change and medical science, as always in war, has advanced so much— huge leaps and I think that has a lot to do with the improvement in health.

Of course, they have cleared out the worst slums too, but in the worst slums in Edinburgh I had patients whose houses were like a new pin. I remember well the sort of big range fireplace, and the high mantlepiece lines, you know the strip of brass round about it polished so that you could see your face in it and everything was absolutely . . . you could have eaten your food off the floor.

DR A C MCLAREN

The improved home conditions, I mean there have been a lot of houses renovated and a lot of the stairs that used to be dismal and dirty are now very nice. I've seen the fitted kitchen arrive in so many homes. Another thing I've seen is that, 25 years ago old people were not able to afford—I'm talking about Tollcross, Lauriston— were not able to afford adequate heating in their houses, there's no doubt about that. I have never in recent years had any pensioners who do not use what I would consider is adequate heating, whether they can afford it or not I wouldn't know, but they use it, and they are adequately clothed to keep warm, and they are adequately fed. There is an improvement in the shopping that comes in and is laid on the table, when I go into the house. That's one thing I've noticed.

People are very well now. You see, I can look back forty years and think of walking along the streets, one occasionally used to see children in the street with a red line down their neck from a chronic suppurative otitis media (ear infection)—

I've never seen one in the past 25 years. But 25 years ago, there used to be children one could see in Lauriston, Tollcross, Grassmarket and so on, who had two red lines on their upper lips from a chronic purulent rhinitis (inflammation of the nasal passages). You don't see any children who aren't well looking children in this part of the town now. I'm not saying this is due to the Health Service, it's just a fact. And the houses are better and cleaner apart from a few disaster houses, where in spite of all that the Social Work Department does to help, the people wish to be happy in their chaos.

Dr W Grant McIntosh

But one characteristic—although perhaps shaken and somewhat diminished by the structural changes that have taken place—continues to play a significant part in the health of the area.

Of course, the great thing which made such a difference in those days was that everybody had neighbours, and the neighbours rallied round. When there was a confinement, you had neighbours in to help to make cups of tea and heat water and all this. When people were ill, the neighbours rallied round and I think that saved an awful lot of people from complete starvation and things like that.

Dr A C McLaren

I think there's still a lot of community spirit about. I notice it with my patients, they tell me how other patients of mine are, there's still a mutual interest in this area. I think it's a great community.

Dr W Grant McIntosh

CHAPTER SIX

In Time of War

Gillean Somerville-Arjat

Edinburgh did not suffer greatly from aerial bombardment in either of the two World Wars, compared with the saturation bombing of London, Coventry or Clydeside during the Second, but people were nonetheless prey to the same anxieties and deprivations and offical defence preparations went ahead just the same.

First World War

First hand memories of the First World War are fading now, but there are still those who can remember the Zeppelin raids. Mrs Plenderleith, who was born in Freer Street Terrace in 1909, recalls the sighting of a Zeppelin one evening when her mother had gone out to the cinema with a friend, leaving the father in charge of three small children:

> Now there wasn't such a thing as a blackout as you would call it, like switching off your electricity, but everybody had to turn out every light in the house. So . . . Lizzie and I and the bairn Patrick . . . were playing, and just then we heard three hooters going in the mill for when there was air-raid . . . My father just grabbed us and brought us in the hoose. It was dark, you see, and he was puttin' a bucket of water on the fire. You can imagine the mess! We heard the noise and we looked out the door at what was happening. It was the Zeppelin above! It was looking for the mill and the Forth Bridges, but they were so low that we heard the muttering of the men, the guttural sound they have, the Germans, and my father thought if we said a word, they'd hear us! And he put his arm round the two of us, over our mouths to keep us quiet . . .

On the night of Sunday, 2 April 1916, several Zeppelin bombs were dropped on Edinburgh. One fell on a house at 39 Lauriston Place where Dr John McLaren and his young family lived. Many years later his son, Alastair, also a doctor, wrote in an article for *The Watsonian* magazine (1987–88):

137

36   Bomb damage at 39 Lauriston Place after a Zeppelin raid in April 1916. Courtesy of Dr A C McLaren.

The 100lb Zeppelin bomb exploded on hitting the roof, causing extensive damage . . . The nose cap travelled down through the middle landing, then the sitting-room and finally was stopped by the stone floor in the kitchen pantry . . . My father called out to everyone in the house to ask if all were well . . . My sister in her bedroom on the top flat, shouted that she was alright and was lying looking at the stars! She added that she could not get out of bed as the roof was on top of her. My father warned us all to stay put until he could find out if the floors and stairs were safe. As the electric light had gone, he called to the maids, also on the top flat, to light a match and candle, but they shouted back that they could not do so as they had dived under their beds . . . While we were waiting my brother amused us by drawing cartoons on the spare bedroom door in the thick lime dust which covered everything. He depicted the Zeppelin dropping its bomb on our house, and also a caricature of the Kaiser. These drawings were photographed by the press, and, I understand, were published abroad as propaganda showing how even youngsters were not frightened of German Zeppelins.

Firemen extracted my sister from her bed. When the bomb had exploded her wardrobe had been blown across the room and leant across her bed so preventing the rafters from actually falling on her. She was unhurt apart from a scratch on her leg! They assisted the maids to come from under their beds and found what a wise precaution it had been as the door of the bedroom had been blown on top of one of the beds. The bed where my brother and I should have been sleeping was deep in heavy plaster and debris from the roof and we undoubtedly would have been injured had we been there.

Such an escape seems little short of miraculous. That nose cap remains to this day a polished memento on the doctor's sideboard. There was, however, a darker legacy from the First World War: the scars from trench warfare that continued to afflict so many of the soldiers who survived it. In many cases their health suffered for the rest of their lives, with corresponding implications for the welfare of their families. Tommy Lang's father was gassed, a condition which affected his breathing and his long-term health. And that was not all:

I can still remember him stripping off at night to wash . . . you could see the marks where the shrapnel had gone in and there were still parts of the shrapnel they hadn't been able to take out. So that more or less put a finish to his boxing career.

But Tommy Lang's father at least could work, first, with effort, as a labourer, later, and more happily, in his own small ice-cream business in Fountainbridge. Betty Lennox's father was not so lucky, but his family put a brave face on it:

My dad had been wounded when he was in the army and his old war wounds had affected him to such a degree that he had to give up the tramcars at one time. My dad had what you call 'trench feet'. During the war when he was in the trenches, his boots had frozen solid, so when they cut the boots off, the result was it affected his insteps. So he was off for a while with that, with the result that my mum couldn't make ends meet. So she had to go to the Parish, cap in hand. There was no shame in it at all.

In a poignantly more bizarre memory John Webster remembers fetching an artificial limb for a war-wounded teacher at Tollcross School:

Mr Atkinson had an artificial leg from the '14 War. Now maybe once a month or every couple o' month he used tae pick a boy in the class tae take his spare leg down tae Rothesay Terrace tae get it changed from the Limbless Association. And ye got two pennies from him. You put that box in front of the tramcar from Tollcross to the West End. Ye carried it along Rothesay Terrace. Ye got it changed. Same procedure goin' back tae school again. It was a light aluminium leg. I got a few times tae do it, but everybody got their chance.

Tommy Lang's father's eldest brother was killed three weeks after being sent out to the Western Front in August 1914, and his younger brother, who had forged his age in order to enlist, died at the age of 18 at Passchendaele. His generation remained understandably reticent about such experiences:

My father never talked much about the war. 'After four years of that,' he says, 'I would never let any son of mine go into any services or do anything for the army again.' . . . My mother never said much about it either. She lived in Colchester. She was a forewoman in one of those factories making uniforms for the soldiers . . . I think the main idea with most of them was that it was such a horrible thing that they wanted to put it at the back of their mind and forget it.

For a slightly later generation knowledge and information came from other media:

We learned about the First World War from cinema, from listening to adults, and we were taught about it at school. We were taught to honour the dead, even as small children, and Armistice Day was a very special day, and every child, however poor, went with their penny for their poppy. They sold them at school and you put your penny in the box and got your poppy. The Armistice was strictly observed. It didn't matter which day of the week it was, people did stop. Everything was silent for two minutes. The traffic stopped in the street. There was no sound at all. We had a book at home, one of the few books we as children were allowed to look at, and it was all about the Great War. All the gory pictures. I spent many hours looking at that.

MB

Preparations for the Second World War

Contemporary cinema newsreels and newspapers showed horrific images of the Spanish Civil War, especially the bombing of Guernica, and chronicled daily the mounting tensions in Europe arising from the territorial ambitions of Hitler and Mussolini. War, despite the 'piece of paper' Neville Chamberlain brought so hopefully back from Munich at the end of September 1938, became increasingly probable.

The early preparations on the home front took the form of defence against air attack and the protection of the civilian population. The ARP (Air Raid Precautions) was formed in 1937. Gas masks were distributed to youngsters and adults alike. Trenches were dug in public parks and air raid shelters built

37   Tollcross Peace Souvenir Calendar following the end of the First World War.
Courtesy of the Royal Bank of Scotland on behalf of Mr Alistair Coull, ex Manager.

in streets, back greens and private gardens. Sometimes, as Alex Kitson recalls, the building of these shelters in the back greens could cause unexpected problems:

> There was a hell of a furore when the war started over the building o' these shelters, taking up their space and what have you. The social life of the community was a' done there, even a' the women blethering and everything, was a' done on the back green. Well, that killed it.

Many of the Edinburgh tenements, which were considered solid enough to withstand air raids, were sandbagged—that is, the ground floor entries, front and back, to a common stair would be protected by a baffle erection of concrete and sandbags.

Civilian volunteers joined the Auxiliary Fire and Police Services and training in fire-fighting was given at public demonstrations of the use of stirrup pumps, sand and sandbags. J Walker Blanch worked with the Scottish Motor Traction Company at East Fountainbridge throughout the war, but he was called up to the AFS on the Thursday night before war was declared:

> As a team we went down to St Anne's Maltings at London Road and we collected our gear. Now there was about 10 or 12 of us collected the pumps and all the equipment, the hoses and the hydrants and all the stuff. I was a fully trained fireman in 1937 . . . in the first September crisis. It was a guddle. Tollcross was our centre. Tollcross School. They called it G7B . . . Now we had a senior officer, Cluny Johnson . . . and one or two ordinary firemen and quite quickly I was promoted to a leading fireman. We had a patrol, No. 2 Patrol. We called them the Jaywalkers. That was my team. We did a good deal of training . . . The janitor of the school was very, very kind. He and his wife allowed us to use their bathroom for a hot bath, and they brought us pots of tea, because we had no facilities. No cups, saucers, plates, beds or anything to lie on. They turned over the whole school.

This was during the early months of the war, while the school was evacuated and there were no children around.

Young men were being mobilised for the forces throughout the late 1930s. By April 1939, young men aged 20–21 were being conscripted and by August military reservists were being called up. Mrs Ruby Clifford recalls her fiancé being called up to the Territorials in 1938. He was kept on standby duties for a year before finally going away in 1939:

> I always mind going down and seeing them all get taken away at Grindlay Street . . . big lorries. It was just ordinary builders' lorries that they were all going away in. There was no army trucks.

He was sent to Burntisland in Fife, but coming home on his first leave:

> there was a big crash and there was sixteen of these Edinburgh lads all in that crash. There was four killed. That was really the first tragedy of the war. And it was a lot

38 Auxiliary Fire Service members in 1939. Courtesy of Lothian and Borders Fire Brigade.

39　Air Wardens, Fire Watchers and First Aiders at McEwan's Brewery at Fountainbridge in 1940. Courtesy of Edinburgh City Museums.

of Fountainbridge lads that was in that thing . . . it was on the Kinghorn Road and they bumped into a telephone kiosk. They were taking a bend and they were all standing up in these lorries and they were all thrown. I was just sitting down in his mother's waiting on him coming home . . . when a padre come to the door to say he was lying seriously ill in the Victoria Hospital in Kirkcaldy.

The Territorials had a big parade through the centre of Edinburgh as part of their military send-off. Mrs Ina Begbie remembers the Sunday war was declared:

I mind that too as if it were yesterday because one of my brothers was a regular and they got called up right away tae report and he played the big drum . . . the one wi' the swirly sticks . . . and he had tae report tae Gilmore Place . . . and of course ma mother's running everywhere tae see everybody's all right. And we went up tae Gilmore Place tae watch the boys leaving and we were too late. We'd missed them. So we took the tramcar down tae Princes Street tae see the parade along Princes Street and there's the brother swinging these big sticks. Here, did the head no come off one o' the sticks and my mother's running along trying to pick it up, no tae embarrass her son . . .

There seemed to be no holding back most young men from joining up. Some, like Mr A A Alexander, were inspired by the thrill of uniforms and marching. He had already enrolled at the age of 13 in the Fourth Cadet Battalion of the Royal Scots:

We were kitted out with uniforms, balmorals, boots and gaiters, and we had real rifles and everything. We had real drills. We went on exercises to the King's Park and to Redford Barracks, and the proudest times were for certain functions we were allowed to march on the Castle esplanade. Guys of 14, 15, you felt six foot tall . . . Tremendous stuff . . . I couldn't get in the army quick enough, all because of that.

For others, leaving school in the middle of the Depression, there were economic considerations as well as the challenge of service life:

I left Darroch when I was 16. I'd done the Higher School Certificate. It was then 1936 and jobs were hard tae get, and the biggest majority o' the young lads leavin' school then joined up, and I joined up myself. I wanted tae join the Scots Guards, which was the family regiment, but there was no vacancies then, and that's when the recruitin' offices were on Cockburn Street. And the big sergeant at the door, he told me, 'Why don't ye go down and join the Navy?' So I went down tae Haddington Place, and as I was walkin' in the door, there were two doors, and outside one o' the doors a big marine sergeant was standin'. He says, 'Where are you gaun, lad?' I says, 'I'm gaun tae join the Navy'. He says, 'You don't want tae join the Navy at your height. Come in here and join the Marines'. So that's how I finished up bein' a Marine. I was over 6 feet then.

JOHN WEBSTER

40   Men queing at the Bureau at Riego Street in October 1939 for the call-up. Courtesy of Tommy Lang.

Others still, unless the case of George Ramage, product of a disrupted and nomadic childhood, is unique, found themselves virtually 'Shanghaied'.

> A couple of months after my fourteenth birthday—my mother had apparently had enough of me and my problems—she took me to Maryhill Barracks and signed me into the Cameronians, for 16 years: four years' boys' service, nine years' regular service, three years' reserve duty. I guess that's one solution to a kid problem. It wasn't until I was 16 or 17 that I started to realise the full impact of what she had done . . . I wouldn't be free until I was thirty years old. And what would I do then? The Army wasn't into teaching trades and job skills as they do nowadays.

Tommy Lang was working as an apprentice printer. He didn't have to rush to join up, but the impulse seemed to be stronger than he was:

> So I, big-hearted Arthur, went down and volunteered because my brother had joined the Navy . . . about a year before the war, and so I thought, well, I'll go—at the time I should've given some thought to my mother bein' there hersel'—but when you're that age you just don't think. You want tae go away and do things.

The same was true of Mrs Netta Thomson's brother who:

> didn't get taken up right away because he was a bricklayer, a reserved occupation, but he couldn't stomach not gettin' away, so he went into the Signal Corps, then he joined the Airborne Division and was taken prisoner at Arnhem.

Mrs Margaret Mowat's brother, however, could not summon up the same enthusiasm:

> My brother was 32 when he was called up . . . and my mother used to say, 'Oh, they'll never catch up wi' Andrew'. They never thought they'd get to 32. And you know the day that he went away he was down to get a haircut, and he fainted in the chair. He wasnae a fightin' kind of fellow. Thirty-two, you werenae a young chap. He had five years in India.

For the young women, who were not at this early stage liable for call-up, there seemed to be, at least initially, a greater detachment. Mrs Netta Thomson, then a young teenager, observed her mother's reaction with complete incomprehension:

> I never gave it a thought. I didn't really give it a thought. But I remember the morning war was declared. My mother was sitting on the seat and although I was that age I couldn't understand why, oh, she was crying, tears started to flow, and she was saying, 'Oh, not again—all these young men going away.'

Provision for Children

One of the most significant events after the declaration of war on 3 September 1939, was the mass evacuation of millions of urban children to supposedly safer refuges in the countryside. Many of the Tollcross schoolchildren were sent to Fife:

> We walked down from Tollcross School to the Caley Station and boarded trains in the Caley Station over the Forth Bridge, which was great fun, to Lundin Links. I hadn't been quite as far as that—I'd been to Leven on holiday. That was the furthest I'd ever been in my life! We were shepherded into the church hall, handed brown paper carrier-bags. I can't remember all the things that were in it, but I do remember that it had a tin of meat and biscuits and a huge bar of chocolate. That was to be kept for a real emergency. We didn't know when we were all going to be bombed out of house and home, and where we would get our next bite!
>
> MB

Allocation to a host family was, apparently, pretty haphazard.

> We went into . . . a village hall, or church hall, a big bare room. We were all sitting about in a little huddle . . . families kept together if possible, and it was like a sort of auction. People came . . . and said 'I can take three' or 'I can take two' or . . . 'here's a boy and girl'. So we were probably, being four . . . not so easy to get placed, two boys and two girls, varied age, maybe about eight to thirteen. So eventually this lady took us and it was the luck of the draw. There might have been some nice little houses in the village . . . but we got the short straw.
>
> ALEXANDER A ALEXANDER

And experiences varied. MB, despite the rituals of social distinction, considered herself among the luckier ones:

> We were chosen to go and stay with a couple who had a guest-house and it was like something out of Hollywood. It was a huge three-storey stone house standing on its own grounds called Manderley! It was the very last house before the road curved down on to the beach. We were put into attic bedrooms with coombed ceilings, carpets on the floor and quilts! I didn't know what a quilt was! Beautiful rooms. Proper furniture. Very good food. We ate in the servants' quarters, but we ate more or less the same as what went through to the dining-room . . . There were maids and a cook . . . and the two daughters of the house were called MIss Phyllis and Miss Helen and we had to address them as such . . . We were very conscious of being evacuees, but I was very conscious of having landed lucky, really lucky. We were well looked after and I loved it. It really was extra special after our room and kitchen in Fountainbridge.

The Alexanders' situation, however, also in Fife, was little short of disastrous:

> We finished up in a . . . small steading, or smallholding, and the people . . . had

goats running about in the back yard . . . goats' milk in the porridge you could stand your spoon up in . . . and you had to walk down the yard and draw water from a well, and the toilets were outside—it broke my heart because I wouldn't even use the toilet—I think I had to get medicine eventually because I wouldna go for days—so it was far removed from what we were accustomed to . . . I don't think we even went to school. We had to do our own beds and tidy up and I've got memories of collecting wood. We had some chores to do in the yard and had to fill so many buckets a day, draw the water and lug the buckets. I remember the buckets being very heavy, too—a bucket of water is heavy for a wee boy to lift. I would be about eleven. When my mother looked at us we were running about happy as sandboys in one sense . . . but we werenae too clean and had nits in our hair, then my two sisters I think had infections and my mother was in tears. It was late at night, and hard to organise transport—she had to get a taxi to Leven and then a train to Kirkcaldy—but she took us straight home there and then. We only lasted a few months.

Even the alleged safety threatened to be an illusion.

One day in Lower Largo we were out in the playground and we looked up and saw a Spitfire and a Heinkel . . . having a dogfight up above, and of course the teachers were trying to usher us back in, but we didn't want to go . . . I suppose it was frightening, but we thought it was a great adventure. And then they dropped a bomb outside Largo harbour, and there was a lot of excitement that day too. That was the time they were aiming for the Forth Bridge. It was a stupid place for evacuees, really . . . They should have had us inland.

MRS IRIS MUNRO

By Christmas, 1939, most of the children had gone or been taken home. Back in Edinburgh, however, many of the schools were not ready for them. Some schools, like Tollcross Primary, had been taken over by the AFS. Others had not been adequately adapted to the war regulations relating to blackout and the provision of air raid shelters, so for a time alternative arrangements had to be made. MB remembers coming back to the Flora Stevenson School (her family by this time having left Fountainbridge).

. . . we couldn't go because they hadn't built the shelters and they hadn't reinforced the hall and plastered up all the windows with sticky tape and we had to go in groups. That suited me fine because school was never my favourite place. It was a case of two hours in St Ninian's Church hall for, maybe, arithmetic and English one day, and a couple of hours in another hall for French and geography. That lasted for a few weeks.

Mr A A Alexander remembers much the same situation at Tollcross School:

I do remember that for whatever reason, they were building the shelters or something, the schooling was done in private houses for a time . . . It didn't last long, that. It may have been when the AFS took over the school . . . they may have thought, well, we don't want three or four hundred kids in one place, so . . . it maybe only lasted till they saw there was no danger of the bombing.

I can't remember actually sharing the school with the fire service, but I do remember at some stage being in the playground along with them. They were at the top end. They did use the playground to park one or two of those, not the huge fire engines with the bells, the auxiliary ones. It was like buses they had. They were really buses converted into fire engines. I remember those old tenders actually being driven out of the playground. But there were also shelters in the school playground and you did the drill once a week. There was only three things you carried, a first aid box, a lamp and a big jar. I always remember a big jar of sweets. That was in case maybe you were in a while. And I always remember in the dark—you did it all in the dark to make it realistic—quietly trying to take the lid off to get a couple of sweets and pass them on, and I'm sure that before many months had gone that jar had went down a bit, and you officially hadn't been using it!

School was just as normal during the war, but every now and then we had an air raid warning and you all traipsed out and into the air raid shelters. In the back playground, in front of the nursery school, there were two shelters. There was one in the front playground slightly in front and to the side of the bicycle shed, and I think there was one in the boys' playground as well. We always carried our gas masks to school and everything. They had the Donald Duck and Mickey Mouse ones and then the black ones, but I was a real toff because . . . they were given to you in a brown box, but I had a leather one for mine's.

                                                                    MRS ALICE BURT

John Wilson remembers the gas masks being given out in a large hall filled with trestle tables at Fountainbridge School. He still has a very clear memory of the various types of mask. The standard mask, for instance, was:

made of black rubber with a single transparent window at eye-level. It was secured by two adjustable elastic straps which were attached at the top . . . and passed through a common metal clip at the back of the head to two points at chin -level. At some time early in the war another filter was fitted and secured by a piece of plastic insulating tape. This was like an open boot polish tin, with holes in both parts and the filter material in between them.

But some time after the initial issue of this mask another type was produced for children:

This was made of a reddish-orange rubber and had two circular eye-pieces. A small flap of folded rubber was attached below the eye-pieces which looked rather like a cartoon nose. When the additional filter was added to these masks yellow tape was used, which may have led to them being called 'Donald Duck', though personally I cannot remember them being called anything other than 'Mickey Mouse'.

He also remembers how jealous he was of his younger sister when she was given one of these colourful masks and he was not!

The Respirator type of mask he describes as being:

> a bit like a circular aquarium with one end open and a bellows pump on one side.
> It was made of cast metal with rectangular windows on the top side and padding
> on the inside of the bottom. The whole thing was painted the dark colour of green
> commonly called British Racing Green. The open end of the respirator was fitted
> with an eyeletted leather cloth skirt fitted with a drawstring—the idea being that
> the filtered air pumped in would maintain a higher pressure inside the respirator
> and prevent the ingress of any gas.

Mrs I D Graham, who worked as a teacher at Tollcross School from 1941–3,
remembers:

> the windows bricked up to about six inches from the top, which meant working all
> day in electric light. In the rest of the school the auxiliary service were in it, with the
> result there were no cloakrooms for the children. The system was—there were two
> long poles, everybody was supposed to have a latchet on the back of their coat, and
> you held the pole out and the boys put all their coats over this pole, and we hung
> it on a hook, and then the girls came and put theirs over the other pole and it hung
> over two hooks. On a wet day, with the windows bricked up and the electric light,
> the atmosphere was awful.
>
> We did fire-watching. All we had was a stirrup pump . . . and a bucket of sand.
> I don't know what we'd have done if the place caught fire. We did this fire-watching
> in rota . . . We didn't sleep very much.

John Wilson remembers the removal of railings from Tollcross School and
the eager spirit of enterprise it unintentionally inspired:

> The way this was done was to cut them off flush with the stone in which they were
> mounted and we soon discovered that a nail and a stone could help us dig out the
> lead which secured the remains to the stone and Asa Wass would buy this lead.

Occasionally there would be the diversion of a new arrival in the class, or an
unscheduled withdrawal, or a special injunction:

> This Polish man brought his daughter to the school. She didn't know much English,
> but enough, I think, just to get by at school. But about a fortnight later her father
> was put into prison, not because he had done anything wrong, but because he was
> Polish. They didn't call it prison; it was an internment camp.
>
> MRS ALICE BURT

> Kids would disappear from the school for a couple of days and you found out that
> their fathers had been killed.
>
> MRS ALICE BURT

> I also remember going into the school one day at Tollcross. We were told to be very
> quiet and we werenae to annoy James. The teacher just said that James's dad had
> been taken a prisoner by the Germans. His dad was one of the first persons to be
> taken prisoner and James was an only son.
>
> MRS INA BEGBIE

Controls, Restrictions, Rationing and Shortages

In ordinary everyday life the state of war brought many demands and inconveniences. There were 'no-go' areas for unauthorised civilians, for instance:

> I remember people going up to the Rubber Mill, especially during the war. Of course, it was all cut off up there. The police used to guard all that. You couldn't go over the bridges during the war. There was one wee patrol bridge. You couldn't go over that, and there were troops in the beginning actually guarding up there.
>
> STAN PLAYER

If you had a big house you could be liable for billeting, whether you liked it or not:

> There was four of us in the family, two boys and two girls. But then there was more in the house, because my mum looked after my grandfather and another uncle as well. It was a big house we had in Lauriston and during the war she had to take in other people. They made you take people in if you had room. They came round and assessed the situation. I can remember different people over the years. We had Polish WAAFs at one time. We had a couple of sailors. We had Rosyth dock workers. You always had to take two, and as they went put another two. So you had to utilise your full rooms. They paid you, but not very much. Same as they took all the railings away from the front of the house. You know they never went back . . . We had service people and foreigners and everything living with us in them days. My mother had to do it all.
>
> ALEXANDER A ALEXANDER

Food rationing, which was introduced in January 1940, affected everyone. At first it was 4oz ham, 4oz bacon, 12oz sugar and 4oz butter per adult per week. In March meat was rationed to 1s. 10d. worth a week for adults (about 1lb in weight) and 11d. worth for young children. In July tea, margarine and cooking fats were rationed to 2oz per week. By the summer of 1941 the cheese ration was down to 1oz a week and the distribution of eggs was controlled. By November, milk too, was under controlled distribution. Then the points system was introduced to supplement rations. By the summer of 1942 there was no more white bread and packets of dried egg powder began to appear. By early 1945 whalemeat and barracuda were on sale in the fish shops. Heavy workers, such as miners, qualified for higher rations and pregnant women were issued with green ration books which entitled them to additional milk, orange juice and cod liver oil. Locally, people made shift for extras as they could. St Cuthbert's issued their members with white cards, but mostly it was a matter of word of mouth or being in the know:

> There was Eddie Brannan, he had the butcher's shop . . . I registered for butcher's meat with Eddie because my mother went there. We'd go in sometimes and he'd say 'Firewatchers today'. Now his mother made the most gorgeous potted head and there was always queues of people for potted head and things that were off the

ration. He'd say, 'Firewatchers'. 'Oh, lovely, I'll have them'. Now nobody else in the shop knew what you were talking about. He was an air raid warden and they'd an empty house in Lauriston Place opposite his shop and they all used to stay there at night, and for that night he made special sausages, almost all beef, and we just called them 'firewatchers'!

MRS GRACE TAYLOR

Two ounces of corned beef a week, but I was never aware of being hungry or anything. My mother sacrificed a lot for us. In Lauriston Park, where the car shop is, they sold horsemeat. We had this butcher round the corner—Eddie Brannan—he was a bit slapdash, but he was a right good-hearted soul and he looked after his own customers, no doubt about it. Someone would say, 'Eddie Brannan's corned beef's in' and we'd all away round and stand in the queue, or 'he's got sausages in', and we'd all go round and get sausages. Everybody told one another

MRS IRIS MUNRO

You used tae go up tae the Store and I used tae try tae find wee Willie—ye didna like the three women that were servin'—because he was on from when I was a wee kid, standin' wi' the basket wi' the handle over like that and my feet on either side, talkin' tae him . . . he was awfy good slippin' ye maybe two pound o' sugar, or . . . he used tae maybe no tear your coupon off—people were all wantin' that, of course—just leave it so you could get more again another day.

MRS MARGARET MOWAT

The bit I mind about rationing was . . . one time Betty and I was out and we were going up Home Street and there was a big queue at Rankins. Well, every person with a ration book was allowed a lettuce and two tomatoes, but we had to stand in the queue. I gets a lettuce and two tomatoes and Betty gets a lettuce and two tomatoes for my mother. So when she comes in frae her work I say, 'We got a lettuce and two tomatoes fir ye'. 'What?' I had tae tell her the price and they were dear. 'Dinna tell me you stood in a queue for that?' She wisnae pleased. She thought it was terrible.

MRS CHRISSIE BORTHWICK

Mrs Munro had the benefit of an uncle in the Merchant Navy and an aunt in New Zealand, but she had to keep an eye on her overly kind-hearted mother:

I remember the sweetie ration. That was a thing that used to get to us. That was terrible! I had an uncle who was at sea on a merchant ship. He used to bring bananas and onions and things, and this was unheard of. My aunt in New Zealand used to send a pack with butter and pieces of mutton in it and she used to wrap eggs in hot fat, sealed in, and you had to melt it off. My mother—she had such a big heart—used to divide it up among the neighbours, keeping some for us. Somebody was always 'an awful poor soul', and I had to watch my clothes because she would say, 'Oh, she was really needing a pair of shoes', and she would go and hand over my shoes! The people in our stair ate well when the New Zealand parcel came in.

And there was often someone in the family whose special needs had to take priority:

> I remember with things being on the ration you were only allowed so much butter, and with my father having a bad stomach he got the butter ration and we had to eat margarine, and I always hated the stuff after that.
>
> MRS ALICE BURT

Lexie Lang, perversely, acquired a preference for powdered egg, because she liked the way her English mother-in-law made it:

> I remember when I used to be goin' to Tommy's mother I'd say to my mother, 'You have my egg this week because I like the dried egg.' . . . And my mother would say, 'Oh, I'll get powdered egg in and do it,' and I would say, 'Oh, but you don't do it as well as she does it'. I preferred it to the fresh egg.

The effect of rationing on wedding celebrations caused particular concern. It was a help if you had useful contacts of some kind or could draw on the pooled support of an extended family:

> All you normally got for catering was what you call a 'tea', so my mother wouldn't have that. So she ordered . . . soup, steak pie, tatties and peas . . . and everyone managed to mump a wee bit off their butcher. Even my grandfaither handed over his ration book to get these steak pies . . . and my mother and dad stayed up all night and everything was carried up to the hall, and there wasnae individual dishes enough to go round all the guests for the trifle . . . And I had a two-storey wedding cake. Willie was on submarines and he got a lot of dried fruit to make up for the things they were deprived of. And my dad managed to get some and someone else managed to get some and a woman in Craigmillar made the cake. And there was enough left over that there was a cake made about the same size as the bottom tier and that went back as a good luck cake. So we had a great wedding.
>
> MRS PEGGY WEDDELL

> The reception was in the Cavendish. We had a meal and Tommy's mother got a firkin o' beer . . . There was a band and dancin' . . . It was well done . . . Things were hard to get, food and that . . . but his mother worked some deal. I don't know what it was, but she got a few extras and I think everybody enjoyed theirsel'.
>
> TOMMY and LEXIE LANG

A later feature of food rationing was the 'Dig for Victory' campaign. In order to reduce as much as possible dependence on imported food people were encouraged to grow their own. The number of allotments in the city rose from 1,500 at the outbreak of the war to nearly 6,000 by the spring of 1942. Many of these were in the Meadows. Mr J Walker Blanch had one:

> That was only five shillings a year, a very nominal sum. What a produce you got. You couldnae eat it all, so you gave it away. . . . We never starved, we used to make banana spread, with parsnips and banana essence.

Clothes were rationed from 1 June 1940. The price, quality and style of all clothing, cloth and footwear were strictly controlled. Frills were banned and two top British designers were commissioned to design fashionable prototypes for women to copy. These were disseminated through the women's magazines of the time. The coupon system was introduced, actually copied from Germany. Everyone had to make stringent economies. From 1943 the government instituted its 'make do and mend' campaign, patronising but patriotic, encouraging women to make the best use of what they had.

These restrictions, too, affected wartime weddings, like Lexie Lang's:

> My wedding dress was white satin, but vey plain. I can't remember where I bought it—the Guinea Shop or somewhere. There used to be a shop called the Guinea Shop, where you only paid twenty-one shillings, at the West End . . . The headdress and the veil was Tommy's sister's from her wedding, so that was borrowed . . . I had to have it and I couldn't get it any other way, because the coupons was a nuisance. There was no special coupons if you were getting married . . . If you were wantin' to be dressed for your wedding you had to borrow or save up your coupons. It was difficult to get bouquets made up, so that was why I just had a white prayer book in place of the flowers . . . My bridesmaid wore the dress from Tommy's sister's wedding also. Now you would say, 'Oh, no, I want something different', but you had to just go with the circumstances.
>
> During the war everybody got married in a suit unless somebody in the family had a wedding dress. My cousin's wedding dress was made out of my gran's curtains. I remember that much because my mother helped to make it and grannie's curtains were used for the lace and that. It was a lovely dress when it was finished.
>
> MRS ALICE BURT

> I was going to get married in my uniform, but my mother wouldnae hear of it . . . So we went up to the wee wife up Lauriston . . . Rachel . . . the Polish Jew, or whatever she was . . . and I got a blue dress because blue was my colour. It was a short dress. There was no way you could have got a weddin' dress. It was blue *crêpe de chine*. My husband had his uniform on . . .
>
> MRS NETTA THOMSON

Stockings, too, were impossible to come by, but fashion-conscious women had their own ways of overcoming this problem:

> You painted your legs with, to me it was like ochre, a liquid, like foundation, which we must have bought in the chemist, and it dried. You couldn't have it patchy. You put it on with your hands. And sometimes you got somebody to help you with it, where they could see. And drew a black pencil mark for the seam. You didn't want to go dancin' wi' white legs.
>
> MRS LEXIE LANG

It wasn't very practical—Mrs Jane Moore remembers that it came off on the sheets—but it undoubtedly served its turn. Real luxury came in the form of gifts of silk stockings:

41   Tommy and Lexie Lang on their wedding day, 12 April 1941, at St Cuthbert's
      Parish Church. Courtesy of Tommy and Lexie Lang.

Tommy sent me silk stockings. I think he sent me a pair and his mother a pair . . . from Iraq, Baghdad . . . the black market. These things were easily obtainable out there for some reason . . . That must have been the end of '41, the beginning of '42 . . . and, oh, they lasted for ages. Of course, I made sure that they lasted.

TOMMY and LEXIE LANG

Lexie Lang also had a keen eye for interesting imports:

You got accustomed to the shortages. Maybe they'd have something come into the shops. For instance, I would get an hour off my work tae go tae Allan's in Princes Street if I heard they were going to have Joyce shoes, American shoes. They were lovely shoes.

Courtship and Marriage, Honeymoons and Separation

Marriages often had to be hastily arranged, sometimes from a distance and often against the possibility of suddenly cancelled leave:

My husband was in Hampshire and I was in Derby. My sister had to do all the arrangin' up here. It so happened the month we had arranged to get married all the leaves were cancelled because they were invading Europe. However, I got a leave and his leave was arranged, but when he went to go and get his pass, the officer wouldn't give him his pass, and I'm sittin' in Grove Street and he was supposed to come in on the six o'clock train from London. Ten o'clock he still wasnae in. We were getting married in Dalry Church. My mother says, 'Go up tae the Post Office and telephone Glasgow tae tell them no tae come through for the wedding, that he's no here.' So I rins away tae the Post Office at the top of Grove Street, and I'm just tellin' the man the telegram tae send when he comes flyin' in, and his hand was cut. He had torn it on the bannisters as soon as he had got in. He had to go over the officer's head who had refused him the pass. So we were married then on the 29th of December 1943.

MRS NETTA THOMSON

Mrs J D Thomson became engaged to a naval man from Buckie who was stationed at Rosyth. While they were courting:

He stayed in the Sailors' Home in St James Square. He wouldn't stay with us because 'people would talk' and 'think the worst'. He used to come and meet me at my work, but while I was working he used to sit in East Princes Street Gardens, where Waverley Market is now. A policeman came up to him. He was recalled. This is what they did. Very few people on phones . . . He came along to Gibson Terrace and told my mother that he had to go back. Of course it was a false alarm.

I think it was after that the Navy would only let them out for 2-3 hours in the afternoons and they weren't allowed to come across the Forth. They had to stay in Dunfermline or Inverkeithing. So we, the wives and sweethearts used to have to go in the train over to Inverkeithing and wait for them coming in on the bus from

Rosyth. One day . . . the porter on the station said he would ask the WVS canteen to give us a cup of tea as there wasn't much in Inverkeithing. We weren't supposed to get served as it was only for the troops and they werenae very keen: 'What do you want to be bothered with sailors for? We're sick of them!' And one woman . . . tore into her saying, 'You wouldnae have any tea to serve to anybody if it wasnae for sailors!'.

When we got married he had leave to come and he wanted me to go to Buckie to meet his people, but I couldn't get off my work unless I was married to him. We couldn't get a special licence at first . . . When he couldn't get it he went back to the Registrar who said he should be able to get one and told him about Mr Maitland, the Minister at St Bride's Church, Orwell Place, who ended up in the Navy as a Chaplain. Mr Maitland was very nice . . . We got it all arranged and we were getting married the next day . . . When we got the licence, we had to go down to the church to have the banns called, and there were two women out in the street brushing their rugs. We had to stay inside at the back of the kirk door and the minister went out and read out the banns in the street. Then he brought the women in because they had to sign the banns. When we got back to the house I had to get changed, then we went back to the church . . . We had our lunch, and then we were going to get the 2 o'clock train to go to Buckie. We walked along Fountainbridge to Lothian Road to get a tram. Normally we would have walked all the way, but we were in a hurry and we both had cases. It started to snow. We eventually got to Buckie at 9 o'clock at night.

Honeymoons, as Mrs Thomson's account suggests, weren't elaborate or even particularly romantic. People didn't have money, travel by train was restricted and servicemen would only be given a few days' leave. It usually meant staying with in-laws, sometimes in very cramped conditions:

We didn't have the cash for a honeymoon and it wisnae very practical. He only had seven days leave. So it was just a case of livin' wi' your folks until it was time for him to go back. Then Tommy went off to India and I didn't see him again until May of '45. I stayed at home wi' my mother and carried on working in the same job I had.

Mrs Lexie Lang

When we got married my sister got a bed put up in this boxroom, because my mother had a boxroom in this house that my granny had. So she had the boxroom and they had the bedroom. So Alex and I didn't have a house, nowhere to stay, so we moved into the bedroom and my sister went into the boxroom. We were there a year and then we got this house round in Grove Street.

Mrs Annie Kitson

Long separations were unavoidable:

During the war you worried all the time when they were away, especially in the infantry. I had regular communications before he went overseas, but it wasn't so easy after that because they could never tell you where they were. You were more or less guessing. You'd hear about a battle here or a battle there and you'd wonder, I hope he's no in that. It was just a sort of tension all the time.

Mrs Lexie Lang

Tommy Lang was taken prisoner during a German raid on the Greek island of Leros late in 1943 and after a hazardous sea-crossing to Athens was imprisoned in a camp outside Munich. Lexie records how she got the news:

> When Tommy was taken prisoner, first of all I got a notice from the War Office to say that he was missing and as soon as they knew anything they would let me know. Well, it was a good many weeks, going into a month or so, and there was two letters came. One was from . . . an elderly man from Peebles to say that he had heard his name over this Lord Haw Haw programme as a prisoner of war . . . The other was from a WAAF who was on duty in the communications and she had heard it . . . It was two or three weeks before I heard frae the army that he was a prisoner of war and what camp he was in and where I was to write and I was not to mention any broadcasts from the Germans. If they'd said that before I would have known, but I had wrote one letter when I got the address . . . That upset me. I thought, 'Now what have I done?' So I wrote to the War Office and I got a nice letter back from them to say that the censors would catch it, but not to worry about it. They said, 'You have enough to worry about without worrying about that'. And Tommy told me he got a letter. It was just 'Dear Tommy' and bits cut out everywhere!

Her efforts to send him clothes and other supplies met with no success:

> He never got any o' the Red Cross parcels I sent him. I was given a voucher from the Red Cross every so often to go and get him underwear and socks and things like that. And I always went to the same place to get them, Hope Brothers in Princes Street. And I sent them regular, but he said he never got them. Once I sent him a pair of glasses, goggles, for the sand, that was when he was still in Egypt, but he never got them either. He was very unlucky. As he says, durin' wartime, people pick these things up. They can guess what sort o' thing that's in.

Bombs, Sirens, Shelters and Blackout

Transport was another aspect of the home front which came under tight government control. In those days Alex Kitson was a vanman with St Cuthbert's:

> For example, the lorry I drove was seconded to the fire service. And if the sirens blew, anytime, it didnae matter where you were, whether you were in the hoose or in the pictures or out in the road, you had to report back to the depot and then you were allocated a fire station. I was allocated one of those auxiliary fire stations up at Merchiston Castle . . . I was only once at a fire. It was when they bombed the distillery at Dalry and I took the pump down there. That was about the only bombing there was in Edinburgh. It was a Sunday morning, at five o'clock. I was going to my work and when I was coming down Viewforth, the sirens blew and then there was an explosion like I don't know what.

This was the bombing of the bonded warehouse in Duff Street in September, 1940. Lexie Lang also remembers it. Her mother-in-law was living in Downfield Place at the time:

> You knew that a bomb had dropped somewhere because I didn't live that far away, but I never thought about it till I went down there and there was the police and firemen. And then of course they wouldn't let you past. They'd hit a distillery. There was whisky running in the streets. Everbody was sayin', 'You see a' the drunk firemen!' But the men were marvellous. It was quite scary at the time, but when you think what they were gettin' down in London you can imagine.

Many individuals remember the sound of the German planes going west for the bombing of Clydebank and the guns on the periphery of Edinburgh firing at them on their way back. Mrs Jane Moore can pinpoint her memory of the raids to March, 1941, because she was ill and confined to bed in her flat in the High Riggs after the birth of her daughter. She heard the planes going over in waves two nights running.

Mrs Betty McAnna was caught out in Princes Street on one of these evenings:

> We used tae do voluntary work in this canteen in Waterloo Place. That was when Clydebank was bombed, because I can remember with the sireens goin' we'd been kept in and I thought, oh, I've got tae get home, and the only way I could get home was walkin' it—so I can remember another girl and I walkin' along Princes Street and duckin' in doors tae avoid the shrapnel, and I thought, Oh, I wish tae God I was home! I wish I hadnae went there the night! We got up tae Woolworths, up Lothian Road, and there was three sailors standin'—I think they must have come oot the Palais—they were rotten drunk, couldnae stand, they were singin', and they'd tin hats on their heads and the shrapnel was hittin' them, and I thought, Oh God, I wish I had half your disease, I wouldnae know what was goin' on!

Mrs Netta Thomson recalls the effect on her bricklayer brother who was sent over to clear rubble after the Clydebank bombing:

> I've never seen him so upset. He definitely was cryin' when he come home. 'Oh, mother!' he says. And he was sent tae a Catholic area, and it was crucifixes and all the dead bodies . . . just a young lad . . . a young civilian man and just dumped in Clydebank.

But if Edinburgh remained remarkably bomb-free there was always the anxiety:

> I used to go down to Port Seton to the dancing with the other girls who worked with me in the rubber mill. Now I'd be coming back on my own and I'd be thinking, Oh, my God, will I get home before they sirens go? Because if the sirens went you had to get in a shelter and if you got caught in Princes Street you had tae go in the Gardens, in the big shelters, and ye never knew how long ye were gonna be. On the road up I'd get the bus to the square and then come running down Princes Street

and catch a tram up to Lothian Road and run along Fountainbridge. I'd say, Oh my, oh, let me get home, let me get home, let me get home to my mother, so that I'd be there, and she'd be safe and I'd be safe.

MRS MARGARET MOWAT

   After a while people didn't bother with the shelters, and some, as a result of their circumstances, took a philosophical view. When Mrs Mowat joined the ATS and her able-bodied brothers were in the services her mother was left at home with only her deaf and dumb son:

42   Margaret Mowat in the uniform of the ATS during the Second World War.
Courtesy of Mrs Margaret Mowat.

Well, my mother having rheumatism, bad with her legs, when I was away and my two brothers were away, and Jimmy might have been on night-shift that week, she never used tae get out o' her bed, and there was no way of getting her down to a damp shelter, she would get her rheumatics more again. And when Jimmy was in his bed he didnae hear the aeroplanes coming. So she would say, 'What's the good o' us gettin' out o' our bed . . . It was 'san-fairy-ann' to my mother if the bomb dropped or not.

But amid all the trials and confusions of the time there were episodes of defiant humour. Lexie Lang recalls her mother-in-law's concern for her insurance policies:

Tommy's mum had this Gladstone bag. She used to take it everywhere with her and she had her insurance policies in it. As soon as the siren went, if she was in the shop and it was during the day, she'd lift this bag, and she'd go runnin' down to where you went for the shelter, and as if the guys in they planes could hear her, she'd be shoutin' and wavin' this bag, 'You lot o' buggers!'—wi' the English accent, 'Eh, you buggers!'.

Blackout was rigidly enforced from the outbreak of the war. Tommy and Lexie Lang were unexpectedly caught up in a 'practice' blackout one evening before war was actually declared:

I remember comin' frae the pictures the night o' the blackout and it was terrible. We said, 'Oh, my God!' I had tae get the tramcar at Tollcross to where she lived at Shandon. And of course it went up to the King's and turned along Gilmore Place, and all you could see was glimmers o' blue lights. This was them havin' a practice before the war started.

Mrs Betty McAnna remembers a comic moment on her way to a British Legion dance at Coates Crescent:

I can remember walkin' past the Police Station one night, and my mother's friend fell, and she stood for about ten minutes apologisin', 'I'm awfy sorry,' she says, 'I don't know who you are, but I've fallen all over you and I hope I havenae hurt you'. And my mother says, 'Who's she talkin' to?' I says, 'I don't know, but it's a sandbag that's lyin' there!'.

Lexie Lang's father was an engine-driver. As she and her husband remember, the blackout was particularly hard on him:

It was the same travellin' on trains durin' the war . . . You were fallin' over people sleepin' in the corridors, the trains were so packed, and all you could see were glimmers o' light. My dad was an engine-driver and the strain was terrible, judging the end o' the platform and that. They had the firebox and of course the driver used to lean out. I remember they used to put canvas hoods over the back o' them so you couldn't see the light o' the fire when they were stokin' the fire. Where the driver stood was quite open. Oh, his eyes used to be, oh, terrible!

43   War time fire at Duff Street Distillery in 1940. Courtesy of Lothian and Borders Fire Brigade.

War Work

In the early days of the war many women had wanted to join up like like their male counterparts, but no real role was perceived for them then. As the war progressed, however, their labour was not merely in demand but actually required. By March 1941 women aged 20-21 were being directed towards essential war work and by the end of that year this applied to women up to the age of 30. By June of the same year there were 100,000 women in the services. By December, conscription of women had been introduced. Those free from family ties and in the prime of life found themselves liable for war work either in industry or the services. By mid-1943 nearly 3 million married women and widows were employed, compared with a million and a quarter before the war. Some women made the transition reluctantly. Others, especially the young and fancy-free, seem to have had an immensely good time:

> Any teenager from 16 or 17 to her twenties who said they didn't enjoy the war years, I don't think they could be tellin' the truth—unless you maybe lived in London or somewhere where you got bombed—you met people you would never have met in a million years. Social life and services both . . . once the Canadians and these people came into Edinburgh and you were meetin' all these different guys, dancin' an' that. It was a good time for teenagers.
>
> MRS NETTA THOMSON

Annie Kitson had started work in 1936 in St Cuthbert's bakery in the High Riggs, specialising in cake decorating. She stayed there until she married:

> Then I had to go to a war effort, of course. I had to go and paint army trucks. And then I was down in Haymarket Ice Rink washing out submarine parts . . . Until I had my family, until I had Irene. I was about 23. I hated that [the war work] because I was just getting into the job I was doing. But then there was the shortage of sugar. That put paid to the decorating of the cakes. I had to leave because that wasn't an essential job . . . I had to leave and go into this painting wagons at Alexander's great big place. And the same in the Haymarket Ice Rink. I was up to my elbows in paraffin, cleaning submarine parts. Hated it! had to wear overalls.

Mrs Betty McAnna worked in Scott Morton's, just off Gorgie:

> It was a place that made furniture, a joinery works of some sort, but the war work we had tae do was, of all things, making bunk beds that were put into the boats for the sailors—you used tae write your name in it, in case a sailor would like to write back! . . . You got the frame. The joiners would put the frame together and bring them through, and you had to—it was a wire, the wire that they lay on—you had to nail it at the one side and then pull it. My hands used to be sore. And you had tae do so many a day . . . And office furniture, in-trays and out-trays . . . what they termed 'war office furniture'. One o' the young chaps that was there said, 'You're no doin' it right', and I thought, 'I'll show *you*! And one of the head ones came down and said, 'Good for you'. And I got an award. I'd beat the men at making the in- and out-trays. I'd done sixty-odd in one day and they'd only done forty.

Mrs Margaret Mowat, too, started in a bakery:

> Some of the girls were leaving and were going into the rubber mill to work. Well,
> of course, it was preparing for war and we were doing the gas masks. I went in first
> because I wanted to learn the sewing machines. I was on the baby gas masks, the
> one with the big mask and the covering over the baby . . there was a lining in it and
> we stitched a khaki-coloured piece on to it, and we just kept stitching all day like
> that.

Mrs Jane Moore had a more 'hush-hush' role. When her daughter was three
or four she put her in the Central Halls wartime nursery at Tollcross and went
to work in Ford and Torrie's hardware shop on Hanover Street. At the back of
the shop was a factory making invasion barges. She was simply told it was a
factory 'doing war work'. She had to stay in the front shop, selling what they
had, which wasn't much, and to keep an eye on who came in. She wasn't
involved in the factory work at all and only met the girls who worked there in
the canteen.

Many firms made their own internal arrangements for fire-watching. This
was particularly important for volatile substances like alcohol and vulcanite.
Lexie Lang worked in the chemical factory in Wheatfield Road, Gorgie, making
up medicinal tablets and saccharine:

> During the war we used to spend about one weekend in five fire-watching at the
> factory. There were so many women, about four or five of us. It was a voluntary
> thing, but once you were in it you had to have a good excuse to say, 'Oh, I can't
> come, when it was your turn. But nobody wanted to do that because we quite
> enjoyed doin' it. They had lovely dormitories for us. We supplied our own food. We'd
> maybe take sandwiches. We weren't restricted that we were stuck in there. We
> could go out to get something and bring it back, although there was always
> somebody there to see that you showed your identity and everything when you
> came back. We had to have fire drill and they'd good recreation facilities for us. It
> wasn't a hard thing to do. The firemen came and showed us how in an emergency
> to put the hoses together . . . and how to come down from the building to escape.
> You had a contraption that went up your back and round your legs, so it was like
> a seat round your back and your thighs. It was like a canvas material . . . It was a
> bit scary, but once you'd done it you'd say, 'Och, I'll go up and do it again'. Of course,
> I don't know what it would have been like in a real emergency. We never had one
> to cope with.

Mrs Betty McAnna was involved in a similar arrangement at Scott Morton's,
except that relevant training seems to have been non-existent:

> When it came to the weekends we had tae do our share of the fire-watchin'. There
> was a room you went into and there was a wee kind of stove thing, and if you took
> a wee tin o' soup you could heat it up, and if you took sandwiches you could make
> a cup o' tea. This was in the buildin', but we had tae go up on the roof o' Scott
> Morton's wi' the tin hat on and walk round it. And I said tae the man one day, 'What

am I supposed tae be lookin' for?' Because you're never told! He said, 'You've got tae spot aeroplanes', and I says, 'But if I see an aeroplane, so what?' He says, 'Well, you're supposed tae know the difference between ours and theirs', which I never ever found out!

Both Mrs Margaret Mowat and Mrs Netta Thomson had a rude awakening from their apparently secure jobs at the rubber mill:

> We were all supposed to be a reserved occupation till there were some days you hadna a lot o' work to do and so you were away early. I went tae the Palais dancin' in the afternoon. And of course this lady came from the Bureau and we were all made a reserved occupation but you had to state what you wanted to go to if you were being conscripted. I'd said the ATS, but when the time came I wanted tae go to the Land Army. But I'd committed myself to the ATS and you couldn't change it. So I remember the one week we were made the reserved occupation and the following week we were paid off. It would have been the early part of 1942 for I hadn't a job after that.
>
> Mrs Margaret Mowat

But both, unlike many, took to the ATS, the discipline and the drills, the comradeship, the technical skills they had to learn (and the fatigue duties that came their way if they stayed out too late and were caught!) with relish:

> It was an adventure, an exciting adventure . . . Margaret and I both, bein' dancers, we loved the drill, we loved the marching. It was absolutely fantastic . . . I think women, or girls, who had a wee sense o' adventure, these were the people who enjoyed it. I mean, you got the ones who cried all the time and moaned all the time.
>
> Mrs Netta Thomson

> The thing I think for ALL girls was freedom. You didn't have your mother behind you.
>
> Mrs Margaret Mowat

Mrs Mowat joined up in spite of strong pressures to stay at home:

> Well, I went and I shouldn't have gone because my mother wasn't a well woman, and the doctor, McLaren, said I shouldn't have been going, but my mother says, 'Well, she's young. She wants to go'. She wouldn't stop me. But I remember the day I did go, my mother and I, she could hardly speak. And I went out to Penicuik. I've still got my train ticket. My mother kept it. My mother kept all these things.

And girls from respectable homes were expected to behave themselves:

> The day I left Newbattle Abbey the officer came in and says to me, 'You've to go outside. Your mother's outside'. Parents didn't get in the grounds, you see. So I went out and I says, 'What is it? I'm goin' away in the mornin'!' So she says, I'm just out tae tell you tae take care of yourself and remember, always remember, that you were

brought up to be a good girl, so don't let this gettin' away from home go to your head and get yourself into trouble'. She thought that was important enough for her tae come to the country from Edinburgh to tell me.

MRS NETTA THOMSON

I got that in all my letters from my brother, the middle one that was in India. He took the place of my father right from when I was a baby. He used to write: 'You stay on the straight and narrow. Never volunteer for out here because I see what happens to them when they come out here'.

MRS MARGARET MOWAT

But she had her own way of shrugging off this moral shadow:

The other one was in the Shetlands. He used tae send me the tin of fifty Capstan cigarettes. That was a' that I used tae look for!

Mrs Peggy Weddell volunteered at $17\frac{1}{2}$ for the Land Army:

I wanted into the WRENS and it was very difficult then, and we didn't want to go to the ATS because we didn't like the stockings . . . so we went to the Land Army. We went for an interview and this woman says to me, 'Are you going in for horticulture or agriculture?' And I said, 'Well, what's the difference?' She said, 'Well, agriculture, you'd be working with the animals'. And I said, 'Coos, and things like that? Oh, I'm no doing that!' So I said, 'Well, I'll go in for the other thing'. So she says, 'Well, that's market gardening'. So I actually thought I would be picking floo'rs! . . . I regret it in a sense because we weren't looked after like the forces. We weren't accommodated or housed. Maybe some were . . . I went to a private place to begin with at West Linton, Carlops, it was, Newhall Estate. It was miles from anywhere. I took the place of the gardener that had been called up and the old gardener had collapsed and died. I lived with his wife and she showed me, nightly, where her man had collapsed and died. Then I went to Musselburgh, to a hostel, and I met some very, very interesting people. But, by God, we worked hard. And we weren't adequately rigged oot and there was quite a few cases of TB. I was in the Land Army for three years. It was just sheer perseverance. I was touch and go with TB as well.

Patriotic Fervour and Home Entertainments

On the home front, despite all the privations, there seems to have been a strong patriotic spirit, especially when it was mingled with entertainment. Back green concerts for the troops were a feature:

My mother used tae run Spitfire dances . . . which was money for the army fund, like tae send parcels. And I remember she had one in what was Maxime's then but became the Cavendish, and I must have been 15 or 16, and the sirens went and we were just in and we had tae come oot, and the tram depot used tae have a shelter and everybody had tae run into the shelter . . . and when the sirens went off you all went back into the dance again.

MRS INA BEGBIE

And then one time I remember that most of the back green concerts were for the war effort . . . and every back green had a concert and they all used to try and outdo each other.

Mrs Betty Lennox

The Palais continued to be a popular place for entertainment, although there were fights and rumours of fights, especially when the American and Canadian servicemen arrived on the scene:

> I remember the trouble we used to have with the American sailors. They said it was usually between them and the Royal Scots. They would retreat to the stair and defend the stair. That's where most of the fights were. But all the time I went to the Palais, I never saw a fight . . . it must have been after the time of the servicemen.

George Robertson

This is borne out by Mrs Betty McAnna's memories of working in the cloakroom there during the war (see chapter 3).

At the outbreak of war all theatres and cinemas were closed for several months. When they re-opened they were to become immensely popular diversions for civilians and service personnel alike. With a seven-year-old son and a husband who wasn't fit enough for call-up, and whose peacetime occupation, glazing, was for the time being not much in demand, AHR took a job at the Lyceum Theatre and fell in love with it:

> There was such a wonderful atmosphere in the theatre. There were big placards telling that entertainment was essential—probably it was about the only thing that people could spend their money on, everything was rationed so much. Now there were so many army personnel came into the theatre, and there was French people who probably had evacuated themselves over here. They came in week after week. We got the same patrons.

MB, however, recalls a darker aspect to demonstrations of patriotic fervour:

> We were brainwashed . . . the cheers if you saw the RAF in the cinema dropping bombs on somewhere. Everybody went mad. When I think of how we cheered when they dropped the atom bomb. I feel ashamed of that—what we were doing to other people.

John Wilson reinforces this with a memory of people running down Fountainbridge smashing the windows of the Italian shops when Italy entered the war in 1940. But he also provides us with a very human encounter with some German prisoners-of-war laying a drainpipe down Fountainbridge during the winter of 1945-46. He was a small boy at Tollcross School at the time. He remembers what they wore:

> Navy blue battledress uniform of the type worn by the Merchant Navy Artillery. The only change was the yellow circles on the back of the battledress tunic and just

above the knee of the right leg of the trousers. They were both made of material similar to bunting used for making flags, the one on the back of the tunic being about eighteen inches in diameter, that on the trousers about a foot.

The prisoners themselves appeared to be a mixed lot, some short and dark . . .the others tall and blonde . . . The latter spoke quite reasonable English with a heavy accent. We were taught a few words of German by our teacher and these we tried out only to be corrected by the prisoners amongst some hilarity. This I can now understand for the phrase we were using meant 'Did you have a good dinner today?' which is a bit pointless when they were fed while sitting on the edge of the trench with sandwiches and mugs of tea. I cannot remember any of the adults who passed us while we were fraternising making any comment other than to give the usual tolerant smile at our efforts.

This seems to have been the only sighting of prisoners-of-war in the area.

The End of the War

When the war ended, the news seemed to come suddenly, taking people by surprise. People reacted spontaneously, spilling out into the streets in an infectious spirit of exuberant release:

We were sitting in the Poole's picture house. There was three of us that worked in Thom's. When all the lights went up we thought the thing had broken down again, and the manager came up and said that the war had ended. Oh, God, I never forgot that. Everybody was up, whooping it up, and they were all screeching, and we were all heading to get into the streets. There was a wee wine merchant's in Grindlay Street, and Nellie Bremner, her man was a prisoner-of-war, we went in there and we got a bottle of White Lady cocktail and went away down to Phyllis's house at Montgomery Street, and celebrated down there. Her sister had just come in from her work and we were all celebrating with the bottle of White Lady. I never forgot that night!

MRS RUBY CLIFFORD

Mrs Netta Thomson, who was living with her mother in Grove Street after the birth of her first child, heard the news on the radio. Immediately they all 'made across to our grandmother's, which was the hub of our family life'. Men selling newspapers came round the streets shouting the news:

All that you could think of was, 'When will the men get home?'.

That evening the neighbours from Grove Street and Brandfield Street gathered in 'the Biggie', the large back green behind the Brewery, for a huge street party. Everybody baked something, scones and cakes mostly, and juice was provided for the children. Those who could sing and make music did so. Accordions emerged. There was a yodeller. People did 'turns', whatever they had a talent for. There was 'a great community spirit' and people danced well into the night.

The Second World War effected many changes in the lives of this community. Some were already in train at the beginning of the war, as in John Webster's memory of coming home to find his home no longer inhabited:

> My family moved to No. 8 Heriot Place at the beginnin' o' the war. I came home and I was never told they had moved. And when I walked up the High Riggs early in the mornin'—because we arrived from London early in the mornin'—I seen all the house barricaded up. But my father had three flower-pots on a ledge on the front window which had orange lilies in them. Well, from 1939 tae the actual buildins were knocked down these orange lilies bloomed every year. I tried tae get one, but I couldnae find anybody tae ask for one, but I was told they were knocked down wi' the buildins when they knocked it down.

Some were faced with deeply personal losses when they least expected them, casting a shadow over otherwise joyful and long-awaited homecomings. Lexie Lang, for instance, found herself with the task of telling her husband of his much-loved mother's death several months before his release from prison camp.

44   Margaret and John Webster in the uniforms of the WAAF and Royal Marines respectively, in 1945. Courtesy of Mrs Jane Moore.

The maverick George Ramage decided not to come back. The healthier and sunnier life he had enjoyed as a soldier in India gave him a desire for something better. Coming home on leave in the middle of the war,

> the smoke-grimed buildings and city smells seemed worse than ever. The only real change seemed to be that with the war in full swing everyone was working, even the women. I ended up entertaining myself by driving a coal lorry until my leave was up.

He was ordered to report to Southampton, to form part of the guard of a convoy of German priosners of war being sent to America. When he got to New York he liked what he saw so much that he jumped ship, found himself a wife and lived, worked and raised a family there as an illegal immigrant for 40 years. Only in 1989, when he had finally legalised his status with the American authorities and found out that he could qualify for the military amnesty granted by Queen Elizabeth II as part of her 1977 Silver Jubilee celebrations, was he able to come back to visit the Edinburgh streets he had been so desperate to leave 41 years before.

One accepts that men who go away to fight in wars will be changed by their experiences. In this war, however, more, perhaps, than ever before, was demanded of women in terms of their positive participation in the conflict. Not merely had they worried and endured and coped with immense privations and loss, as they always had, but they had been required to work and assist the fighting in considerable numbers as well. Even those who stayed at home acquired a spirit of independence, together with skills that previously they had depended on their menfolk to provide. The potential for radical changes in their lives could be said, therefore, to be in place. Unfortunately, the immediate post-war years were to see a retreat to domesticity for married women and a reduction of childcare provision that was to inhibit their growth into greater independence for the best part of a generation.

One can, therefore, understand the view of women like Mrs Margaret Mowat and Mrs Netta Thomson when they describe the war years as 'the greatest years' of their lives. That view reflects their response to widened horizons and to comradeship intensified by the shared experience of a common national danger. Both acknowledge, however, that their lives were neither blighted by the Blitz nor exposed to the loss of their nearest and dearest in the fighting. For others it was a different story—one that even yet they can't bring themselves to tell. The memory of Royal Marine comrades crying out as they went down with their sinking ship in a distant corner of the war at sea still haunts John Webster, and he wonders how many of the young men he knew as a youngster growing up in the High Riggs ever returned—and if any of them did, where, if they are still alive, they might be now.

CHAPTER SEVEN

Entertainment

Allison Young

Home Entertainments

For the majority of local residents in the first half of the century, entertainment began at home. Although there was an abundance of places to go and things to do, there was not always the money or time available to spend evenings at the cinema or theatre, with more time being spent in the home, or, in the case of the men, outside.

> The lives of the boys and men were very much outwith the home. We never spent much time in the house at all. We were always out . . . Well, there was nothing really to keep you in the house because it was just a matter of—you have your tea or your dinner . . . and you just went out because there was no TV, no radios or anything like that. You might have had one of these old-fashioned gramophones, you know with the big horn, 'His Master's Voice' and the old bow-wow beside you! But other than that, there was nothing to keep you in.
>
> TOMMY LANG

Evenings spent at home could be quiet, but occasionally turned into full-scale parties.

> It was always surprise parties we used to have. that was our entertainment.
>
> MRS FRANCES WEDDELL

> At one time, as often it happened, you could get a sing-song going. Go into a house and get a sing-song going. It would be a case of, 'Right, roll back the carpet. Right, get up and do this sort of song'. Somebody'd get up and do a song, and dancing. There was a party spirit. And when we got a bit older, you could go into a pub and start a sing-song and *everybody'd* join in! There was none of this disco with the flashing lights and the rest of it!
>
> MRS BETTY LENNOX

When radio became popular in the late 1930s, it began to provide a means of being in contact with the wider world, and became very much a family pursuit. Everyone had his or her favourite programme, and listened intently, without the radio simply being background noise.

There was no TV. There was only the radio—Dick Barton Special Agent! Housewives' Choice in the morning, that was a great favourite, and when I was much younger, the childrens' programmes were a super thing! Auntie Kathleen and Howard the Hare! My father had a little case which he kept under this cabinet underneath the radio, and I used to pull this case out and sit on it and listen to the Childrens' Hour. it was absolutely wonderful!

MRS IRIS MUNRO

I can remember when we first got radio, and we thought it was wonderful, and we were sayin' to my dad, and I can remember him sayin', 'Ah, but one day you're goin' to see pictures through all that.' And we thought, 'Aw, haw, ha.'

MRS LEXIE LANG

We got our first radio about 1934 or '35. And the radios in those days were antiquated. You had to run it off a wet battery similar to a car battery, and they had to be charged up every so often. So usually the newsagent at the end of the street, they'd take the batteris in and send them away somewhere so they were charged up.

TOMMY LANG

You didn't get news reports . . . You'd get perhaps thrillers. You got a play. 'The Man in Black' and things like that. And you used to get the dance bands. That's where they got the expression for that dance hall: Henry Hall.

TOMMY and LEXIE LANG

Back Green Concerts

Stairs and streets were communities in themselves, and nowhere was this demonstrated more than in a back-green concert, when all the residents overlooking the green took their turn to entertain the others to the best of their abilities. Shows were often fiercely competitive, with 'guest appearances' being made by local 'celebrities' like Willie Sives on his spoons.

There used to be that singer that went round . . . Bing. He used to go round the back greens and some people used to heat up pennies and chuck them down . . . What a bloomin shame!

GEORGE ROBERTSON

There was a group came from Glasgow . . . They came all the way through here to perform up in Grove Street. Oh, Codona, the one-man band! That was a very famous

45   A party to celebrate the Coronation of Queen Elizabeth II in 1953, held at the end of Brandfield Street. Seated on the left is Edward Simpson. Courtesy of Mrs Betty Simpson.

one. In fact we had relations of theirs living next door to us although they would never admit it.

STAN PLAYER

Profits from concerts were donated to charity, and occasionally stalls were set up in the garden to provide refreshments and increase funds.

And we used to do back-green concerts in No. 10 Freer Street, and that was to help the troops that were in hospitals and we gave the money that we got to them. This was after the war.

MRS FRANCES WEDDELL

All the mothers would get all the chairs down. Somebody would bring a table down, and there'd be a flask of tea or a big pot of tea and sandwiches, and mothers would do baking. There'd be someone at the entrance who would charge you thruppence to get in, and all that money went to charity, the hospital.

MRS BETTY LENNOX

And then at one time I remember that most of the back-green concerts were for the war effort . . . and every back-green had a concert and they all used to try and outdo each other. Somebody'd put on a better concert than somebody else, but it was all the same people. All the kids would get up and do their own turn. They'd dance and sing and tap-dance. You'd maybe get mums and dads going up and doing a turn. Somebody'd get up and recite poetry. Somebody'd perhaps do magic.

MRS BETTY LENNOX

But despite the main purpose of the concerts being fund-raising, participation gave immense pleasure, as Mrs Plenderleith recalls:

Mr McLaren had the pub facing the Coliseum Picture House. He used to come along that way—you had to walk along the banks. We used to charge a ha'penny for tuppence worth of old teabread, and whoever paid a penny got a choice o' what they wanted oot o' the bag. We were all in skirts wi' different coloured tissue paper— crêpe paper—and bows in our hair. Better dressed when we had a ha'penny concert than any time! But my speciality was the Irish Jig, and one day Mr McLaren came along. He was going to open the pub at three o'clock, and I was doin' the Irish Jig and I was gien' it laldie! Pat McLaren came along and he stood and watched. There was nae stoppin' me. It was like I was wound up, and when I finished he clapped his hands and they all looked at him, and they clapped as well. It was rare! I was the only one that got a clap, and I got a half-crown as well. And there was a big discussion with the mothers—it was ha'pennies we were supposed to get for the hospital—where were we getting the half-crown? I don't think the Infirmary got it either. I think it was divided amongst the mothers!

MRS J PLENDERLEITH

Street Entertainers

The locality was home to many characters who made their living by touring the streets and entertaining the residents. Many became almost living legends, such as 'Monkey Mary' who is remembered by many of the interviewees.

> She used tae have a barrel organ and a wee pony. She actually stayed in the Grassmarket, and she'd a wee monkey.
>
> JOHN WEBSTER

> It was a wee woman—a wee Italian woman, and she used to play this wee hurdy-gurdy . . . and this monkey took it's hat off to you and held out the wee plate where you put your penny or your ha'penny or whatever you had.
>
> MRS JANET DOW

46   The Ritchie Brothers, Alex (16 years) and Hughie (20 years), in 1932. The brothers often played in back green concerts. Courtesy of Mrs Helen Fraser.

The entertainers were not regarded as beggars, and many were highly respected, performing high quality acts to an appreciative audience.

Oh aye. I mind this guy, I think he was a Glasgow chap, what a rare singer he was, and he had a pin leg. We hadnae much money, but we used to laugh at this lassie who always threw him thruppence. 'Oh, I couldnae have him singin' for anything less!' He was a smashing singer. What a waste!

MRS ANNIE HEPBURN

Then you'd old Holy Mary, she should've been in the Opera House with the voice she had. Her favourite tune was 'The Old Rugged Cross' and 'Abide With Me' and 'Amazin' Grace'. She stayed in the Salvation Army Hostel at the bottom of the West Port, and that's how she got the money tae stay in there. She went round the streets on a Sunday singin'.

JOHN WEBSTER

One thing that sticks out in my mind was a Christmas morning and it was snowing and there was a man come into the stair, and he sung in the well of the stair . . . and I remember my mum and dad going oot and leaning over the balcony and listening.

MRS PEGGY WEDDELL

There used to be a clog dancer come regular, and they were good dancers. They brought their own piece of wood and a wee platform, and a man played the melodion and another played the spoons. Then there was Willie Sives, he played the spoons. He stayed in Newport Street, and he tried to keep up wi' the man. And then there was a man came round wi' a roundabout, and for a ha'penny, you put the bairns on it and he gied it a shove, and the buskers were wonderful. The brothers that stayed in the Grassmarket, and each one was accomplished with the instrument he played. The accordion, the fiddle and the sax, and one sang, and they walked in a row, and it was marvellous! You'd pay money now and never get the like.

MRS J PLENDERLEITH

Not all the entertainers were of such high calibre.

There was thon wee wifie that came roond that had all the hundred coats on her. She never really sang. she just went 'A dewha, dewha . . .' like that.

MRS PEGGY WEDDELL

One particular man, I remember, used to stand stripped to the waist and ripple his muscles and say, 'I am the man with the body and the muscles!' And he'd have his cap on the ground and if you had a spare penny you'd throw it in, and . . . I stayed well back because he also had white mice that he had trained to run over his body, you know, round from one hand over the shoulders on to the other hand. I was always terrified in case one of the white mice jumped off and got me!

MB

Most, though, were welcomed and enjoyed by the local residents

> There used to be a chap, Miller, and he had one of these melodions, and every Saturday night that chap used to come out and play the box and it used to be marvellous. A' the folk dancin' and singin' in the street. there was no harm done. No arguments or anything.
>
> MRS CHRISSIE BORTHWICK

> Ye got different other characters gave ye a wee bit turn. The streets were full o' colour, plenty entertainment and everything.
>
> JOHN WEBSTER

47   Skiffle Group in the 1950s at the back of Fountainbridge.
Courtesy of Mrs Christine Roberts.

Dancing

Nowhere in Edinburgh is there a higher concentration of entertainment centres than in Tollcross, and this has almost always been the case, from the early days of Cookes Circus in Lothian Road to today's multi-screen cinemas and night clubs. Venues have changed purpose, with the Palais in Fountainbridge going from dance hall to bingo hall, and the meatmarket becoming a restaurant and discotheque, but overall, the amount of nightlife in Tollcross has increased, bringing with it the problem of late night noise, due to ever later licensing.

Although today, the majority of those seeking entertainment come from outwith the Tollcross area, this was not always the case, with each part of Edinburgh supporting it's own cinema or dance hall. In Tollcross, different venues gained popularity at different times, as fashions changed.

> There was always plenty dancin' and plenty cinemas, because that's where you done your courtin'. Then you'd Maxim's for dancin'. You also had the Palais de Dance. That's where you done your jiggin'.
>
> AHR

Certain venues were considered the 'place to be', whilst others were completely out of bounds. This was especially true of dance halls. For some, the Palais was the only place to be seen in, but for others, it seemed too posh. In later days, things were reversed, and the Cavendish in Fountainbridge was seen as the most fashionable nightspot.

> I couldn't afford to go dancin', but the Palais was the main place—tails and bow ties . . . Really well-dressed.
>
> J WALKER-BLANCHE

> We went to the Palais de Dance, but at the time you had to be in evening dress . . . I was dressed to kill in black chenille velvet. I remember, it was the Theatrical Ball.
>
> MRS GRACE TAYLOR

> Well, we danced at the Palais, the Plaza. We didn't really dance at what became the New Caveindish—Maxime's. It had a reputation. It was the sort of place one didn't go somehow. *The* place was the Palais on Friday nights. You had to be in evening dress, dinner jackets and so on.
>
> DR A C McLAREN

> When we were young, we used to go along to the side o' the Palais and peep in because it seemed so high class and fancy.
>
> MRS NANCY BARCLAY

> The Cavendish was where the dancers went, and I used to do a bit of ballroom dancing, and that's where I headed. To dance, you went to the Cavendish. To pick up a girl, you went to the Palais.
>
> STAN PLAYER

48   Bertini's Dance Band, playing at the Palais de Dance, around 1940.
Courtesy of Huntly House Museum.

49   The Melody Three singing trio who performed in the Palais in the 1950s.
Courtesy of Mrs Christine Roberts.

Or if you wanted really high class you went to the Plaza—that's where the nurses and that went.

GEORGE ROBERTSON

Both Stan Player and George Robertson have fond memories of the Palais and the Cavendish:

The Cavendish was two halls . . . It was all ballroom dancing there. I was quite heartbroken when it actually turned into a disco-type place . . . I think the Palais had the best floor. One thing I remember about the Palais, when they had the dance at Christmas and New Year, you couldn't get in. The queues were miles long. I remember there were a lot of fights especially in the Teddy Boy era at the Palais . . . and I remember riots in there . . . literally riots and that's one of the reasons it was actually closed.

STAN PLAYER

It [the Cavendish] had big mirrors on the wall and was always very dark.

GEORGE ROBERTSON

Dancing was considered a major social skill, and was seen as a step into the adult world, as Tommy Lang describes:

Our first real effort into the dancin' world was the club in Fountainbridge. This was run by the unemployed who were allowed to use the top flat of Fountainbridge School, which was only used for makin' school dinners. And at night, twice or three times a week they ran these dances. And all that the band comprised of was an accordion player named Miller, and he went under the name [in those days they called an accordion a box] of Boxo Millier. He was a very small man but he could play the accordion and he *was* the band. This was quite a cheap way . . . and it gave itself the nickname of 'Are you goin' to the Ball?' And they used to end up sayin', 'Are you goin' to the Henry Hall?' And everyone knew that you meant the dancin' in the school. And it was quite popular. I would say 80 or 90 people in this top flat and we thoroughly enjoyed ourselves. I graduated later on, but this was my first step towards dancin'.

TOMMY LANG

The dance halls were the hub of the social circuit, giving a reason to get dressed up, and a means of encountering the opposite sex. Many a 'click' was made in the Palais de Dance.

The Palais . . . all the Yanks comin' . . . the good times we had! And lots of fights too. This was after the war.

MRS FRANCES WADDELL

I made what they called a 'rhumba skirt'. This was a straight skirt with pleats round the knees. It cost me one and six. I got three yards of linen material and made myself this skirt. I wore it the night, I washed it, and I had it on again the morn's night.

MRS ANNIE HEPBURN

I remember there was an organist came up out of the floor.

MRS ALICE BURT

When we first started to dance, we went to the Westfield, with the knots on the floor, and . . . this is how naive you are . . . I saw this fellow, lived in Grove Street, and I went up to him and I said, 'Will you give me this dance, please?' because I couldnae dance. But the Palais was the best place . . . You used to go and stand and hopefully you would get a dance, and you could go and break in. As you go around, you touched the girl that was dancing, and you danced with the fellow, or somebody comes up and touches you. When you came roond again, you could touch them back.

And of course, the Yanks used to come as well. I mustn't have been the type that attracted Yanks. Thank God for that, because what were they? They were either skinny, or they were big and flabby.

Mrs Nancy Barclay

For some, the dancing itself became almost secondary to the problems involved in getting there. Great cunning and persuasion had to be employed to secure a night at the 'late', and was not always successful.

I liked the dancing . . . I had a dress for the Charleston with rows and rows of fringes, and my mother knew nothing about this because I went out with my skirt and jumper on, and went up to my pal's, and I put a band round my heid, and a silk garter wi' a big bell on it, and when you did the Charleston, the bell rattled. And this night, we must've clicked wi' two fellas in the dancin', and they wanted to see us hame . . . and I looked at the time and we had to be in by ten. Ten a Saturday, nine a Sunday, and it was ten past ten. I took to my heels to run around Ponton Street, and the fellas were shoutin' after us. We knew we had to get up to her house, and I tore off the band, took the dress off and put my skirt and jumper on, and I took off my shoes and put them under my arm. 'Please God, let my mother be sleepin' . . . and I'll put tuppence in the plate on Sunday!' And I was askin' a favour and tellin' a lie at the same time, because I only had a penny. However, I got in the house, and I tried to shut the door, and I couldn't shut it . . .!

Mrs J Plenderleith

I remember goin' tae ma first late night ever, ma first dance that I wis goin' tae . . . And, oh, I was goin' tae be the whole cheese and ma ticket was standin' on the mantelpiece . . . and ma brother came in in his Navy uniform and he says, 'Where dae ye think you're goin'?' And I says, 'I'm goin' tae the Westfield, I'm goin' tae the late night.' He says, 'Ye're no goin' . . . because *I'm* goin'.' And it ended up that we had a fight and I pulled the ribbons off the Navy uniform. Well, he went and told my mother and I had tae sit and repair the ribbons tae let him go to that dance, and I didnae get, for after all, 'he was a fighting man and he wis home on leave and he didn't want tae see his wee sister at a dance'.

Mrs Ina Begbie

Dancing today in Tollcross is virtually all 'disco with the flashing lights and the rest of it', but still, practically every night, the area is thronging with people dressed to kill, in search of an evening on the dance floor, with perhaps only a little less romance than the 'dance hall' days.

Cinema

Going to the cinema was a favourite pastime for local residents especially since there were several picture houses in the area, all showing different films.

> We used to got to the wee cinema down the road. The King's Cinema. They used to keep you standing outside, and the place was half empty when you got in . . .
>
> J WALKER-BLANCHE

> There was . . . plenty cinemas, because that's where you done your courtin', in the back seats, which was then called 'chummy seats'. Then you'd the King's Cinema where you got sprayed in scent on the way in, if you knew how to work the machine!
>
> JOHN WEBSTER

> I remember before that cinema was built (the Regal) at the back was a whole lot of rubbish because it was the canal bank or something, and the King and Queen— King George the Fifth and Queen Mary, I think it was—were coming at one time. They tried to do everything up nicely so's they wouldn't see the dump at the back. They put up flags and what-nots so's they wouldn't see it when they were coming up the road.
>
> MRS NELLIE RODGERS

Despite evidence that one could gain entry to the pictures using jam jars as currency, the cost of seeing a film was still prohibitive. However, in the early days of the Palladium Cinema formerly Cooke's Circus, there were ways of seeing a film cheaply, even if it *was* from behind.

> Now the screen then was brought down from the centre of the ring, for a penny, you got to see the picture on the wrong side but for thruppence, you got to see it on the right side. But the screen was put in the proper place after that. Then it turned into a theatre.
>
> JOHN WEBSTER

> You got sixpence out o' your wages, and it was thruppence for the pictures, tuppence for a quarter o' boilings, and a penny for the plate on Sunday mornings, and that was your sixpence.
>
> MRS J PLENDERLEITH

Saturday morning was the childrens domain, and amidst the cowboys and Indians, chaos ruled.

> It was silents then, and in those days, of course, everybody could talk and shout and yell, because when the baddie come on behind the goodie, you used to shout 'Watch your back!' and all these things, you see. 'Shoat! Shoat! Mind your back!' This was the general converstation.
>
> Well, I could only have been five or six at the time . . . and I needed to go to the toilet and my father had to take me out, and we came back, and it was one o' these

parts where it was grippin', and everything was quiet, and I turned round to my mother and shouted, 'Mammy, I pee'd an' daddy pee'd!', and she says, 'I was mortified. I just didn't know where to look!'.

There were special shows for the kids, *Fu Man Chu* and *The Green Arrow* and things like that, and these were all serials of course, where the car or the girl's on the railway line and the train's comin' thunderin' down and—'See the episode next week!'.

TOMMY LANG

We used to smoke cinnamon. Yes, actually lit it, at the back of the picture house at a Saturday matinee. And if Mr Albin caught you, you were out.

You went to the matinees on a Saturday, and they had a singing contest, or reciting, or anything you could do, and big dolls for prizes—never just wee bars of chocolate—big prizes, and a lucky draw.

MRS GRACE TAYLOR

Cowboys and Indians, the only movie to see! We had Buck Jones, and who was the space guy? Before all this new space stuff, we had that back then too. But in your dreams, you transferred yourself to the Wild West.

We used to try and scrounge something we could sell, like pieces of wood we could break up and sell for kindling. Got half a penny or a penny and bottles and things like this and we'd turn them in to the scrap man down the road and try and get that few cents that it took to get in on a Saturday afternoon. And if we couldn't get in we used to wait outside until one of the kids we knew went in and we'd ask him to go round to the back door and let us in.

GEORGE RAMAGE

Occasionally, the stars of the films visited the cinemas on a promotional tour.

There was an English star. She was presented with a box of chocolates. Now the children of Glen Street, the one's who played there, Mr Albin lined us up inside the place to greet her, and she opened up her box of chocolates and passed it round so that every kid got one of her chocolates.

Tom Mix . . . came to Tollcross Picture House, and we all got to try his hat on. We were thrilled to bits. Remember Drummond Shiels, the photographer who was up in Lauriston? Well, Mr Albin's grandson, his photo was in that shop for years and years, dressed up as a cowboy with Tom Mix's hat on.

MRS GRACE TAYLOR

The cinema retained its popularity into the early 1960s, but was still very different from today's multi-screen complexes.

The cinemas was alright. The newer ones were fine, the likes o' the Blue Halls, that come into existence round about 1928 or '29, an' that was beginning to get posher wi' the tip-up seats, the cushioned seats. Whereas if you went to the Palladium, that was a real kingpin. I remember when I was a kid at that time, when you went, you paid your money and they gave you a big metal thing made o' lead and that was

50   In July 1954 the film star William Boyd (centre)—Hopalong Cassidy—visited
Edinburgh with a group of American teenagers who had won a competition relating to
their paper rounds. Gladys Kilpatrick (second from left) heard of this through relations
in America and learned that a cousin, Richard Kesel (second from right), would be in the
party. A surprise meeting was arranged at the Regal Cinema, along with Gladys's
husband George (first on left) and Hoppy's wife (first on right). Courtesy of George
Johnstone Kilpatrick.

your admission ticket. You took that up the stairs and handed it to the commissionaire,
and he dropped it in a big box and it come right down to the box again, so they'd
be re-issuing all the time. It was just like a big metal slug.

TOMMY LANG

Today, Tollcross is home to three of Edinburgh's five cinemas, with the
Cannon showing mostly general release films, and the Cameo and Filmhouse
both presenting more *avant garde* screenings. Even now, queues for the Cannon,
on the corner of Morrison Street and Lothian Road, can still wind all the way
round into Fountainbridge and back along Semple Street, dispelling the idea
that cinema-going in the 1990s is on the decline.

Theatre

Whilst a visit to the cinema was quite a regular occurrence for local residents, a trip to the theatre was much more of a special occasion. Few actually went to see plays or opera, but variety shows and pantomimes were popular for a special night out.

> It was always variety. sometimes the local Palladium—and we've even been to pantomimes in the King's Theatre in them days. We had a lot more theatres in Edinburgh of course.
>
> ALEXANDER A ALEXANDER

> We went to the Garrick Theatre at the foot of Grove Street. It was variety, and I can always remember one song—I must have been tiny. Why it stuck in my head all these years I'll never know. They must have been dressed as minstrels and they sang, 'God Bless Mammy, God Bless Dad. Make them happy, make them glad. I'm in heaven down in Tennessee.'
>
> MRS GRACE TAYLOR

As with the dance halls, everyone had their favourite place to go. Certain theatres were considered to be too high-brow and expensive by local people, but each one had regular visits from particular 'stars' who attracted their own audience.

> The King's Theatre was a little bit classier. It always tended to be for the well-to-do people.That was always big stars, and people used to attend there wi' evening suits and women wi' long dresses. It was always beyond us. Our entertainment in that line would be either the Empire or the Royal. We used to go for the variety turns, these old time stars, the big bands like Harry Roy or some o' these comedians like Dave Willis and Harry Lauder or Will Fyfe.
>   We liked the sing-songs and stuff like that, things where you could join in. We used to go to the King's for the pantomime as kids, like they do now. You either went to the King's or the Royal for the pantomime, but never for an ordinary show.
>
> TOMMY LANG

Despite the high price of a theatre ticket, there were ways of getting in, if you knew the right people.

> I went to the Palladium. Hamish Turner . . . a friend of mine, he was the manager. I knew Hamish, so I could go in any time . . . I'd just kind of say, 'Is it alright to go in and have a seat?' 'No problem, Walker. Backstage and up you go.'
>
> J WALKER BLANCHE

The large number of theatres in the area also provided employment.

> I loved the theatre. I started off in the seats as an usherette, then I was in the bar for a spell . . . [We] met many of the actors and actresses. Originally we had to go in

through the stage door, and you signed in, and you met all the famous actors and actresses: Vivien Leigh, Laurence Olivier, Marlene Dietrich, John Mills when he was young, I can remember him. There was a wonderful atmosphere in the theatre.

AHR

But not everyone's foray into the world of the performing arts lasted as long as this employee's 43 years. For others it was over before it had properly begun.

Then there was the Garrick Theatre in Grove Street, Now Joanne Gallagher and I were 13½, just before I left school, and they were wantin' lassies for the chorus. So we went, and of course, we got the job. The two of us. But our mothers were waitin' to grab us when we came out at night. It was 'Mother's Sailor Boy'. I'll never forget the title o' that thing. And they said they were goin' to London, and we were to ask our parents. If we went to London, we would have tutors to give us lessons. But we just started to tell them that we were goin' to London, and the baith of us got leathered all the way hame! And they said, 'London! Don't mention that place to me again!' And they never let us go back to the Garrick!

MRS J PLENDERLEITH

Today, both the Lyceum and the King's Theatre host shows from all over the world, but variety is practically unheard of, perhaps due to television's virtual domination of the 'light entertainment' scene. Nevertheless, the annual pantomime has remained practically unchanged, and is still a major crowd-puller for the theatres, even though they rely upon the added attraction of TV personalities to ensure a full house.

Billiards

Billiard Halls were seen by many as being dens of iniquity, but for others, they were merely a way of escaping into a male-dominated smokey atmosphere for an evening. Their bad reputation was earned largely because of the number of unemployed people who spent their time there, rather than on the street corners. This encouraged the idea that billiard-playing was for those with time to waste, and was not something to be indulged in on a regular basis.

There was billiards at the top of the canal basin. The laddies that went there were idle. It was never their pleasure. They went there to get out o' the road. A dark place.

MRS J PLENDERLEITH

We used to nip across to this billiard saloon, the Trevelyan . . . it was free to go in. You had to pay to play on the tables, if you wanted to play billiards, or snooker as it was then. But most people in the winter [the only place that had a fire], most people, like the unemployed, they used to go in there and congregate. Then they used to try and make out that it wasn't allowed. The guy that owned it was always chasing them. they used to sit there with the paper and make their lines for the betting on the horses.

TOMMY LANG

51 The Trevelyan Billiard Team taken at Bob Martin's Saloon in Fountainbridge, in the late 1930s. Courtesy of Mrs Margaret Mowat.

Despite the bad reputation of the billiard hall, no serious trouble ever seemed to take place there, and it was as much the appearance of the place as anything else that led to rumours about what must go on inside.

> It was a den. It was a low roof and it had only four billiard tables. It was very small, and it was a terrible place . . . Oh, I had a misspent youth! . . . My biggest bugbear was the Trevelyan. It was quite a well-known place in those days. It was a reconverted bakehouse . . . and it was smokey and dusty and very dingy. There was big poles in it, and when the balls landed in certain parts of the table you couldn't play right. You had to go underneath and here there was a billiard cue about 18 inches to two feet long, and you had to use that to play your shot.
>
> TOMMY LANG

The Trevelyan was a great place for studying local characters as Tommy continues:

> They all had their nicknames. There was one called 'Swerver'. He used to play this game and he always used to try and make the ball go round and whenever you seen him you said, 'There's Swerver.' And there was another one, his name was Pettigrew, and he used to try and make the ball come back, and we used to say, 'There's Screw, there.' And that guy that owned the place, his arms were only about the length of our elbows . . . and his hands were malformed . . . but he owned the place, and he was one of the topnotch players around there. He had no thumbs, and he just grasped the cue and run it across his knuckles. He was an amazing player.
>
> TOMMY LANG

The only place to get a game of billiards in Tollcross now is Marco's Leisure Centre in Grove Street, which has considerably more than four tables and requires a membership to gain entry.

Gambling

Up until 1960, betting outside a racecourse was illegal but this was overcome by the bookie's runner, who took bets in the street and then delivered them to the course. Betting was largely frowned upon as a waste of money, but was still very popular.

Mother used to hurry past. 'We don't approve, but we're going to co-exist'.

Ms Liz Allen

We went to the Sacred Heart Church up at Lauriston. Father Gill used to come up to the house. He was a Dutchman—and he used to leave a bet with my mother, would Father Gill. And he and my Auntie Mamie used to pick the horses. He was one that I liked.

Mrs Mary Cruickshank

There used to be a street bookie's at the corner of Ponton Street, not that I ever used him, I couldn't afford to. And there used to be one at the corner of Tarvit Street.

Mr Munro

The police attempted to control the street bookies, but largely to no avail.

The bookies used to ken when they were getting lifted. They used to get the squeak, just go up and pay a £20 fine and away again. Oh, the runners kent when they were all going to get lifted. 'Oh, it's ma turn to get lifted this week', and a' this patter.

Andrew Laing

Tommy Lang describes the system of the bookies' runners:

They had nothing like Ladbrokes or Corals or Mecca or anything like that. He (the runner) used to stand—the police knew who he was too—but he always used to stand at the corner of Grove Street and Fountainbridge, and you'd walk up to him and you'd hand him your little line with your thrupenny bet or your sixpenny bet on it, and he used to take it, and he was only a front man for one of the bigger bookmakers. There were still big bookmakers then, but it was illegal, and these big bookies used to bet mostly at the racecourse, but they took bets in the street on the side, and these street runners used to watch a clock and when it got near two o'clock for the two o'clock race, they'd a little canvas bag wi' a lock on the top of it, and they put all their betting lines in here, you see. Your betting lines were written on any type of paper, and nobody gave their name. You used to give a *nom-de-plume*: 'Smiler', or any sort of name you could think of. You never put 'Thomas Lang' or 'Jimmy Clark' or anything like that. He used to put them all in a bag just before the two o'clock race and lock it and put a key in, and it was all on a time clock so's he couldn't put any more bets in there after the race was run. A lot o' them were at the twist, or 'hurry up' as we used to call it then. They'd try to keep the clock out but the clock registered two o'clock, and if anyone tried to get there after two o'clock, then the bookmaker wouldn't pay out.

TOMMY LANG

Gambling was not, however, an exclusively male pursuit.

I can remember the bookie in the back green . . . There was one of these horse races on, the National or something, and . . . we had done a horse called 'Sheila's Cottage'. And here, there had been as many people on this, and I can remember standing in the back green in a queue at the bookies to get our money.

MRS ANNIE KITSON

And betting was not confined to the horses.

But then we got into the gambling craze. There was gambling schools in Freer Street, and there was gambling schools down in Brandfield Street . . . It wasn't the big-time, like the Mafia or anything. It was just five or six of you getting together and you'd play cards, similar to how you'd played younger with cigarette cards, but this time you were playing for money. We used to play in Brandfield Street, and they had all these back greens, and they all led into the 'Biggie', so what used to happen is: the police used to know that it would go on and they used to occasionally come down and try to pick you up or chase you. But you always had somebody, and you used to always pay him, and they used to call him the 'Shoatwatcher' because the expression 'shoat' means 'scram', 'get out of it', see? And the shoatwatcher is standing at the top of Brandfield Street, and we'd be at the bottom of the stairs, playing cards and all, and he watching and see the police come up and right away he'd shout, 'Shoat, shoat!', and everybody vanished, over the walls! It was an easy exit. They could never catch us because there were five or six back greens and you all went over different walls, and they knew it, too, theirselves. It was just a matter of saying, 'We know it's going on and we're just here to say "watch it"', style. And that's what used to entertain us on a Sunday. They were never big stakes. Only 1*d*. or 2*d*. If you bet 3*d*. you were the man that broke the bank at Monte Carlo!

TOMMY LANG

Despite the descriptions of shadowy figures on every street corner pretending to be doing absolutely nothing, then bolting at the sight of a policeman, the area was not such a haven for the gambler when compared to Tommy Lang's description of the big-time in Silverknowes.

What they did down there, they had big gambling schools. They were organised ones. They used to come from Glasgow on a Sunday, because the place was absolutely heaving with people. They'd play these old games they used to play in the Navy . . . 'Crown and Anchor' . . . and one day the police did raid them, and, oh, they arrested about twenty or thirty of them.

TOMMY LANG

Pubs

The large number of pubs in the locality was, and still is, a controversial subject. Today, many people come in from outside the area to visit the cinemas and theatres, and enjoy a drink before or after the show, whilst ever-later opening hours means groups of night-clubbers spilling out onto the streets at 2 a.m. or 3 a.m. in the morning, bringing with them the problem of noise. Between the wars, and up until the late 1950s, pubs were seen as male territory, with few women going out merely for a social drink.

> Women never really went to these places, I think, till after the war. You would get the odd woman, you know . . . on a Saturday night.
>
> MRS ANNIE KITSON

It was still possible to go out, though, without drinking, as most dance halls and cinemas did not sell drink, and provided tea as a refreshment. However, there are conflicting opinions about the role of alcohol in the lives of the residents.

> Up until 1939, the pubs shut at 9.30 p.m. as I always remember my father saying, 'Come on, it's time we went for some lemonade!' That was his euphemism for a pint of beer. And you had to be in by 9.15 p.m. otherwise it was hopeless.There was never any drunkenness either.
>
> MR MUNRO

> I'd say that many, many people, many husbands spent all their time in the taverns, all the time. So what does the woman have to do to raise three kids, four kids, five kids? She has to find some way to do it.
>
> GEORGE RAMAGE

> On a Saturday, it was a great thing to see men in their working clothes, and still hadnae been home, and they were drunk
>
> MRS ANNIE KITSON

Only a few took drinking to extremes.

> I don't recall many drunks in the street, but I do remember the meths drinkers who went into the stairs to get gas for their drink. They didn't bother anybody . . . They mostly stayed up by the canal. I think one fell in and drowned, once.
>
> MS LIZ ALLEN

In general, though, the local pubs were places for working men to enjoy a sociable drink, reinforcing the idea of men's lives being very much outside the home.

> I must have been about fourteen when I started drinking, when I started at the brewery, like . . . Rutherford's, which they called the Vietnam Bar. There were always fights in it . . . They were brewery pubs, actually. Likes o' that Foy's Pub,

right across from the brewery, where the Tun Room is. Every week his beer pipes used to go to the Tun Room and get drained and cleaned and back ower again. A lot o' people thought that that pub had pipes leading into the brewery, thought that their beer came right fae the brewery, but it didnae.

ANDREW LAING

But even before traffic really engulfed the area, it was still hazardous to 'drink and drive'.

I got run ower in Fountainbridge by a horse and cairt, and I was on a bike at the time. Naw, I wisnae badly hurt. Actually, I was drunk on the bike. And I ran into the horse and cairt. Luckily it was a sensible horse. It sort o' stepped ower us.

ANDREW LAING

Holidays

Holidays were something of a luxury for the majority, with caring for the family and staying at work often taking priority. Holidays were taken relatively close to home in comparison with today, and had to be saved for.

You had to put something away every year for your holidays. Down in the mills in Gala, they had what they called the 'Fresh Air Fund'. They put so much away, and at the holiday season, they got their money.

MR J WALKER-BLANCHE

When I was a wee lassie, my first holiday was with wir Auntie Kate. I used to get her messages in the morning before I went to school, and I got sixpence. She saved it up for me . . . and she took me my first holiday to Anstruther for a week. I was only nine year old.

MRS ANNIE HEPBURN

A holiday was something to look forward to, and to remember, sometimes for painful reasons, as Mrs Munro recalls.

We didn't have a lot of holidays because there wasn't the money, but I remember going to Leven for a holiday, and I got very badly sunburned with big blisters on my arms, and I was all bandaged! I remember that holiday fine!

MRS IRIS MUNRO

Many had a favourite place to which they returned year after year.

Kinghorn! One year, my mother couldn't get booked in Kinghorn so she went to Burntisland, which you can walk to in less than half an hour. But she had to take the bus because I think she thought she was in a foreign country!

MRS PEGGY WEDDELL

I went over to Burntisland or Kinghorn. I had a wee hoose over there that we got every year. Or Port Seton. We bought a wee hut over there, and then we sold that off. That was our life and we were quite happy with it.

MRS RUBY CLIFFORD

We never went up to Oban or the Highlands. what they used to do, just like they do now, they'd rent a little house and go there for a week or a fortnight . . . Blackpool was catchin' on a wee bit.

TOMMY LANG

Renting a house was one way of having a holiday, but as Mrs Borthwick describes, the pleasure of 'doing it yourself' was immense.

My mother came in one time and said. 'I've heard about a place that's selling off old buses'. I think it was only twelve pounds and she went and she got this bus, and somebody told her about this man that would tow it down to Port Seton for her. Now, we were down in Port Seton for over twenty years.

She recalls the personal touches her mother added to their holiday house to make it a 'home-from-home' by the sea.

And we went down, and, oh, it was beautiful . . . It was like a little palace. She got the joiner to come down, and he added a bit on to it—it was a single decker bus— and I'll tell you what she had in it. In the bus she had a three-quarter bed. She had a full-sized table at one side, and she had a small table to hold a bunch of flowers at the other side.

There was a chair in front of the bed and then there was a big cupboard where she kept her pots and pans . . . Then outside the door, she got steps up to it and a wee verandah where you could go out and wash the dishes. Then she got fencing right round. In fact she was growing lettuces and everything . . . We went there for years—that's where we went for our holidays . . . But then they said they were taking the buses away and were putting just caravans . . . but it was a marvellous, marvellous holiday.

Getting away was often difficult, whether due to financial reasons, problems in getting away from work, or simply family responsibilities. For many women, there was a welcome holiday at the Tired Mothers' Home at either Humbie or Leadburn, depending on the age of their children, designed to give them a welcome break from the hard work of being at home.

For holidays, I can remember going to Humbie Home. I was always meaning to go back. It was a village with about six or seven different cottages, with a woman in charge. There was treacle pieces and sitting outside. On a Sunday, you went to church, and you were provided with a red cloak with a hood like a Red Riding Hood cloak, for the express purpose of going to church.

AHR

And I wis put tae Humbie for a whole fortnight, and I gret the whole fortnight. I didnae like it. Tae me it was like being in a home.

MRS CHRISSIE BORTHWICK

The Guildry also organised camps to give children a chance to get away from the city in the summer.

The one camp I can remember . . . was in Nine Mile Burn, and it was only a long, long house and I don't know whether the church obtained it or the Guildry Office . . . And rationing had started so ye had tae take yer coupons so the teachers could buy what have ye. So we all arrives at the Nine Mile Burn and gets a' the thing unpacked, and it was all the palliases on the floor. So it came to the first meal and the tables are getting set and all of a sudden, Miss Brown says, 'Who unpacked the sugar?' . . . And we'd let the sugar go back on the lorry. Well . . . I would say at a guess there would be at least forty of us there and not a drop of sugar in the place!

MRS INA BEGBIE

An ideal solution to the problem of escaping the city was to fill the summer weekends with daytrips.

I remember going up the canal, on a flat-bottomed boat which was pulled by a horse. I don't know whether we went to Meggetland or where we went, but this horse pulled the boat on the towpath. We had a label on, and we were provided with a tinny. When we got there it was races and different things to entertain us. We looked forward to it for weeks before we went and it was spoken about for weeks after we returned.

AHR

As bairns, we used to go to Cramond on the train. The men went round the night before and stayed all night, and there was tents, and you all had your dinner at Cramond. And you got the train for three ha'pence. We used to shove the wee ones up in the luggage rack. Packed like herring in a box.

MRS ANNIE HEPBURN

When we were younger, my mother couldn't really afford to take us any holidays. She used to take us to Portobelly. She used to take Wullie and I down, and she'd buy us a wee spade and a wee pail and we used tae sit, and she used tae take sandwiches down wi' her. Then maybe other Sundays we would take a run down to Cramond.

MRS CHRISSIE BORTHWICK

Although most of the trips were only a few miles out of the city, going away without one's parents turned the journey into more of an adventure.

The kind of places we went to . . . we thought was far away. You'd go in the bus with your streamers and that.

ALEXANDER A ALEXANDER

And that [the canal] took us to Ratho once a year on a trip. We thought we were goin' miles and miles . . . We used to go on that boat, and it had been all hosed. It was coal it had carried. You sat doon and you thought it was clean, but it wasnae, it was dried dust, and what a mess you were in! And that was another doin' when you got in, 'cos you were all dirty. and the horse walked along the side of the canal and dragged it along, and coming back, we saw dear old Edinburgh again, as if we'd been away for year. It was only a mile and half down the road!

Mrs J Plenderleith

52   Men relaxing at Johnston's Boathouses at Leamington by the Union Canal in the 1920s. Courtesy of the Royal Commission on Ancient Monuments, Scotland

Children's Games

Children rarely seemed to be bored, despite a lack of expensive toys, spending most of their free time playing outside. Pocket money was in short supply, so games and expeditions had to be cheap, if not free, with much more imagination being used than cash.

> When you were a child you were out all the time. You had plenty o' places to choose from for your activities. If you couldnae afford a ball, ye got a lot o' newspapers and wrapped them up till they were the size o' a football and ye tied it together wi' a piece o' string and that's what ye kicked about the street until it burst.
>
> JOHN WEBSTER

> It cost us nothing to play. Mind, you used to make up music boxes out of your matchbox . . . a button at one end and a string through it, and you'd thingmy the button up and down.
>
> MRS RUBY CLIFFORD

53   Tollcross 2nd XI football team in 1914, taken at Tollcross Primary School. Oliver Watt is seated in the front row on the right. Courtesy of Oliver Watt.

There was nothing to take you into the house. If you went tae the house, all ye could do was go to bed. You didn't have anything tae really amuse there. So we used to stay out till nine, ten, sometimes eleven o'clock at night, especially . . . when you got the long days. You just made do wi' what ye had. Ye didn't have a lot o' cash. If you'd got a penny or tuppence you were well off. Ye didn't know what tae do wi' yoursel'. Just a penny's worth o' sweeties, or somethin' like that, an' share them out amongst all the lads. Ye never made plans for the next day, or anything like that. Ye just went through that one day.

All I can remember was good summers, playing on the back greens. Statistics prove that they were as bad then as they are now, the summers, but ye never thought on the rain or the winds.

Tommy Lang

Toys and games could be created from almost anything.

When we got cherries we used to take the stone out the cherry and leave them till they dried, then, in the street . . . we used to have a bit of chalk, and you made a long strand and a round and six different wee squares, all numbered. Well, you'd saved up a lot of cherry stones, and you took your cherry and you flung it and if you went to three that other person had to give you three cherries. I liked that one.

Mrs Chrissie Borthwick

We used to tie a rope round the lamp posts and swing round . . . Crack your head when it went back!

Mrs Grace Taylor

We played champers. Bit's o' newspaper . . . cat's dirt came up very well for brown sugar! Broken glass an' all that. And sittin' doin' our crochet or exchangin' scraps. You had your book with all your scraps in it. 'I'll give you a fairy for an angel', or something like this.

Mrs Nancy Barclay

Right there in Gardner's Crescent in the winter time, the bread truck used to come out of St Cuthbert's Bakery, every night time usually, and as the truck came out there would be frost and ice on the ground and we used to run out behind the truck and just let it pull us so as we were able to slide on the ice.

George Ramage

We used to play games like 'A Levoy' or 'Hessie'. 'Hessie' was just an expression for someone who used to hide their eyes and lean against a wall and everybody would run away and you'd try and catch them and bring them back to the den. Or 'A Levoy' was you'd all go away and hide and somebody'd catch you and you'd go back to the den, but while they're looking if someone else come running through the den, they released all them that were captured before.

In those days, you used to get little cards in the cigarette packets, you know, football players, cricketers, and we used to get a pack of cards and we'd play a game called 'Banker'.

Tommy Lang

I remember I had a hoop and a stick thing. I used to go round the street with this great thing, and a whip, and a peerie and a diablo, you know, throwing it up in the air and catching it. A diablo was a sort of diamond-shaped wooden thing, and you had two sticks with a piece of string or whatever, and you threw it up in the air and you caught it, and I was quite good at it! And that was certain seasons of the year. One time . . . it would be the whip and peerie and the diablo, another season, it was all peevers you played. Another time it was all skipping ropes, and that was how it went on.

Mrs Iris Munro

For a few pennies, it was possible to have transport.

I remember the shop in the West Port that hired out bicycles. They used to have them hanging outside, and lined outside on the pavement, and you could hire a bike. They had an awful lot of bikes with the message boy's basket on the front, so I took it that a lot of shopkeepers hired them for the day. I think it was only about thruppence for the day.

Mrs Janet Dow

They used to hire bikes out, but we were threatened, 'Never go on these boneshakers. They've got no brakes'. And they were dreadful things. Now they'd be arrested if they tried to put them on the streets.

Tommy Lang

We used to go boating on the canal. That was when the canal was clean, no like it is now. We went up the Gilmore Place side of it, and there was a boathouse there with a picture of the Loch Ness monster on it. And we used to hire boats there and row up and down between the Rubberworks and Fountainbridge. That was the only bit you could do.

Mrs Alice Burt

Living in the city may have meant a lack of fresh air and green fields, but there was no shortage of space to play. The streets, back greens and canal banks were all that was needed, with the close-knit community meaning that there was usually someone your own age to play with.

We played opposite in Semple Street, just outside where the Regal Cinema was. There was a nice flat bit where you could roller-skate, or make peevers on and things like that.

Mrs Alice Burt

We used to play in the canal basin, or, further afield and more adventuresome, we'd take the train down to Cramond . . . or fishing in the local canal with rods and glasses for minnows. That's the extent of it. Anything that didn't cost much

Alexander A Alexander

You went down to the back green and you always had somebody to play with. You just joined in. A Levoy, or you played on the clothes poles.

Mrs Nancy Barclay

Everybody used to play together. That's when we used to play 'kick the can' in the street and it went on to eleven . . . or really only when it got dark you were shouted in and you still got your jeely piece thrown oot the window in these days. Ye would shout up to your mother.

Stan Player

Sexes were largely segregated, with occasional concessions being granted to the girls, who might be included in games requiring 'extras', like Cops 'n' Robbers or Cowboys and Indians, but were always on the 'wrong' side, and were always killed off first. Games were seasonal—Chasey, tig and hide and seek were usually played in the winter. Skipping, playing 'houses', champing stanes, dressing up and crochet were saved for the spring, whilst in autumn, girls played with scraps.

These girls didn't have dolls and prams like they've got now. One of their favourites that I can remember was scraps—angels and things like that! Whereas we stuck to the cigarette things that we got out there and it was mostly cricket or football or things like that.

Cuddywaits. This was a game for the boys, not for the girls. Somebody stood up against the wall and then another four or five of them. The guy'd put his head into the stomach of the one against the wall. The other one'd get behind him and you'd have a sort of chain of them. Then you'd come running across the road and try and leapfrog up and get as far up as you could, and then the next one, until the thing collapsed under you. You know—'horsie', 'cuddie',—the old expression for a horse. That's where the name came from.

And by the time we were twelve or thirteen we were away frae these childish games. Everything was football . . . We thought we were adult, you know, and we wanted to play the more macho games. We didn't call them 'macho' in those days, but we thought we were 'he-men', and we used like to play that. Nothing with the girls or anything like that. That was no-no. They were just nobodies.

Tommy Lang

Perhaps one of the greatest pleasures came from doing something which one knew was not allowed.

There was one stair [in Glen Street] in particular. I don't know why it was always that one stair. We used to go to the very top (mostly the boys), and they threw all the doormats down the well of the stair, ran down and rang all the bells. Then we used to go to Lauriston Park, climb over the dyke. Now, we used to peep over the dyke first because there was a man in the first flat and if he saw you climbing the dyke, everything that was on the windowsill he threw out. He must have gone through an awful lot of bars of soap and scrubbing brushes and what have you.

Mrs Grace Taylor

Entry to the flat [at Freer Street Terrace] was from a walkway on the canal side of the building. A stone wall topped with iron bars separated the walk from the canal towpath topped with a barbed wire canopy that attatched to the side of the building. We used to climb the iron bars and hang upside down from the barbed wire, working the wire apart until we had a hole big enough to squeeze through and climb down to the canal.

We'd just throw rocks in the water, or jump on the barge, nothing great. It was just the excitement of, 'Hey! That's out of bounds!' We'd hope to God the watchman wasn't there because, if he were, we'd have to run like hell and get through the barbed wire again. He just yelled at us; he wasn't going to chase a bunch of kids, and couldn't catch us if he tried.

GEORGE RAMAGE

Despite not having today's sophisticated toys and leisure facilities, children made the best of what they had, never allowing lack of money to get in the way of having fun.

She got fed up with me yelping and yelping to have roller-skates because one of the girls who used to sit at the foot of our class was an absolute wizard on roller-skates, and there was a short stretch of road between the cobbles in Fountainbridge and the cobbles in Gardners Crescent, and it was tarmacadamed and we called it the New Road. It was beautifully flat and any children who had roller-skates used to go and skate there. And my mother said, 'Where do you expect me to get sixpence for roller-skates out of Woolworths?' So I was given thruppence to buy *one*. It was rubbish and didn't last long, but at least it was a roller-skate.

MB

I cannie say the children are worse off nowadays other than they have too many material things frae ma point o' view. I've got spoilt grandchildren like everybody's got nowadays and ye wish they werenae spoiled. But as my oldest son says, he went away and worked abroad tae make money and make life better for his children.

MRS INA BEGBIE

Showgrounds

The earliest showground site this century was situated at Lochrin, in the vicinity of Arnold Clarke's Car Showroom. It is remembered by Dr Alistair McLaren, who was born in 1907.

John Evan's Carnival used to come to Tollcross. That was a great thing. This was round by the old Wash House where the garage is now, and as far as we children were concerned, it was a super place to go. We could just drop down there, and we used to just walk up and down at night . . . and never give it a thought.

Later in the 1930s, a showground is well remembered at the the corner of Gardner's Crescent and Fountainbridge.

> We had the shows on the corner where the Telephone Exchange is. [They] used to come every year. Codona's. Oh, we were always that excited about the shows. You had this music going all the time. That must have been awful annoying for people in these houses. It always seemed to be winter, so it must have been Christmas, round about that time. There was the Waltzer, there was the Cake-Walk. And they had side-shows and things like that. And of course, they had the boxing booths. I can remember them setting that up. The crowds that used to go to that—the men.
>
> Mrs Annie Kitson

Stewart's Boxing Booth hosted many well-known fighters, but it was often used by local men to settle old scores, as Tommy Lang recalls.

> People used to drink on a Saturday till ten o'clock at night. Then everything closed . . . you couldn't get a drink anywhere, so they used to fill theirselves up as much as they could before ten o'clock, and they used to come out, and they'd argue . . . So this pair were always fighting . . . they kept fighting on a Saturday night, so they said, 'Alright, why don't we put it on at the boxing booth' . . . and, oh, this was hyped up. 'Boxing Match', 'Grudge Fight', but none o' the two o' them had any idea about boxing. What they knew of fighting was the rough and tumble where you hit each other and hugged each other and pushed and fell to the ground.
>
> Anyway . . . the announcer comes up and announces it, 'Now the Grudge Fight!' he says. And the biggest part o' it was that they took facetious names . . . 'Stoker Freer' and 'Billie Kid Gertie'. They must have been in their thirties and one of them had big varicose veins, and the other had a pot belly! . . . They were just throwing their hands any old way and trying to hit each other . . . and by this time, Gertie was getting a wee bit on top of Stoker Freer . . . and he's shoutin', 'Oh, my operation!'. He'd had an appendix operation, and in the middle o' the second round, he collapsed wi' exhaustion! There was no real mischief . . . There was nothing vicious about it.
>
> Tommy Lang

The very existence of boxing booths may actually have helped to keep violence off the streets, by allowing agression to be burnt off within the confines of the ring, but as Tommy Lang's story confirms, little harm was ever done.

CHAPTER EIGHT

Church Connections

Margaret McArthur

The Mission in Freer Street, that wis our life, if we hadnae had that, what would we have had? . . . Nothing!

Mrs Annie Hepburn

The churches of Tollcross and Fountainbridge have played a large part in the shaping of the lives of the people of the area. Nearly all of our interviewees had had some connection with a church, for some it was only nominal, but there were many who echoed Mrs Hepburn's sentiments above.

During the first half of the century, the church provided education and entertainment, carried out social work, encouraged saving, taught practical crafts as well as all the usual youth organisations with which we are so familiar today. From written evidence, it is clear that most churches in the area were involved in this work, but from our interviews, one church and mission—St Cuthbert's and Freer Street—were mentioned over and over again. For this reason, the first half of this chapter will be about general memories of the churches and the second half will concentrate on the work of St Cuthbert's.

In the majority of the cases, church connections were made when young and for a variety of reasons, although some were not made willingly.

I went to All Saints School. The headmaster of All Saints was the choir master at the church. At that time everybody that went to the school went to All Saints Church; we were all members.

Mrs Grace Taylor

I went to the Band of Hope a few times, my brothers and I. But it was just something to do in the wintertime, to get out of the rain. We never got anything out of it. As far as any other church, we never went to church at all. We used to get religious instruction, at school, an hour every Monday morning in school. As far as I know I never set foot in a church until I was in the Army, and then it was compulsory, at least while you were in the Boys' Service.

George Ramage

54   Freer Street Mission Hall. Courtesy of Mrs Margaret Cooper.

55   The cast of The Midship Mite which played in Freer Street Mission Hall for three
nights in 1932. Courtesy of Mrs Margaret Mowat.

56   A Freer Street Mission Mothers Meeting drive in the 1930s.
Courtesy of Mrs Margaret Mowat.

57   A Sunday School Picnic arranged by Freer Street Mission in the 1930s.
Courtesy of Mrs Margaret Mowat.

We had to go to church; it wasnae a case o' whether ye wanted to go—ye had to go, but I don't think it did us any harm. We went to the Sacred Heart up at Lauriston.

MRS MARY CRUICKSHANK

When you were a kid, the only way tae get a picnic was tae join as many Sunday Schools and Band o' Hope's as you could think of.

There used tae be Barry's down in the Grassmarket, the Salvation Army, the Tollcross Gospel Halls, the Reigo Street Mission, and it was a wonder when you went the day trips, they never clashed with each other . . . they always seemed to have their trips on different days. That's where the old enamel tinny came in wi' the tape around your shoulder. And that's how ye got your summer picnic and also your Christmas Treat as well. The trips usually went to Colinton Dell . . . they kept within the Edinburgh area, so it was within easy reach by either tramcar or bus. They supplied the food and then you'd your races and games and all the rest of it. You made a complete day of it. You looked forward tae these trips every year.

JOHN WEBSTER

Oh no, we didn't belong to any Sunday Schools. We only went to the ones that were giving away free tickets for trips. It didn't matter if they were Catholic, Protestant or Nigerian—it didn't matter as long as they were giving away tickets, and it was always to the Grassmarket we went—to the Undenominational thing. We went there and they used to gie us mugs o' tea and pieces and treacle.

MRS J PLENDERLEITH

I went to Chapel in the morning and we joined the Freer Street Sunday School in the afternoon, so we got to the pairties o' both—we were a bit o' a cheat. And I went to the Band o' Hope in Grove Street at Dicksons—that's where Clan House is now—it was good, plenty songs and there was entertainment as well, and there was a friendliness among the kids that you don't get now . . . they wanted to play with each other, now it's a' what ye've got.

MRS MARY CRUICKSHANK

We went to three Sunday Schools every Sunday. We went to Lauriston Church, we went to one, I think they call it Tollcross Halls, right at the top of Lauriston opposite Glen Street, up the side stairs above the cinema. They had an afternoon session. And then we went down—because we liked singing hymns I think—to one in the evening in Shandwick Place, up a stair again, that was like a mission hall, and it was just singing hymns. And when I got a bit older, maybe fourteen or fifteen, we used to go up to the one in the High Street, Carrubber's Close, because it was the one you got a cup o' tea and a bun.

Sunday School Picnics—I'm sure the kind of place we went to, what we thought was far away, you'd go in the bus with your streamers and that, I'm sure we went down Queensferry way, somewhere with a park like Dalmeny. Davidsons Mains was another one and Spylaw Park, and we may have went as far maybe as Dalkeith. I remember going to them all and running the races and having a form . . . you took everything with you and the bigger lads had to help to carry the stuff, and you'd bring it all back to the church.

ALEXANDER A ALEXANDER

And even those who weren't allowed to go on these trips often envied those who were.

> Opposite us in Lauriston Place, there were shops built out in front of the houses and at the end of that was a little passage that went to what had been a main door and that was a Mission Hall, I think it was called the Edinburgh Denominational Mission or something like that. But I know that the great thing was that in the summer they had picnics and we would see all these children gathering there and marching along the street to the bus or tram or something like that, all with a tape round their neck and the tin mug on it. We children sort of envied that because we never went on these picnics.
>
> Dr A C McLaren

And some of the interviewees even thought that todays children are missing out on all the fun they used to have.

> All Saints Church had its own little school in Glen Street. There were two schools in Glen Street, St Ignatious, the Catholic School, and All Saints, the Episcopal School, and All Saints belongs to the church and the Brownies met at the top of the school which was called the Mission Room. I don't know why it was called that. I went to the Brownies there myself when I was seven, and I went from Brownies to Guides, to a Pack Leader to a Tawny Owl, then a Brown Owl, and then I was in Rangers as well. We taught them semaphore and that kind of thing, but the badge system was different then. There was a second class badge and a first class badge. For the second class you had to polish your shoes for a week, and dry the dishes for a week, and then, later on, in first class, it was a wee bit more adventurous—you had to grow cress and make milk puddings—household tasks really. And we had sports days, races and stuff like that. We went on hikes and Sausage Sizzles to Corstorphine Woods. We had skipping competitions and all sorts of things like that. I went to camp at a wee place called Spott. That was my first camp. This was the adventure to end all adventures! You had to take your gas mask with you, of course. We had a week camp there and my mother came out on the Wednesday with cakes and stuff as if we were starved; she brought all this food. We had what you called a palliasse, like a downie cover that you filled with straw from the farmer's barn. You filled this thing like a mattress. Oh, it was rare! It was great! We were pleased with much less then.
> We didn't feel we had to take the television with us.
>
> Mrs Iris Munro

> There was a little side door into All Saints Church and we used to go from school to the church. Then the Sisters of the Church—well, they dressed like nuns, you know, but they were Sisters—they lived in the big house next to All Saints School and they were really good. The kids were all collecting bonfire wood and the sisters had a cellar which went under the road and they used to keep our bonfire wood for us. The kids from Lauriston Park or Panmure Place would come trying to steal our bonfire wood and the Sisters would come running out with their brushes to chase them away. And the bonfire—everybody took part in it.
>
> Mrs Grace Taylor

And there often seemed to be no specific allegiance to any particular church in the youth organisations.

> We used to go to Baillie Dixon's in Grove Street to the Band of Hope on a Friday night. Sometimes you got a lantern slide or whatever. Then I was in the Brownies, I went to Fountainbridge Brownies, then I was in the Guides and then I was a Ranger for a while, but I discovered the dancing so that was the end of the Rangers. And then Nan McKay and I were in the Lothian Road Choir—Church Choir.
>
> Mrs Peggy Weddell

> We went to Sunday School at Castlebarns and Scrivenors Hall. Castlebarns belonged to St Cuthbert's on Lothian Road. We used to go to the Good Temperance thing—that was at Scrivenors. We used to go to another place down at the bottom of Morrison Street where these women with the blue hats on and the big ties. Some Mission. I think it's still there, just round the corner from Torphichen Place. Just a Hallelujah thing to get you on the road.
>
> Mrs Ruby Clifford

> I fell oot wi' my pal, so I went tae the Guides in St David's, Morrison Street, but ye see I was a Guildry girl through and through, and I mind o' getting a couple o' badges from the Guides but I went back tae the Guildry again. I think at that time, quite a few of us were friends, and one kept picking on my chum and I picked on her one night and I got put oot o' the Guildry for picking on this lass and that wis me in the huff.
>
> Mrs Ina Begbie

> Oh, I was a member of every church in the district. We were actually members of St David's Church in Morrison Street, but it was too far to go on a Sunday morning, so we used to go to Lothian Road Sunday School in the morning which was just across the road and down the Chucky Pend, and St Cuthbert's Mission Hall at Castlebarns in the afternoon, and the family went down to St David's at night. I went to the Brownies and Guides in Lothian Road Church. The church wasn't important for a lot of people but it was for us, because my mother was always a church person, my father to a certain extent but not so much as my mother. I mean my mother had been brought up in the church in Dundee and she was in the Guildry and everything, she really was church.
>
> Mrs Alice Burt

Parental habits and attitudes towards churchgoing also had a somewhat mixed effect.

> My mother and father were not churchgoers, my mother had belonged to Carrubber's Close when she was younger, but my father didn't bother about church. But we went to the Sunday School and we went to the lantern lectures at the Barclay Church, and of course there was always the soiree and things like that.
>
> AHR

I never remember my mother and father going to church, but it didn't mean to say that they didn't have a religion of their own. But we always went to Sunday School. I think in these days the church did play quite a big role because there wasn't much else. I think everything we did seemed to revolve around the church or the mission or whatever.

Mrs Peggy Weddell

We were made to go to Church—the Sacred Heart in Lauriston. At that time the women wore big hats. Some had birds in them. And we always seemed to get at the back o' somebody wi' a big bird in their hat. And we were always put outside for laughing, and when we got outside, we didn't want to laugh, and when we came in we wanted to laugh again. So they kept us out. We never went to Sunday School. Never any social church things.

Mrs J Plenderleith

I was the only regular churchgoer in the family. My mother went occasionally, but my dad never ever stopped us going. I gave a lot of time to the church. At one time we were nearly running the place. I was at All Saints from when I was seven. They had a lot of activities. There was the Little Guild, that used to meet downstairs . . . Mrs Hammond's guild. That was for us the junior people. There was also the Light Bearers. This always seemed a spooky kind of thing. It was just a girls' meeting. I was in the choir and the Sunday School, and at that time at All Saints, there were nuns, we called them sisters, and they lived in the house by the church building. They did an awful lot to hold everything together. They got us interested in the Sunday School. It was a huge Sunday School and I think it was largely due to their influence. They would come to your house to visit, they really did a lot. I remember going up there to do sewing. You had to go up there one night a week to do sewing. It was quite a wonderful time. I'd been there such a long time that I was really in with the bricks, but I found it a very happy time. We were married in All Saints.

Mrs Iris Munro

Different religions did not appear to cause problems in the community.

In Keir Street, of course, or Graham Street, they had the synagogue, the original synagogue in Edinburgh, so there were a lot of Jews lived round about . . . I think Professor Daiches' father was the Rabbi, then in Graham Street. I think the Daiches lived over in Marchmont or somewhere like that, but the boys were brought up there and they went to Watsons and their father was the Rabbi for a long time.

Dr A C McLaren

There was a family of Jews. Now my grandmother, who was a staunch Catholic, she used to go down on a Saturday, which was the Jews Sabbath and do the cleaning for them. Light the fire and do anything that was necessary that the woman wasn't allowed to do.

Mrs Grace Taylor

It also seems that in the main, different denominations caused very few problems.

In Tollcross you were in the minority if you were in the Episcopal Church. Mind you, all my pals went to the Church of Scotland, and I used to go with them to the Band of Hope. I also had pals who were Roman Catholic and I went with them to the Sacred Heart. I was a very liberal minded person! I went to everything, I didn't bother. Edinburgh is one of the few places you could do that. In fact, for a while, I used to go to All Saints Guides on a Wednesday night and on a Friday night, I went to the Catholic Guides. I was in two companies. Nobody bothered and it didn't do me any harm.

MRS IRIS MUNRO

I remember taking Communion Classes at St Cuthbert's and that was hilarious, we used to go on a Thursday tae Communion Classes and the old church elder used tae take us, and ye had tae wear yer hat, so ye had a wee tammy on. And a' ye done was watch the clock tae see what time it was. And we used tae come out o' there at Lothian Road, and we used tae run like blazes right up Lothian Road tae the Sacred Heart, because there was dancing on in the Sacred Heart on a Thursday night and I think it was aboot thruppence to get in or something and I used tae say tae masel' this is sacrilege, but that wis just what ye did.

But years and years after that, I had a neighbour who went tae the Sacred Heart and I used tae go with her tae their social evenings, and I'd been going for two or three months and I won the raffle this night, a pair o' stockings or something, and when I went over it was the priest that was handing out the raffle prizes—and I was so embarrassed—he says to me, 'I haven't seen you in church for a few Sundays'. I was shaking in my shoes, you know, and I remember going back to see Nell and telling my neighbour and she just roared and laughed, she thought this was hilarious. I says 'I'd better no come back to yer Socials' and she says, 'Oh dinnae be silly, he's getting tae know yer face with ye coming every week.' And I think that's what we were in these days, even religion never came into nothing at all . . . other than your Scotch and Irish where you used to have your fights wi' yer bit paper and stick, Scotch and Irish Day, ye know, for St Andrew's Day or whatever it was, I couldnae even tell ye what it was for. But that never came into nothing, I mean some of my friends went to St Thomas o' Aquin and I went to Boroughmuir and I used tae meet them at Tollcross and we linked up and that was it, there was no sort of bigotry then. I couldnae have told ye up until about ten years ago whether it was all Catholics that played for a football team or all Protestants, I mean you always knew that green was the Catholic colour and that's all there was to it.

MRS INA BEGBIE

The stair was a windin' stair and there were four flats altogether. there were five houses on each landin'. We stayed on the first landin', and to put it bluntly we were the only Protestants in the whole stair, the rest were all Roman Catholic, but then everybody all mucked in together. If anybody was ill or wanting anything done, they all mucked in. Religion was never spoken about or argued over.

JOHN WEBSTER

We, at All Saints School, weren't allowed out to play at the same time as St Ignatious School, but on Scotch and Irish Day, St Patrick's Day, we used to make big balls of hard paper, tied them with string and everybody went about with these balls and then you would go up to one and say, 'Scotch or Irish?' Well naturally you lived in the place, you knew who went to the Catholic school and who went to All Saints School or Tollcross School, so you knew what to say. If they asked me and it was the Catholic school people who were asking it, I'd say, 'Catholic'. But if they caught somebody unawares and they said it wrong, well they got battered with the paper thing.

MRS GRACE TAYLOR

However, official attitudes were not so accommodating.

I went nursing at the beginning of the war. I went to Bruntsfield. Now in these days when I did my training, you had to do an extra year at Bruntsfield for gynaecology and then you had to leave Bruntsfield and go to another hospital for general training. I was down to go to the Deaconess, and it was so funny, I was on night duty, Matron came in and she said, 'I'm sorry you won't be allowed to go to the Deaconess'. I says, 'Why not? They accepted me'. She says, 'Yes, but you know it's a Protestant hospital and they returned your birth certificate'. I said, 'It's Scottish Episcopalian that' but the Rector had signed it 'Baptised by me, Canon somebody or other' and whoever had looked at it had said, 'Oh Roman Catholic, she's not coming here'. So they did accept me but I didn't go because I decided to get married. Well, at that time you weren't allowed to marry and train. One or other.

MRS GRACE TAYLOR

Nowadays most of the church's social work is carried out by their administrative headquarters, but in earlier days local congregations were involved in social work.

The Churches—like even the Catholic Church that was in Lauriston Place—they used to give out vouchers, and you went in there, you got the equivalent to maybe . . . everything was loose, of course . . . but you got your barley and your peas, lentils and porridge oats and things like that. You know you got all these things on this voucher, I think it would be the equivalent of five shillings, but with that five shillings you got enough cereals to dae the whole week, probably more than a week.

I went to the Sacred Heart Church, but the Catholic Church was more . . . they didn't have the social activities they have now. You know, now it's more modernised.

MRS JANET DOW

My mother's dad, my grandad, was an elder in the church over in Fountainbridge, and she used to say, 'When I was brought up, I was never out of the church, I had to go to Bible Class and everything.' And I remember there was something wrong with our carpet, she said, 'I mind when I used tae carry carpets—when they were having a sale of work or something you had to put so much into the church—and many a carpet I carried up there that I could dae wi' now'.

MRS CHRISSIE BORTHWICK

I'm still in the same church! . . . they had the holiday home for Tired Mothers in Leadburn—I only had three at the time—but I went there for a week, that was through the church. And naturally they had the Girls' Guildry, but my family werenae old enough for me to deal in that. I only went to the Mothers' Meeting, you could take your children in the pram and sit in the hall, just every week, and it was just a matter of maybe the head minister would come, do a sermon and sing a hymn, it was just for you to go out—broke up the time a bit.

Mrs Margaret Downie

None of our interviewees appeared to be connected to the Methodist Mission but it is clear from the booklet *For The Making of Good Men & Women*, which was published in 1988 to celebrate 100 years of their mission, that they were involved in just as many activities. The following is a list of all that was going on in the Mission in 1933—Sunday Schools, Bible Class, Conferences, Saturday evening concerts, Young Men and Girls Clubs, Wesley Guild, Rambles and Recreational Clubs, Cubs, Brownies, Scouts and Guides, Ladies Sewing Meetings, Play Centre and Roof Garden for little children daily, Bright Hour for Women, Girls' League for Missionary and Social Effort, Band of Hope, Temperance and Social Welfare Work, Drama Club, Fellowship and Group Meetings.

As this is a very similar list of activities to that given by so many of our interviewees about St Cuthbert's and the work at Freer Street Mission, perhaps we should now let them paint their picture of words and bring life to the list.

St Cuthbert's Parish Church

St Cuthbert's Parish Church, as the name had developed at the end of the nineteenth century, was the West Kirk outside the city wall for so long. It had this great sense of its parish and that we were responsible for all the people in the bounds of St Cuthbert's Parish—that was a very real thing.

Rev Dr S Louden

This awareness of 'parish' had caused St Cuthbert's to purchase a house and garden at Castlebarns in Morrison Street in 1849 and set up an 'industrial' school, which in point of fact only gave elementary education for 'a class of children, the outcasts of society'. New buildings were erected in 1862 and the premises were also known as St Cuthbert's Mission and were used for general mission activities and financed by the congregation. In 1902 the number had dwindled so much that the school was closed, but the premises continued to be used for congregational activities until 1967. The activities were many and varied—Mothers' Meetings, a Gymnastic Club, Dressmaking and Millinery Classes, a Work Society, Brownies, Guides, Cubs and Scouts as well as Sunday Schools.

I went to Brownies and Sunday School at Castlebarns but we just knew it as Morrison Street. You had to go up a pend in Morrison Street and I always thought it was dark and creepy when I used to go to Brownies, I think that's why I eventually left. You went through an opening in the wall on the left and then up this flight of open stone stairs with railings, then along this corridor to the hall. Sometimes the Scout Pipe Band was rehearsing outside when we were in at the Brownies and there was an awful din. It was a really big Sunday School and we were all crowded into the hall, so it was hot . . . I didn't like it much.

MISS MARGARET WILSON

All the organisations were spread round the Mission Halls as well as the Church, and it was the Brownies I was in all the time, so that was Morrison Street and then when I was beginning to be a Tawny Owl or something, first of all I had to do so long at Lothian Road, but then I landed up in the Congregational Pack for a while, and then I got married so I wasn't there very long—but to this day you still meet the odd person that you were at Guides with in Morrison Street or Freer Street and it is very interesting how it created links, very warm links in fact.

MRS HELEN LOUDEN

Then we put on a play in Morrison Street, a musical—'The good Old Days' or something, because I remember I was supposed to be the equivalent of Queen Victoria . . . that age group . . . and we all sang in a concert there, we had to scrub all the hall first, but we just done it.

MRS INA BEGBIE

But Morrison Street had no pattern of weekly services or a weekly concert. In some ways it might have been a second set of church halls to King's Stables Road because quite a number of things at Morrison Street were congregation rather than Mission.

REV DR S LOUDEN

Thus the great missionary outreach of St Cuthbert's to the area was through Gilmore Park Mission, or Freer Street Mission as it was more commonly known. The premises in Freer Street were first leased from the British Rubber Mill in 1903 and soon very practical services were being offered to the area.

But when my brother and I were wee, Freer Street was different. There used to be a bank belonging to St Cuthbert's the church doon at the bottom of the street. And we both had a pink bank book and my mother used to say, 'Now Chrissie, there's your thru'pence. Willie there's your thru'pence'. Now we used to go down to the bank and we would put that in and if she could afford fourpence we got it. And whenever we needed shoes or Willie needed pants or anything, she used to give us a wee note down to the Mission to give us the money out, and they were always very very nice to ye.

MRS CHRISSIE BORTHWICK

But it was the arrival of the Very Rev Lord George Macleod of Fuinary in 1926, then simply the Rev George Macleod, Associate Minister of St Cuthbert's that appears to have given greater impetus to the Freer Street Mission. The Rev Dr S Louden, who was himself a student assistant minister at St Cuthbert's from 1934 to 1936, with special responsibility for Freer Street recalls:

I think the Mission was a very modest sort of place they could go to until George Macleod . . . that was his main sort of thrust in St Cuthbert's, to bring Freer Street into a new vitality. He put a student assistant in charge of the Mission and roped in all sorts of West-End types . . . and certainly it was from that the flowering of Freer Street was achieved.

Well, I think they all had money—you know the Wilkies in Shandwick Place, it's a drapers, well, they were involved, the daughters of that, they were involved in the things that we did.

And there were elders' daughters and things like that. It was all people that came and sort o' gave their time, to make it a better life for the kids that were living round about there. It was people that were connected with St Cuthbert's Church. George Macleod, he came there as a young minister, and I can remember getting a prize from him, we used to have a prize-giving and you loved to get a prize for perfect attendance, and I remember him coming there and he was presenting the prizes to us, we always got books. And he said to me, Macleod—well, our name was Macleod you see—and he says to me, what was my father's name, and I said George, and it was the same name as him. And he said, 'That's for having very good attendance and for having a very good name!'

MRS ANNIE KITSON

It's awfully difficult to remember—I think if I'm right I was thirteen when George Macleod came and I only remember that because I was in the Junior Choir at the Sunday School, that was when the congregational Sunday School was a huge afternoon service and they needed the church. It's fantastic to think of it now and they had their own choir, that's how I remember my age . . . yes I would be thirteen and he was starting things up.

MRS HELEN LOUDEN

The first club we went to was the Guildry but we was just wee lassies. Aye, the Mission that was wir life, if we hadnae had that, we'd have nothing . . . Holidays and picnics? Well, the first time I remember anything like that was when Miss Hole, the Sunday School teacher—you would say she was a Flapper—she used tae bring all these young people and they all had cars and I remember she took us to this big house in the Carlops. I thought I was in heaven, because we went upstairs and it was an attic and the toys! Big, big pram! Oh I can remember it as though it was yesterday. Never forgot Miss Hole—or Mrs Frackleton as she became—for that, she was good to the kids in the Sunday School in Freer Street, you had competitions and you won prizes. I can say as much of the Bible because she used to make you word perfect, she was good. And I used to sing in the church choir at Freer Street.

MRS ANNIE HEPBURN

Guildry—Miss Herdman—they owned the Herdman Flour Mills and she was brought up real class. She spoke as well educated people should speak. But she used to come up to our houses and see how your mother was, and come into the old but and ben with the pulley hanging up with all your washing on it.

MRS NANCY BARCLAY

I was a member of St Cuthbert's, right through the Sunday School, Bible Class and
in those days you joined the church quite early, I think I was fifteen or sixteen. But
after the Bible Class, my sisters were already involved at Freer Street . . . we lived in
the Marchmont district, so Freer Street . . . we walked it all in those days . . . more
our side of the town. I got involved with the beginners Sunday School, which was
the under fives and my memory was that it was an absolute hive of industry . . . the
Sunday Schools, there was so many children they couldn't all meet at the same
time, there was a Sunday School for the older ones after probably the beginners and
the primary. Then most of the helpers were staying on to do something else so there
was always a tea party at Freer Street on a Sunday in the kitchen, and those involved
the people who had been at the later Sunday School and then there was always an
evening concert for the local people, every Sunday and that was St Cuthbert's people
finding musicians, singers, speakers, but looking back it was super entertainment.
There was a five o'clock service and the concert was about eight, and you paid—
it was quite a lot of money, eightpence or something as you went in the door . . .
some of the people were famous in the music world, but there was a complete
mixture, maybe if they were short, it would come to the assistant minister showing
films of Palestine, but they always had entertainment.

MRS HELEN LOUDEN

Well as I say, all our entertainment was down in this Mission Hall in Freer Street,
everything happened about there. And we were in plays, and the teachers—looking
back now—they were really good with us, they spent quite a lot of time, and
teaching different arts, like sewing and different things to make. We were there
nearly every night, there was something on, I remember on the Monday night there
was the bank, the penny bank—if you had a penny, you went down with the penny.
And it must have been the elders that were sitting there taking your pennies from
you. I mean it wisnae much but it was encouraging the kids about the place to make
something of themselves. My parents never managed to save, no until we were
working, they never had that kind of money.

We went to the sewing class on Tuesday night and on Wednesday night there was
a sort of playschool thing that we went to. And there the teachers taught us how
to make doll's furniture, wee bits of things out of matchboxes and things like that,
which was quite good and we'd play some games. And then Thursday night was the
Guildry night. We did marching, they taught us how to march to music and all this
sort o' thing. And they taught us how to do skipping to music and we played with
balls, and games with beanbags and things like that. And we had the uniform with
this big daft hat, a felt hat, you know, that we hated. And a white blouse and your
sash. You had to take care of it or your mother had to take care of the laundering
of your blouses and the navy blue skirt. And I remember we had a thing every year
in King's Stables Road, that your parents could come and see all the work you had
done over the year. And you done a display for them, which was quite exciting for
us. I think Friday was Boys' Brigade night. But there was a Boys' Club as well [as
the girls'] so there must have been different times. The things we went to that was
all the girls things, so I suppose maybe we had from 5 to 7 and the boys had 7 to 9
or something like that. But that hall, it never seemed to be shut. And then Saturday
was a sort of free day and then of course Sunday was the Sunday School again, we

58 Girls' Club at Castlebarns Mission, Morrison Street, probably in the early 1950s. From the album of Phyllis J Bain (1912–1978). Courtesy of Miss J Winnert.

59   Reunion of the Girls Guildry at St Cuthbert's Church Hall in the early 1960s. In the
centre of the picture is the Rev Dr R L Small. Courtesy of Mrs Nessie Hood.

went to Sunday School there. We just went to the Mission on a Sunday and then
maybe special Sundays, some festival thing or something, we'd march down to
King's Stables Road, to the church, to St Cuthbert's Church.

Mrs Annie Kitson

I went to the Tired Mothers' Home, again through the church—that was at
Leadburn and it was for mothers only and children under five, children over five
went to Humbie, but if you had children under five you went to Leadburn for ten
days. And we went, it was through the Grassmarket Mission I think originally, but
we went through our church, Miss Bain being our church sister. Well, we went
there and the stories I could tell you about people, the really poor people we met
there. I mean all we done from when we went there—when we werenae walking
the kids—was knit or teach people how to knit or Annie would show some people
how to sew. That was between 1948 and 1952 that I went . . . but it's no the first
woman that's come there really destitute and needing the holiday—mind we
needed it too because we had a family and worked hard and our husbands didnae
make that much money that we could afford to take the children away—but it's no
the first time that we've actually taken women there and between the matron and
the women ourselves, have shown her how to wash hersel' and cleaned her and
cleaned her children's heads and things like that. Well, I think if you hadnae been

brought up in a caring society, which I felt mostly came from St Cuthbert's Church, then we couldnae have learnt to do these things. The matron there was something else, because she would go and dig out clothes for them because obviously she got clothes handed in to her, but we've met some very poor people there.

MRS INA BEGBIE

But the relationship between the members of St Cuthbert's and the people of the Mission was not at all patronising, as the Very Rev R Leonard Small, Minister of St Cuthbert's from 1956-75, points out.

There was a two-way mingling of the actual members of St Cuthbert's and the people who went to the Missions. First of all there were all the people from the church, who went and supplied the skilled and caring running ability for all the organisations.

For example there was a great old lady, Mrs MacRobert, whose husband had been the Solicitor General for Scotland, and she ran—during the very difficult years of the depression,—she ran a girls' sewing class, because if a girl in those days wanted a party dress, she couldn't afford to go and buy it in the shops, she had to go to a remnant shop and buy a remnant and then get a pattern. And Mrs MacRobert taught them how to sew it. And she went on, this is one side of the relationship not at all patronising but entirely family, she gave a party in her house in the Grange area for her girls and she was still having parties when the girls were grandmothers. But that was the kind of relationship, there was no, you know, 'doing the slumming' as I've heard people contemptuously say. It wasn't that at all.

REV DR R L SMALL

Others too felt there was a happy mingling which has stood the test of time.

But it was a wonderful place . . . the one person I know is still there, is Cissy Boyle . . . she's still living about Tollcross . . . now she grew up in that area, they were Fountainbridge . . . she and her older sister grew up through the Guildry, then she became a helper. She and I did the beginner's Sunday School together at one point. But this is what I meant, so many people who started as the local people for whom the Freer Street things were available, then themselves became the helpers . . . and this went on over and over again. It wasn't all just outsiders from the big church going in, it was quite amazing the number who became . . . and then the mothers, of course, at Freer Street, there were always special things for the mothers of all these children.

MRS HELEN LOUDEN

But what was happening in Morrison Street and Freer Street was terribly impressive as the gospel and the life of the church among the residents of an area and it wasn't two-class Christianity, it was just that the church was there in the real sense of a community. And it was a real community which they were sorry to leave. Wasn't it in the thirties that Stenhouse was built and some of them came into the 5 o'clock service from Stenhouse, and the one thing was the hope that they would one day return to the Fountainbridge area.

REV DR S LOUDEN

This was Edinburgh's first Company—Freer Street. There was Miss Herdman and Miss Margaret Brown and Chris Brown—we still send Christmas cards to each other. Unfortunately Miss Herdman's dead now. She lived until she was about 90. They treated us so well and we learned an awful lot.

MRS NANCY BARCLAY

But yes, it was a very different world and yet when you think of all the different things that took place . . . we had a friend in Perthshire who until very recently, she had a bus load of what had been Freer Street mothers going up for their outing and she gets local people in her village to help her with tea and that sort of thing, but that all just went on and on. I don't know how many generations would do it

MRS HELEN LOUDEN

The other side of the mingling was that it became really the accepted thing for people in the Mission to join the Church . . . a very high proportion of them went on to do so, much more than most people imagine. We know it now, because with the whole area being cleared out, entire elders' districts were moved away, far away and lost their connection. To be completely honest, sometimes being a member meant simply coming to Communion, but they all enjoyed coming to Communion, wouldn't miss coming to Communion, one of the two big Communions in the year. But for the rest, the Mission was their church. But it was a live connection.

REV DR R L SMALL

The majority of them went on to become members of St Cuthbert's—most of the choir for the 5 o'clock service at Freer Street were in their teens and they had already been confirmed or made communicant members. I think we had a class for first communicants at Freer Street and, of course, joining the Church was joining St Cuthbert's. They kept up their very active church work and association with Freer Street, but they were definitely members of St Cuthbert's and knew they were.

REV DR S LOUDEN

I was married at St Cuthbert's Church down in Lothian Road, mostly I went to Freer Street, but for a wee while I used to go to Communion at the church with my daughter-in-law.

MRS CHRISSIE BORTHWICK

I was married in St Cuthbert's Church and my two daughters were married in St Cuthbert's and when I came oot here I started up a Girls' Guildry at St Andrew's Church, and so I lifted ma papers from St Cuthbert's.

MRS INA BEGBIE

Freer Street Mission was demolished with the rest of Freer Street in 1967, but that was not the end of the story.

And the last surviving activity of the two Missions, after Freer Street was closed first and after all its surviving activities were transferred to Morrison Street, . . . the Women's Fellowship was moved down to the church hall . . . and it was very funny, if there was any kind of snobbery between the church people and the mission people, it was nothing compared to the snobbery between Morrison Street and Freer Street . . . 'What was she? She was only Freer Street' . . . so any way, people said, 'It won't work, they'll never come down to the church'. But that is the one organisation which is still going strong after all these years; they quite happily moved down to the church hall and integrated properly. There was a gradual integration beginning with a joint Christmas party between the Woman's Guild and the Women's Fellowship—this was Congregation and Mission joining together very, very happily.

REV DR R L SMALL

Another of St Cuthbert's organisations which has survived is the 40th Boys' Brigade Company, which on 1 February 1990 celebrated being in existence for one hundred years. Mrs Mary Cruickshank has fond memories of the company.

I remember standing at the top of Freer Street watching the BB marching up and down, long before I had boys and I used tae think, 'Oh, I wish I'd been a laddie', just to get into the Boys' Brigade, and ma two sons both went tae it, but unfortunately by that time Freer Street was finished and they had tae go to St Cuthbert's, but Alec was the last of the Fountainbridge crowd tae be a BB officer. He still is an officer and attached to St Cuthbert's, but their meetings are now held at Tollcross School until the church is renovated—I think it will be nice when it's finished but I don't know if they'll ever capture the crowd back again because Freer Street was a great place.

60   The 40th Edinburgh Company of the Boys' Brigade, who have been part of the Fountainbridge scene for many years, celebrated its centenary in February 1990. Attached to St Cuthbert's Parish Church at the West End, the Company also attracted many recruits to its premises at Freer Street Mission Hall where it also met for a spell.
Courtesy of Mrs Mary Cruickshank.

Unfortunately it does not seem likely that 'They will capture the crowd back again'. There are probably several reasons why the membership and organisations of St Cuthbert's has declined over the latter part of this century. The Very Rev R Leonard Small points out one or two.

> When we went there in 1956, it was still in a real sense a family, a very large family—at that time the membership was 3,500—but it was still a family and you felt that when they were brought together, like Communion. But the congregation has become fragmented, not because of anybody's fault but just because of social changes. Families have moved or have been moved out of the area. For a while people kept up the sentimental connection, but gradually as their children started going to Cubs or Brownies locally, then the parents rightly and properly went there too.
>
> Thinking back there was a lot of poor housing, Reigo Street, for example, in behind Earl Grey Street. We had a number of people there and we had a lot from that whole area, Morrison Street, Fountainbridge, up to Tollcross itself. A high proportion of St Cuthbert's came from there, but you see that was already changing. I can give you an indication of how it was changing.
>
> The first time we did a Parish Visitation would be about 1959 and we went into every home in the Parish and we were very thorough, we had lists of boys of Boys' Brigade or Scout age and girls of Guide or Guildry age and so on and so forth, and in the whole of that area there were only three boys of Boys' Brigade or Scout age. You see the younger folk were moving out and what were left was often the Grannie who had survived everybody else.

However the influence of these early days still carries on.

In another chapter Tommy Lang tells how recently he was approached by a stranger, who told him that his father's coaching at Freer Street had made a great difference to his life. Mrs Ina Begbie also feels that St Cuthbert's Church was a good influence in her own and her friends lives.

> I think St Cuthbert's Church was good for us, because we had moneyed people that were members there and they were very good to the poorer people. I just always mind that being part of St Cuthbert's Church, No so much in ma day but I remember my sister saying there's something special on at the Guildry—a Guildry parade or something—and a lot of the lassies didnae have white blouses, but they would get told to come and they would go there to the church. And for the ones that didnae have white blouses, there would be a box wi' white blouses—all right they had to give them back—but there was always the stuff there to rig the girls out and that was only done by the church women, the members of the church. And the result was that it came out on tae a lot of us, I think that's why you'll find that Fountainbridge women, especially women that were connected to St Cuthbert's Church and the Guildry have got that 'thought for other people's feelings', because I think they learnt it there.
>
> Looking back on it I feel St Cuthbert's must have been good for us, it must have been a good influence.

CHAPTER NINE

Waiting for the Bulldozers

David Fisher

If I go near Tollcross now and I look along that street I just think, what a shame. What a lovely, bustling, busy area it used to be. An awful lot of folks say it's progress. I look up there and I think the area is awfy desolate.

MRS PEGGY WEDDELL

It breaks my heart tae see what's happened tae the Tollcross area now. It was a thriving community. But now—I couldnae describe it. It's took the atmosphere away completely. All the good things have been destroyed.

JOHN WEBSTER

For over a century . . . there was no direction in planning in Tollcross and this area grew up on civic jungle principles. It is, frankly, an ugly area.

JELLICOE and COLERIDGE,
A plan for the Tollcross area of Edinburgh 1965

Previous chapters have described a close-knit, largely working class community, as it existed in the first half of this century. This chapter looks at some of the changes this community went through in the years following the Second World War, with its focus on those resulting from various planning schemes. Mainly it's the story of things that didn't happen. The post-war history of the area is studded with the jargon of town planning—comprehensive development, local plans, structure plans, relief roads, pedestrianisation, zoning. In the inner city areas of Glasgow, Leeds and Birmingham the 1950s and 1960s saw this jargon transformed into reality. In Tollcross it was different. The development axe has hung many times over the community but has never quite fallen, at least not with the finality that often seemed to threaten. Yet, in amongst the abandoned plans and projects, important changes have taken place.

When former residents like Peggy Weddell and John Webster look at what the area is like today, their main feelings are ones of loss and nostalgia. They would have had a lot more to lament if Jellicoe and Coleridge had had their way. If their plan (produced in line with the Tollcross area's designation as a Comprehensive Development Area) had gone ahead, Tollcross would have

survived in name only. The tenements and streets where John Webster and Peggy Weddell worked, played and grew up would have been replaced with a huge shopping and leisure complex, surrounded by a motorway and overlooked by tower blocks.

How could such a scheme ever have been contemplated? Part of the answer is that planners saw areas like Tollcross in negative terms—to them it was simply raw material, a series of planning problems to apply their skill to. This negative attitude is revealed in the language they use. To the planners it was 'an ugly area', a 'civic jungle', a jumble of buildings that had grown up haphazardly over the centuries and that now needed to be straightened up and put in order. It was a challenge that gave rise to grandiose historical comparisons.

> Edinburgh's twentieth century planners are facing the city's biggest architectural and planning challenge in 200 years—the redevelopment of hundreds of acres of the southern central area around the Old Town. Most of this project—or rather series of interrelated schemes, between Holyrood Park in the east and Tollcross and Haymarket in the west—is scheduled for completion within the next 20 years . . . According to the 1965 Quinquennial Review of the City Development Plan, the proposals for the area present an unrivalled opportunity to lay the foundations for a major project in 20th Century civic design comparable in scale to the Old Town and Georgian New Town.
>
> *Scotsman*, 8 December 1966

It is clear from the proposals put forward by the town planners that few of them knew anything of, or put any value on, the rich, supportive lively working class culture that thrived in the areas they so blithely planned razing to the ground and replacing with ring roads, shopping piazzas and high rises. Previous chapters have described this culture in the residents' own words—the neighbourliness, the menages, the women gossiping in the back green, the colour and variety of street life. But as these chapters also make clear there was another side to this way of life—over-crowding, insanitary living conditions, appalling health problems.

> Society was a different thing then and an aspect of that is the housing situation. Housing in Freer Street, and worse, Freer Street Terrace, was simply unspeakable, right into the 1930s at the time I was a student there.
>
> Rev Dr S Louden

> Conditions were appalling. Maybe Fountainbridge was a wee bit better than other parts of the city, a wee bit better, but nevertheless if people were asked to live in conditions like that nowadays, there would be rebellion, yes, certainly. But that went on. It wisnae until, oh, I would say, they were into the 1960s that was still

---

61   (Facing page) Aerial view of the Fountainbridge area about 1912. In the top right hand corner one can see the Union Canal basins at Port Hamilton and Port Hopetoun. Nearly all the tenements in Fountainbridge and neighbouring streets were removed in the 1960s. Courtesy of Eric Newsome.

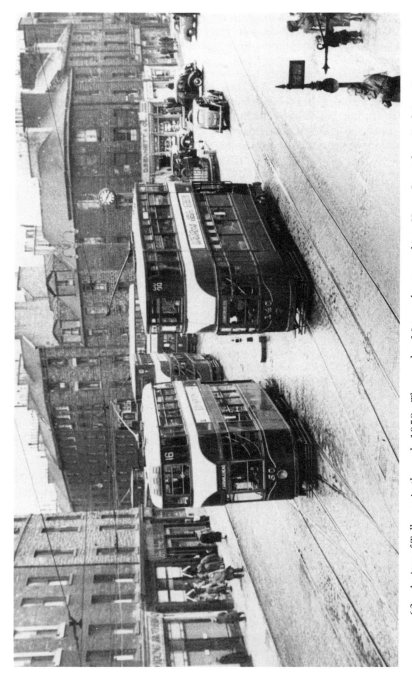

62   A view of Tollcross in the early 1950s. The number 16 tram has turned into Home Street from Earl Grey Street and the number 29 tram will pass the clock to turn into Lauriston Place. Courtesy of the Royal Bank of Scotland on behalf of Mr Alistair Coull, ex Manager.

going on. Well, if you take, for example, they had pends there, and one was called Asa Wass's Pend. And in this Asa Wass's Pend he had a scrap business. Right through there, the rats, and the smell in the place. And that was right in the middle o' this big tenement. But, well, it was just accepted.

ALEX KITSON

In the post-war years however these conditions were less and less accepted. Demand was increasing that the slums should be cleared and decent housing provided in its place, usually in corporation-built schemes on the outskirts of the city. And there were to be no more scrap merchants like Asa Wass carrying on their trade in amongst where people lived—residential areas, industrial areas, shopping areas, were all to be 'zoned', kept tidily apart from one another.

The first task then was to do something about the so-called slums. And the area that seemed to cry out for immediate attention was Freer Street and the neighbouring tenement blocks. People who lived in that area now look back with fond feelings on that time in their lives, and rightly emphasise the warmth and neighbourliness of that close-knit community. However, by the early 1960s the physical condition of the housing there was causing increasing concern. In January 1964 a Methodist minister, John Ashplant, protested to Edinburgh Corporation about the conditions in Freer Street and Freer Street Terrace—and about the fact that the landlord for ten of the properties there was the Church of Scotland.

He said that on a recent visit he had seen a family of seven living in a single room 'no bigger than my vestry'. This family was not provided with running water and had to share a 'disgusting communal lavatory'. Mr Ashplant declared 'One got the impression that every room in the area was occupied by large families'.

Scotsman, 31 January 1964

The Church of Scotland stressed it had not wished to become the owner of these properties, which had come to it as a result of a debt settlement. They were 'very unwilling owners', and wanted to sell the houses as they became vacant. The Corporation's answer to Mr Ashplant was that Freer Street and Freer Street Terrace were part of an area to be redeveloped. All the houses in the two streets were classed as unfit for human habitation, and they hoped to get rid of them under a three-year clearance programme due to start in 1965. Not surprisingly, the Church of Scotland wasn't finding it easy to sell its houses.

Media attention was again directed at Freer Street in March 1964 when Harold Wilson, then leader of the Labour opposition, visited Edinburgh and was taken on a tour of some of its worst housing areas, including Freer Street Terrace.

After completing his trip Mr Wilson told a press conference, 'I think all of us who saw these conditions were shocked by what they saw. Clearly the fact that so many people, and so many children, are living like this in 1964 is an intolerable affront in a so-called civilised society'.

Evening News, 21 March 1964

63   Harold Wilson visits Freer Street Terrace on 21 March 1964, accompanied by
Councillor Pat Rogan. Courtesy of Richard W Cowell.

In an earlier chapter Betty McAnna describes her disappointment on hearing Wilson speak at a public meeting and making no reference to the actual problems faced by local people. The publicity surrounding the visit did, however, provoke debate about the issue, and gave ammunition to those Labour councillors who were calling for the area to be cleared as quickly as possible. But it took two more years for the process to get under way. In April 1966 the first steps were taken when two clearance areas taking in parts of Freer Street and Fountainbridge were announced. Councillor James McInally welcomed the news:

> All we need now is confirmation of the third area and the whole street will be wiped away. I hope the Secretary of State announces his decision quickly, and that we can get cracking.
>
> *Evening News*, 27 April 1966

In preparation for the clearance, people now began to be interviewed for council houses. By August 1967 the 508 people who had lived in Freer Street had been re-housed and demolition work on the area had begun.

Freer Street was not the only area to fall victim to a Clearance Order. Many other streets were affected also—Riego Street, Earl Grey Street, West Port, Lauriston Street, High Riggs, Wrights Houses—all suffered onslaughts of varying intensity. But only Freer Street and Terrace vanished without trace— the houses, the streets, and the names.

Not everyone was willing to go:

> My grandmother always vowed she would never move from Freer Street. I always said the bulldozers would come before she moved out of her house. But she died the year before it was pulled down. And she never had electricity in her house, she always preferred the gas mantles. It must have been the only house in the street by then without electricity.
>
> I didn't see it being pulled down. I was living out at Broomhouse by that time, and anyway I didnae feel I wanted to see it come down.
>
> MRS BETTY MCANNA

But this 'Blitz on Slums', as newspaper headlines of the mid 1960s referred to it, was to be the last of the major clearances in the area. The slum clearance programme was only one part of a much larger development plan for the Tollcross area. The centrepiece of this plan was the inner ring road. In one form or another this was on Edinburgh's planning agenda, from the Abercrombie Plan of 1949, until the late 1970s. The inner ring road, 'travelling for most of its length through areas needing to be rebuilt', (*Glasgow Herald*, 23 August 1963), would encircle central Edinburgh, running through Tollcross, Haymarket, Comely Bank, Canonmills, Leith Walk, St Leonards and the Meadows. It was intended to ease traffic pressure on the city centre and allow the centre itself—including most of the Tollcross-Fountainbridge area—to be entirely reshaped. Most of the residential areas remaining in the city centre would be cleared. Major institutions, such as the University and the Royal Infirmary, would undertake expansion into the cleared areas.

The Jellicoe-Coleridge plan, mentioned above, was one of the first detailed expressions of this programme as it affected what had now been designated the Tollcross Comprehensive Development Area. The programme went through many revisions and reviews over the years, but the underlying vision remained the same. The aim was to create, in the area stretching between Holyrood Park and Tollcross, 'an academic and cultural zone containing university, college, teaching hospital, cultural and residential facilities.' (*Evening News*, 30 January 1967). The order in which the priorities are listed is not accidental.

The University's slice of this pie was to consist of much of the South Side area around the Pleasance and George Square. The area between Lauriston Place and the Grassmarket, opposite the Royal Infirmary, was to be developed by the University as a new Dental School. The Infirmary planned to expand west practically as far as Tollcross itself, turning the whole area west of Chalmers Street into a 'health service centre . . . including family doctor centre, community health centre and many other health facilities'.

The six-lane inner ring road would run along the line of Melville Drive to Tollcross. Earl Grey Street was to be widened to accommodate traffic coming from or going to the West End and Princes Street. From Tollcross the inner ring road would continue in more or less a straight line to Haymarket, joining the Western Approach Road, which was to extend to the M8. The development would have meant clearing more than 30 acres centred on Tollcross junction.

64, 65, 66   Three photographs of 137 Fountainbridge before and during demolition in the 1960s. Courtesy of Andrew Macnab.

At the junction, an 8 acre shopping centre was to be built, enclosed by a roundabout feeding on to the inner ring road. The inner ring road itself would pass through a tunnel underneath the shopping centre. The centre would include multi-level car parks, a series of big stores and a large number of smaller shops. The clearing of the surrounding area would involve knocking down the Cameo and Palais de Danse, but a new cinema and dance hall would be provided within the shopping centre. Escalators would take pedestrians from road level down to the shopping centre, or the 'romantic centre piazza', as the Jellicoe-Coleridge report termed it. There was to be complete segregation of pedestrians and traffic. Just over 3 acres of the 30 acre redevelopment area were zoned for housing—Lochrin Place and the immediate area round Drumdryan Street. This housing would probably have been 'high density'—tower blocks, in other words.

So this was to be the new Tollcross—an 8 acre shopping and leisure complex and a six-lane motorway. How did residents react? The *Evening News and Despatch* reported a public meeting held at Tollcross School in April 1964 to discuss these far-reaching plans. John Millar, Deputy Chairman of the Planning Committee, addressed the meeting.

> Stressing the importance of the overall road plan for the city, Councillor Millar said that a reasonable estimate of its cost would be in the region of £80m–£100m . . . Tollcross, he said, was No. 1 of the areas for redevelopment which could be carried out within the next 5 years.

If there was any hostile reaction to this 'redevelopment' it wasn't recorded.

However, as plans for the ring road became more public and more official, resistance to the project began to take shape. Action groups opposing the road sprang up, drawing their support mainly from the middle class areas through which the ring road was to pass. In December 1966 the Meadows and South Edinburgh Group was formed at the home of architect Paul Newman in Warrender Park Terrace. The MSEG argued that, 'the road will not be able to cater for the amount of traffic. Slums will be created around the road where there was once a residential area' (*Evening News*, 15 December 1966). The group was evidently successful in attracting support—by January 1967 it had 600 members and was increasing at the rate of 100 every four days.

In 1967 a public enquiry, provoked in large part by the opposition of groups like the MSEG, effectively froze the plans for an inner ring road as they then stood, but without actually abandoning them in their entirety. The southern section of the road, including the part affecting Tollcross, remained on the planning board. The entire area was still zoned for comprehensive redevelopment. This combination of plans with inactivity was popularly known as 'planning blight'. No one wanted to buy or improve property in an area scheduled for demolition. Property values in Tollcross plummetted and the area as a whole went into decline as uncertaintly mounted over what the Corporation's plans actually were.

On 23 April 1972 the *Evening News* published photographs showing the dereliction that resulted from the chronic planning blight imposed by the Corporation.

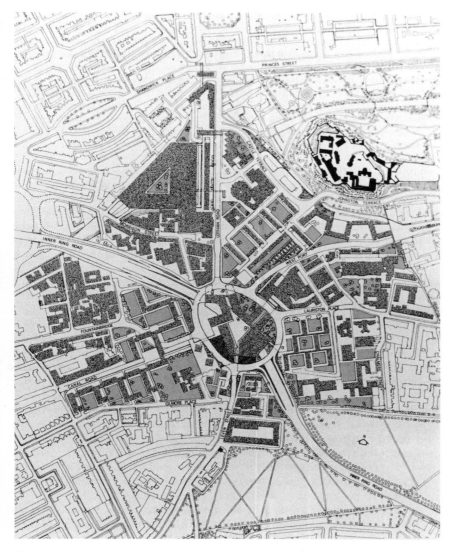

The proposed roadway system in Tollcross, prepared by the Architects Jellico and Coleridge in 1965. The rough shaded areas are buildings and the flat shaded areas are landscaping. Courtesy of City of Edinburgh Planning Department.

These are scenes behind the crumbling façade of houses in Riego Street, where the gaunt and empty buildings cast shadows on this local waste-bin. The residents claim the dirt accumulates because of the dithering; the change of plan; the waiting for another plan before one can go ahead; and the indecision all linked to the Corporation, who are undecided on how Tollcross, including Riego Street, is part of a comprehensive development plan, 'very much tied in with a land use and transport study'. The study, said a town planning department official, should be ready by 1972, and then they could get cracking on what to build in Tollcross. Meanwhile the old mattresses in the Tollcross waste-bin are quietly rotting away with old household debris decaying beside them.

While the planners were preparing to 'get cracking' onTollcross, what was to be done about conditions in the area as they actually were? Residents were no longer prepared to allow planning decisions to be made on their behalf, as the MSEG had demonstrated. Battle lines were being redrawn in the planning sphere. At one time the enemy was easily identified. 'Slum landlords' were the cause of the problem. They were responsible for the appalling conditions in which so many working-class people were forced to live. In this battle, it was the Corporation that appeared as saviour, buying up the slum landlords, tearing down their tenements and resettling their inhabitants in council housing schemes. Now, however, it was the Corporation that was cast as the villain, and people were less ready to believe what the planners and councillors chose to tell them.

All the districts were angry at (the inner ring road). It was going to affect the Meadows, and Brougham Place was all coming down, and my side of Lochrin Place was all coming down. People were very, very angry, and these meetings I was at were well attended. People did band together at that time, because property was involved in it, they were going to lose money. The councillors did just the same as they do now, trying to tell you it was the best thing that could happen: it would relieve the traffic problem, and everybody would have lovely houses, somewhere in the suburbs. Because at that time, of course, they were trying to take all the residents out of the centre of town, just as they've done in Fountainbridge, Lauriston . . . But nobody believed what they were being told, that it was for the benefit of the people of Tollcross, this inner ring road!

I wouldn't honestly say the area was run-down prior to these plans being made public. Once they were public people were out of Tollcross as quick as they could. Because they were frightened that if they held on too long the Corporation would come along and knock their houses down and they would have nothing, they would have to take a Corporation house at Gilmerton or somewhere like that. But they were selling their houses to the District Council who did not put anybody in the houses, did nothing to them, and that's when the area became more run-down.

MRS JOSEPHINE BLACK

It was a vicious circle—the development plans meant the area went into a physical and social decline, which made redevelopment even more likely, and so on. There were many who believed, and still believe, that this was a deliberate policy on the part of the Corporation. There was also a belief that ultimately the only group that would materially benefit from the redevelopment plans were the property developers. The *Tollcross News* highlighted some of these issues in 1975. It pointed out that at a time of acute housing shortage there were 150 empty houses in Tollcross. 'Flats which were structurally sound and perfectly habitable have become neglected and rotting shells'. It reported that according to one (anonymous) council official, 'many of the empty houses are managed by property companies, who use them as an investment. Once Tollcross is freed from its planning blight, the houses will rise in value and be sold at a tidy profit.' The *Tollcross News* discovered that three property companies were factors for thirty of the vacant houses, 'some of which have been standing for several years.' One of the companies denied that they were engaged in profiteering and that their policy was to resell empty houses 'as soon as possible'.Many of the remaining empty houses were owned by the District Council, though owing to some impressive bureaucratic stonewalling *The Tollcross News* was unable to unearth any details, and commented:

> The new (i.e. post-1975) councils seem to have brought a blossoming of ridiculous red tape and inefficiency—or perhaps they have something to hide . . . We can no longer tolerate inefficient, bureaucratic councils and monopoly playing property speculators. Tollcross must fight to stay as a thriving, living community. We need homes, not offices and opera houses.

Local residents, concerned and angry at the developments the Corporation had in store for them, began to join together to see what common action could do to save their community and their homes. In 1970 the Tollcross Residents' Association was formed. The TRA was not so much concerned with the specific issues of the ring road as with the consequences for them of the council's development plans in general. Whether or not some, or all, of the ring road plans went ahead, the triangle of tenements between Home Street and Brougham Place was scheduled for clearance and redevelopment. It was in this area that the TRA emerged. Its aim was to put pressure on the council either to implement a definite Compulsory Purchase policy, or to declare their area a Housing Action Area, thus entitling them to rehabilitation grants. A Compulsory Purchase Programme would at least have meant that dispossessed owners could have got a good price for their property, and would also ensure that they were adequately rehoused. In the absence of such a programme the council had been able to pursue a policy of buying up property as and when it fell vacant, at knock-down market-led prices.

Grace Suttie, a founder member of the TRA, remembers the early days of the Association:

> We hadn't a lot of people, so we had to go round every night of the week, I and somebody else, we had an area, went up every stair, knocked at every door. Well, some people didn't understand, these people were frightened. But the more people we had, the more hearing we had.
> So we got to the stage we had meetings. We got the people themselves, like the

architects—oh they came because *they* were frightened, they started being frightened of us then. And then we got in the paper and all sorts of things . . . I just used to phone up the council and say, 'We're having a meeting, we'd like you to come'. And there they would be. Because there must have been questions flying about in the City Chambers, what we were doing. And maybe how they could stop us. But they found out they werenae able to stop us . . . I know we made ourselves very, very clear. In fact at one of the meetings that I was at I told them, 'Well, if you want to come with your bulldozers you'll just have to bulldoze me in the house, because I won't be moving.' That's how firm I was in my mind.

Fortunately for Grace Suttie, and for Tollcross, the bulldozers never arrived. By the mid 1970s a number of factors were coming together to ensure that the planned redevelopment of Tollcross would never go ahead. Community opposition of the type represented by the TRA was a crucial element in this. It's also likely that the CDA plans had simply been on the books too long, had been subject to too many revisions and had lost even such contact with reality as they originally possessed. Reality for the residents of Tollcross, Fountainbridge and the West Port included neglected, decaying tenements, gap-sites that seemed to have no other use than to be turned into car parks, and a general demoralisation of the community. Councillors were now beginning to emerge who realised that the real problems of the area were not going to be solved through large-scale, no-holds-barred redevelopment. Councillors like George Foulkes and Bob Cairns, along with local MP Robin Cook, became active participants in the community's fight against redevelopment plans. In the early summer of 1975 this campaign won an important victory when the most dilapidated parts of the Home Street-Brougham Street triangle were declared Housing Action Areas. The council had already admitted that any redevelopment of the area was unlikely to take place within the next ten years. It was difficult to argue for a redevelopment scheme that seemed an increasingly remote possibility, in the face of a rehabilitation programme that promised immediate benefits. The council could still (for a while) maintain the fiction that the rehabilitation policy was only an interim one, until the 'real' development of the area could take place, but the Housing Action Area programme meant that those campaigning against CDA plans had a foot in the planning department's door and were now unlikely to be budged.

    There were, however, other interested bodies, besides the council, who had to be taken on if the fight against redevelopment was to be won. The development plan which had hung over most of south-central Edinburgh since the 1950s was essentially based on the needs of professional institutions—the University, the Royal Infirmary, financial and cultural interests. All these groups had plans for expansion in the Tollcross area. The Art College was busy buying up and clearing property in its immediate vicinity. In 1975 *The Tollcross News* commented that:

> People who have lived near the Art College for the past few years might be forgiven for thinking that their artistic neighbour seems to be better at creating car parks than works of art.

Around 1969-70 the College began buying up property in the West Port, where it had plans for expansion. However, financial problems intervened and they settled for their present site on Lauriston Place instead. 'West Port meanwhile was left to rot'. In 1973 the College demolished the old church at the corner of Lady Lawson Street and the West Port. The north side of Keir Street was also demolished by the College, leaving a gap-site, 'which seems likely to remain as a car park indefinitely'.

Expansion on a much grander scale was envisaged by the Royal Infirmary, as noted above. In 1965 the whole area west of existing Infirmary buildings, down as far as Brougham Place, was zoned for hospital expansion. This expansion was to take place over three phases: 1975-80, Archibald Place to Chalmers Street, for a reproductive biology department; 1981-5, Chalmers Street to Lauriston Gardens, possibly for a burns and plastic surgery unit; and finally, some time between 1986 and 1995, the land between Lauriston Gardens and Tollcross 'might be needed'. Naturally the inevitable planning blight descended on the area as a result of this zoning for hospital use of land which the Infirmary 'might need'. The TRA launched a campaign against the Infirmary's plans. At a public meeting held in Darroch School, the TRA, together with local councillors and Robin Cook, called on the Infirmary not to expand further west than Chalmers Street (*Evening News*, 13 June 1975). According to Geoff Dukes, an architect and planner living in the area:

> About 350 houses would be affected by the board's proposal and more than 1,000 people would be made homeless . . . If a brewery or a school wanted to expand they would have to have a full investigation by the town planner, but the hospital has statutory powers which apparently allow it to bypass stringent investigation.

Nonetheless the campaign against the proposed hospital expansion ultimately proved successful. In December 1978 the District planning committee told Lothian Health Board they intended to allocate the Lauriston Gardens/Lonsdale Terrace site for new housing, because of the Board's failure to come up with detailed plans of its own for the area. Then in January 1986 the Secretary of State refused permission for the Infirmary to expand by knocking down tenements on the south side of Lauriston Place. The Infirmary was told to find a green field site for any future development. Phase 1 of their planned expansion was as far as they were to get.

There was a further victory in the 1970s for the anti-CDA campaign when the University was refused planning permission for its proposed Dental School on Lauriston Place. The University sold the properties it had acquired there to the Lister Housing Co-operative.

By the mid 1970s the tide was turning against the CDA philosophy. Local sentiment had found its voice in campaigns of the kind mounted by the TRA. The importance of Tollcross as a residential area was being established. In 1971 the TRA organised a survey of the 100 or so inhabitants of 'sub-standard' houses at 1–63 Home Street, which the council was considering clearing as part of its redevelopment plan. The survey showed nine out of ten residents wanted to stay where they were—another boost to the rehabilitation argument.

Housing Associations were beginning to establish themselves in the area. They too spoke up for rehabilitation rather than redevelopment. The Fountainbridge Housing Association was founded in May 1976, and by 1988 it had over 500 flats to rent in the Fountainbridge area. Castle Rock Housing Association took an early interest in rehabilitation work in the Tollcross area. Edinvar Housing Association carried out the development work for the Lister Housing Co-operative at Lauriston Place. When the development was completed in 1982 it had transformed the frontage of the south side of Lauriston Place, resulting in 122 rehabilitated houses and 14 new flats. In 1984 Castle Rock Housing Association completed a 32-unit sheltered housing scheme at the foot of Lauriston Park. Sixty-two Edinvar flats will be part of the Burrell Company's development at the SMT triangle.

This movement at ground level also found expression in changing planning priorities at District and Regional level. In 1976 the new Lothian Regional Council, in its Green Paper on transport, formally abandoned the inner ring road concept—though a major relief road for Tollcross remained a possibility. Yet the move was now away from all-embracing ring road types of proposals and towards solutions based on traffic management systems, utilisation of existing road systems, and better public transport. The District Council published the Tollcross Local Plan in 1982, which replaced the old CDA proposals. Its main recommendations were:

> —housing needs to be met primarily by new building and by rehabilitation and building on green field sites to be severely restrained;
> —new shopping investment to be encouraged only in established shopping areas;
> —inner housing areas to be protected from office development;
> —traffic problems to be dealt with by making better use of road space already available.

The last gasp of the old transport plans for the area was the proposed Western Relief Road. Designed to relieve traffic pressure on Corstorphine, the Relief Road would have meant 55,000 vehicles a day spilling out on to Lothian Road, from where they would then have had to squeeze through the unreconstructed road system. There were forty objectors at the inquiry which opened in November 1984, including British Rail, Edinburgh District Council, Tollcross Community Council, the Cockburn Association, and BEWARE, a local pressure group under the presidency of Pam Scott. Locals feared both the immediate consequences the road would have on their area in the form of vastly increased traffic, and also the prospect it opened up of a revived Southern Link Road through Melville Drive and Tollcross to cope with this increased traffic. The issue never came to the full-blown fight that had seemed likely. In May 1986 Labour won the regional elections and, in line with their manifesto promise, the Relief Road was unceremoniously scrapped—or as Councillor James Cook put it, 'consigned to the deepest, everlasting tomb'. There are many Tollcross residents who certainly hope it will remain there.

Although by the late 1970s plans for the wholesale redevelopment of the Tollcross area had been abandoned, this did not mean there were no more planning battles to be fought. One aspect of the Tollcross Local Plan that seemed to have a positive impact since the first drafts appeared in 1976 was its opposition to new office development in the area. In 1977, for example, the District Council ruled against an application by James Grant and Company to bring in a change of use from shops to offices at 22-84 Earl Grey Street, on the grounds that there was already plenty of unused office space in the city centre (*Scotsman*, 10 March 1977. In 1982 the District Council refused Alexanders permission to build a 7-storey shop and office block on the $1\frac{1}{4}$ acre site in Semple Street, where their garage and showroom used to be, on the grounds that the scheme was contrary to the council's policy of restraining office development in central Edinburgh.

By the late 1980s, however, council policy seemed to be switching back in favour of office development. In 1987 the District Council issued its West Central Edinburgh Development Strategy, in response to the 1984 Regional Structure Plan which required more offices in the city centre. Answering local residents' criticisms of the plan, which it was feared would replace the Tollcross Local Plan, David Wilcox, District Community Planning Officer, stated:

> Edinburgh needs ten acres of office space near the existing office core, so as not to miss out on the prospect of economic growth in the financial sector.
>
> *Tollcross Times*, June 1987

However, locals continued to be worried by the District's new emphasis on offices and car parks. The District's concern over the need for office expansion has been mirrored by David Murray, of Murray International Holdings, the man behind the Port Hamilton development. Speaking of the importance of office facilities in his overall plans for the former canal basin, he said:

> It was obvious to me a year ago that Edinburgh would run out of office space and that companies would start going to Glasgow. Edinburgh is in danger of losing its identity.
>
> *Scotsman*, 30 March 1987

Of course 'losing its identity' was exactly what Tollcross residents feared would happen to their area if the kind of office development he proposed went ahead.

Planning in the Tollcross area has been a constant tug of war among a variety of interests and functions—offices, houses, shops, traffic, parking, residents, non-residents—and the area's gap sites have been one of the principal arenas for this. In the case of the SMT triangle, Port Hamilton, Lothian Road and the Morrison Street Goods Yard sites, community groups, planners and developers have argued and negotiated over the last twenty years about how best to utilise these derelict waste-grounds. Now it looks as if these negotiations are going to start taking on physical reality as the builders finally get to work. The buildings that will result from all this will reflect long processes of consultation and debate that have won a number of specific gains for the local community. The Laing plans for the SMT triangle, first made public in 1975, were for a massive (125,000 sq ft) department store, with offices and parking for 2,000 cars in six basement layers. This relic of CDA gigantism has, however, after protests by community groups and local councillors, been replaced by a scheme much more in harmony with the area, under the new developers, the Burrell Company. The department store has gone, replaced by small shops along Earl Grey Street, combined with sixty-two Edinvar flats, a medical centre where seven Tollcross doctors will hold their surgeries, a pedestrianised High Riggs, and open space in the centre of the triangle. Office space is to be 'minimal'. At Port Hamilton, again after a criticism voiced by local groups, the original plans have been amended—plans for a hotel have been dropped, the height of the complex has been reduced, there is to be a creche and a landscaped city park with safe play facilities. There are still, however, reservations over the amount of office space (60,000 sq ft) and a dispute over whether plans for housing, once part of the development and then dropped, are to be reinstated. At the Lothian Road site financial interests predominate. This 'flagship' financial and conference centre will include 1.1 million sq ft of office space as well as a conference and exhibition centre capable of hosting 1,200 delegates. There are also plans for fifty-four houses on the site. At the Morrison Street site outline planning permission is being sought for a development that would include hotel accommodation, office space and 275 houses for sale and rent, including sheltered housing. However, Dalry Colonies residents are expressing concern over inadequate parking facilities for residents, while the Grove Street Residents' Association is worried about the Grove Street homes being dominated by the 6-storey eastern side of the development.

As far as the community is concerned, the present planning situation seems to represent an uneasy compromise between the developers' financial concerns and local needs. Community groups still have to be prepared to fight their own corner and only time will tell if the compromise turns out to be a workable one. As far as the planners themselves are concerned, the last 25 years or so have been a slow learning process for them, but the consultation message is perhaps getting home now. Andrea Shaw of Tollcross Community Council was, 'pleasantly surprised' by the willingness of the Burrell Company to engage in dialogue over plans for the SMT site: 'The architect consulted with us from the start, came along to Community Council meetings to show us his plans and models'.

In the end, what has been the effect on the Tollcross area of all this planning and development? What kind of community is there now in Tollcross, and how does it compare with the earlier community described in previous chapters?

The first impact of the post-war clearances was inevitably one of dislocation, when the clearance and resettlement of most of the original community left a void that could not be filled as long as planning uncertainty continued. The Very Reverend Leonard Small, who worked with St Cuthbert's Missions in Freer Street and Morrison Street in the 1950s and 1960s, remembers the deep roots that continued to link those who had moved away with the area they left behind.

> What used to happen was that a daughter from Freer Street would get married and acquire a family, and on Sunday, the regular pattern was that they came in from

their house in the housing scheme, could be Saughton Mains or somewhere like that, and spent the day with granny. And the kids went to the Sunday School, that got them out of the road of granny and the parents, and they spent the day where they belonged, then picked up the kids and went home again.

I think the total decline of Tollcross as a community in the deepest sense was when the grannies were moved away. I'm quite delibeartely using that as a picture of the past—that granny was the centre of the community. She had brought up the family, often with very great toil and many great sacrifices, and they realised that and they kept coming back. But once granny was away, the attraction to Tollcross was gone, so they stayed out in the housing scheme.

Once the grannies, along with the close-knit, family-based ties they represented, had gone, what was to take their place? By the 1960s the old settled way of life, revolving round close attachment to a particular street, was becoming a thing of the past. People now thought of themselves as belonging to a larger and more diverse community than in the old days, though some of the old attachments linger on, as Josephine Black describes:

I was born in Tollcross. Now there is no way I would have considered Gillespie Crescent a part of Tollcross. Neither would I have considered Lauriston, West Port—I mean we were a district all on our own, which was more or less to Valleyfield Street, a part of Gilmore Place, Brougham Place, Panmure Place, but not Lauriston Gardens, that belonged to Lauriston. You know, Tollcross covers a very big area now . . . I mean, people in Fountainbridge would *die* if you said they came from Tollcross, even to this day! I know people that stay up here [Gillespie Crescent], the same age as myself or older, and they would be horrified if you said they came from Tollcross. 'Cause this was a better area, of course, Bruntsfield!

Tollcross Community Council, of which Josephine Black is a member, now takes in a much bigger area than the Tollcross of her youth, and deals with the problems that affect everyone within this area, whether they are from Valleyfield Street or Fountainbridge: late licences, traffic, shopping facilities, planning proposals. There is now perhaps less of the old 'stair-heid' solidarity, but greater cohesion betwen areas that might once have seen themselves as separate and distinctive. The population has become more transient and more mobile, both physically and socially, and association is now more likely to be based on common interest than on neighbourhood. Proposed developments like the Inner Ring Road and the Western Relief Road brought together community groups from all over the area, involved in the same cause because they saw themselves as being faced by the same threat. The Port Hamilton Development requires a response from residents all around its boundary, whether they are from Gardeners Crescent, Morrison Street or Fountainbridge. Areas that might have once felt they had little in common are united by the developers' plans. And these developments are themselves potential centres for any sense of community that might emerge in the future, though it will be one based on an entirely different pattern of work, leisure and family life from that described in previous chapters.